New Practical English

2

新编实用英语 拓展教程

XINBIAN SHIYONG YINGYU TUOZHAN JIAOCHENG

Extended Book

本书编写组 编

高等教育出版社·北京
HIGHER EDUCATION PRESS　BEIJING

内容提要

　　《新编实用英语》（黑龙江版）系列教材在《新编实用英语》（第二版）的基础上，结合黑龙江省的实际情况进行编写。本套教材贯彻了"学一点、会一点、用一点"、"听、说、读、写、译并重"和"边学边用、学用结合"的原则；注重听说技能训练，注重实用文体阅读能力培养，将应用语言基本功的能力与实际涉外交际相结合。

　　《新编实用英语拓展教程2》（黑龙江版）包括《读写教程2》单元拓展练习（阅读、语法、应用文模拟套写等）、单元主题扩展语料库和全真模拟自测题等部分。

图书在版编目（CIP）数据

新编实用英语拓展教程：黑龙江版 . 2/《新编实用英语拓展教程》编写组编 . —北京：高等教育出版社，2011.7
ISBN 978 - 7 - 04 - 031231 - 7

Ⅰ.①新…　Ⅱ.①新…　Ⅲ.①英语—高等职业教育—教材
Ⅳ.①H31

中国版本图书馆 CIP 数据核字（2011）第 131981 号

策划编辑　闵　阅	项目编辑　张慧勇	责任编辑　赵凯锋	封面设计　张　楠
版式设计　刘　艳	责任校对　赵凯锋	责任印制　尤　静	

出版发行　高等教育出版社
社　　址　北京市西城区德外大街 4 号
邮政编码　100120
印　　刷　人民教育出版社印刷厂
开　　本　850×1168 1/16
印　　张　15.25
字　　数　384 000
购书热线　010-58581118

咨询电话　400-810-0598
网　　址　http://www.hep.edu.cn
　　　　　http://www.hep.com.cn
网上订购　http://www.landraco.com
　　　　　http://www.landraco.com.cn
版　　次　2011 年 7 月第 1 版
印　　次　2011 年 7 月第 1 次印刷
定　　价　35.00 元（含光盘）

NEW Practical English

Extended Book 2

新编实用英语

拓展教程2

（黑龙江版）

《新编实用英语》系列教材编写指导委员会

主　任：李志宏　王　伟

副主任：孔庆炎　刘鸿章　刘　援　李津石

委　员：姜　怡　安晓灿　余渭深　向前进　伍忠杰　周　龙

《新编实用英语拓展教程2》（黑龙江版）

总主编：王利民　顾世民

主　编：林铁成　李　才

编　者：陆　姣　钱双双　史艳丽　裴　玉

策　　划：闵　阅

项目编辑：张慧勇

责任编辑：赵凯锋

封面设计：张　楠

版式设计：三月天地

责任校对：赵凯锋

责任印制　尤　静

前　言

《新编实用英语》（黑龙江版）系列教材是由黑龙江省高职高专院校外语教学研究会，结合黑龙江省地方经济和社会发展的实际，在《新编实用英语》（第二版）系列教材的基础上，组织本省高职高专院校具有丰富教学经验的一线教师编写的一套高职高专英语教材。

《新编实用英语》（黑龙江版）系列教材由《听说教程》、《读写教程》和《拓展教程》组成。每种教程由2册书组成，每册书10个单元。另外，使用者还可以在中国外语网（www.cflo.com.cn）上免费下载各教程的《教师参考书》。

把《听说教程》和《读写教程》分开，主要是为了避免每个课时都"面面俱到"的课堂设置，更方便教师安排授课重点，使学生在每个课时内更加有效地学习相关内容。《听说教程》每个单元包括2个部分——"说"（Talking Face to Face）和"听"（Being All Ears）；《读写教程》每个单元包括3个部分——"读"（Maintaining a Sharp Eye）、"写"（Trying Your Hand）和体现黑龙江特色的阅读文章"黑龙江简介"（Glimpses of Heilongjiang）；《拓展教程》包括《读写教程》的单元拓展练习、《听说教程》和《读写教程》的主题扩展语料库以及4套全真自测题（含答案）。

上述教程各部分的具体内容如下：

1. Talking Face to Face：包括5个短小的交际话题模拟练习，使学生边学边练，以增强学生的实际英语会话能力，并配有2个紧扣交际主题的对话样例，供学生学习模仿。

2. Being All Ears：本部分是对Talking Face to Face的扩大与补充，以体现听力训练的范围要广于会话训练的原则，并为阅读作铺垫。

3. Maintaining a Sharp Eye：包括2篇阅读文章，旨在使学生通过阅读开阔眼界，进一步提高语感和交际能力，为自主学习创造充分的条件。

4. Trying Your Hand：包括应用文写作（Applied Writing）、句子写作和语法回顾（Sentence Writing and Grammar Review）2部分。第一部分培养学生阅读和模拟套写常用应用文的能力，第二部分通过句子写作、技能写作和篇章写作等层次训练学生的写作能力。

5. Glimpses of Heilongjiang：以短文的形式介绍黑龙江的自然、社会、经济、文化等，增强学生学习英语的针对性和实用性，激发学生的学习兴趣。

6. Self-assessment：选编了4套高等学校英语应用能力考试A级和B级的试题。

《新编实用英语拓展教程2》（黑龙江版）由孔庆炎、刘鸿章任总主审，哈尔滨学院王利民、哈尔滨师范大学顾世民任总主编，黑龙江农业职业技术学院林铁成、齐齐哈尔工程学院李才任主编，黑龙江农业职业技术学院陆姣、黑龙江科技学院利民校区钱双双、黑龙江农业工程职业学院史艳丽和哈尔滨学院裴玉参加编写。

由于本书是一种新的尝试，实际编写中恐有不当和疏漏之处，希望广大使用者批评指正，以使本教程为黑龙江高职高专英语教学做出更大贡献。

改编组

2011年6月

CONTENTS

Unit 1   Making Reservations

Unit Goals

❖ What You Should Learn to Know About

1. Hotel services in the USA
2. Relative clause

SECTION I

Maintaining a Sharp Eye

Read More by Yourself

Lost and Found Items *Perplex* the Hotel Trade

Housekeepers at all large hotels are well aware that **departing** guests leave things behind them. The lost property **cupboard** at one particular hotel in the United States is **overflowing** with socks, ties and **underwear**, and it also contains more unusual **leftovers** such as a mini dress, a Korean fan, a music box, etc.

Almost everyone in the hotel has heard about the **live** lobster discovered in the mini-bar. There have also been forgotten **pets**, including a pet mouse, though the owner was a little **shy** about mentioning this. **Apparently** he asked if they had found a little **garment** in the shape of a mouse. Among the interesting items ending up as lost property in London were **DNA** samples of a disease, several oversized tins of **baked** beans, and a little rabbit left in a shoebox under a bed.

Each hotel has its own **peculiar** tale to tell. The housekeeper of one Sheraton Hotel is at a loss to explain a rise in the sets of false teeth left behind. Four sets were left at the hotel in a single month; two sets had yet

| |
| 困惑 |
| 离开 |
| 壁柜 |
| 充满；内衣 |
| 遗忘的东西 |
| 活的 |
| 宠物 |
| 害羞的；表面上地；衣服 |
| 脱氧核糖核酸；烘烤的 |
| 奇怪的 |

to be **reclaimed** two months later. "You would have thought once they started **chewing** into breakfast, they'd realize something was **missing**," the housekeeper says, with a laugh.

Most hotels hold on lost property for three months and, if it is not reclaimed, give it to **charity**. Some hotels give the person who found the item the opportunity to keep it. This encourages them to hand in the items they may find while cleaning rooms. Usually, hotel managers will wait for guests to claim things unless an item is of great value. They prefer not to do the contacting.

If what guests leave behind is interesting, so is what they choose to steal. Some hotels spend as much as US$10 000 each year **replacing** wooden coat **hangers**. "Guests take anything that's not **nailed** down," says one manager. "We've lost irons and **bathrobes**, and pillows are starting to become more popular. Hotels have found that items with **logos** are more popular than **non-monogrammed** items.

It seems guests take them as a **memento** of their stay. Some hotels have printed cards in the bathrooms saying bathrobes can be bought. The **ashtray** is a popular souvenir for those who stay at Hong Kong's Royal Pacific Hotel. The **motivation** for the guests' **light-fingeredness** is often more than mere **nostalgia**. As the Sheraton Hotel's public relations manager says, some guests think hotel rates are so high that "they should get something for nothing."

索回
咀嚼
丢失的
慈善机构
代替
衣挂；钉
浴衣
标识语
无标识语的
纪念品
烟缸
动机；扒窃
怀旧

1 **Read the passage carefully and check your understanding by doing the multiple choice exercises.**

1) Which of the following is NOT mentioned as items left in hotels?

  a. Suitcases.   b. Socks.   c. Ties.   d. Underwear.

2) When he asked about a garment in the shape of a mouse, the guest was in fact asking about his _____.

  a. clothes   b. pet lobster   c. pet mouse   d. DNA sample

3) The word "over-sized" in the second paragraph means _____.

  a. much larger   b. too small   c. of the usual size   d. larger than usual

4) The housekeeper of one Sheraton Hotel couldn't explain why _____.

  a. underwear was usually left behind

  b. so many sets of false teeth were left behind

  c. live lobsters were left behind

  d. samples of a certain disease were left behind

5) In most hotels, if the lost property is not reclaimed, it is usually given to _____.

  a. the person who found it

  b. charity

  c. the manager

  d. the housekeeper

6) Which of the following is true according to the passage?

  a. Guests are allowed to take away anything interesting from the hotel as a souvenir.

  b. Items with logos are more likely to be stolen than non-monogrammed items.

  c. Pillows, bathrobes, irons are not the things that guests would like to take.

  d. Hotels have to nail down everything they don't want to be stolen.

7) It seems that guests take away items with logos because they want _____.

  a. to have something to remind them of the hotel they stayed in

  b. to express their dissatisfaction with the hotel services

  c. to have something special to present to their friends as souvenirs

  d. to own something they cannot buy elsewhere in the market

8) According to what one public relationship manager says, one of the main reasons for guests' light-fingeredness is that _____.

  a. the services of hotels are poor

  b. the things that hotels provide are so attractive

  c. the rates of hotels are too high

  d. people are more likely to recall the past

2 Choose the proper word or phrase in the box to fill in the blank in each of the following sentences, changing the form if necessary.

public relations	reclaim	property	aware	live
souvenir	nostalgia	popular	depart	great value

1) Knowledge of English and the computer is of _____ to this job.

2) A wallet has been found and can be _____ at the Lost Property office.

3) Many people look back with _____ on the places where they once lived and worked.

4) If only you were _____ of all the facts, you would immediately change your mind.

5) Mrs. Patel has shown her talent for _____ from the very beginning of her work in the company.

6) There are still some problems with broadcasting the concert _____.

7) He keeps an astray with the hotel's logo as a _____.

8) Fred's good nature makes him the most _____ boy in the school.

9) Before you _____, let me give you a word of advice.

10) The police found some stolen _____ hidden in the thief's house.

3 Put the following sentences into English, using the words and expressions given in the brackets.

1) 大厅挤满了人，有些人不得不站到外面。(overflow)

2) 有人认领你捡到的公文包了吗？(claim)

3) 警察们不知该如何解释这个事情。(at a loss)

4) 父亲鼓励孩子们学习绘画。(encourage sb. to do sth.)

5) 他尝试过几份不同的工作，但后来还是当了律师。(end up)

PASSAGE II

General Information of Reservations at Motel 6
RESERVATION POLICIES

- All guests registering must be at least 18 years of age and present **iden-tification.** 身份

- Check-in time: any time based on **availability**. Check-out time: 12 noon. 可用性

- Children 17 and younger stay free when occupying the same room with an adult family member.

- **Occupancy** may be restricted by local **ordinance**. Generally, a room with one bed may be occupied by one or two persons. A room with two beds may be occupied by no more than four persons. If your party consists of five or more, an additional room or rooms must be rented to accommodate the additional people. 占用；法令

- An **infant** may be added to the total number of persons permitted in rooms, **provided that** the Manager has a portable **crib** available which is adequate for the weight of the infant. 婴儿 以…为条件；儿童床

- Sleeping bags, **cots** or furniture of any kind may not be placed in a Motel 6 room by any guest. 帆布床

- Motel 6 **locations** offer **facilities** for the **disabled**. Please confirm availability with our Reservation Center or with the Motel 6 you plan to visit. 场所；设施；残疾的

INDIVIDUAL RESERVATIONS

- Reservations can be made for all Motel 6 locations by calling our Reservation Center at 1-800-4-Motels 6 (1-800-466-8356).

- You may also reserve rooms by phoning or writing to the Motel 6 you plan to visit or simply stop by any Motel 6 and they will call ahead for you.

- If **guaranteed** with your credit card, your reservation will be held all night for your arrival. If you are unable to guarantee your reservation, your room will be held until 6:00 p.m. (at most locations). 担保

General Information of Reservations at Motel 6

- If it becomes necessary to cancel a reservation which you have **prepaid** or guaranteed with your credit card, you must **notify** the Motel 6 reserved by 预付

通知

6:00 p.m. on the arrival date and receive a **cancellation** number.

取消

- Please cancel reservations made through the Reservation Center by telephoning the Center rather than the Motel 6 reserved.

GROUP RESERVATIONS

- Call our Group Desk at 1-800-544-4866.
- Outside U.S.A./Canada Fax: 614-601-4052 or to make an **inquiry** online, send to _groupsales@motel6.com_

查询

- Group reservations (ten or more rooms) require an advance payment deposit of the total charges for the first night's lodging. This deposit must be made at least 30 days before the arrival.
- Contact our Group Department for specific policies on Children's Groups.
- **Notification** of cancellation must be made 30 days prior to the arrival date.

通知

4 **Are the following statements true or false according to the passage? Write T or F accordingly.**

☞ 1) Guests under 18 are not allowed to stay in the hotel.

☞ 2) Guests can check in at any time they arrive at the hotel.

☞ 3) A room with one bed may be occupied by a family of three.

☞ 4) Even though the manager can provide a crib, an infant must still be included in the total number of guests.

☞ 5) Facilities for the disabled are available at any Motel 6 hotel.

☞ 6) Any Motel 6 hotel can make reservations in any other Motel 6 hotel for the guests by telephone.

☞ 7) If you have guaranteed your reservation by credit card, your room may only be held until 6:00 p.m..

☞ 8) If you want to cancel the reservation you have made through the reservation center, you have to telephone the hotel where you made the reservation.

☞ 9) Group reservations can only be made on the condition that you pay a deposit 30 days ahead of your arrival date.

☞10) You have to notify the hotel a month ahead of time if you want to cancel a group reservation.

5 **Fill in the blanks with the right form of the word provided at the end of each sentence.**

1) I have had two _____ already this morning. I wonder why people want to _____ their seats in the theatre. (cancel)

2) You can't _____ any more people. The infants are already _____ to the total number. (add)

3) If you want to cancel a _____, you have to telephone the hotel where you _____

before 6 p.m. on your arrival date. (reserve)

4) I would like to _____ my reservation by e-mail, but the hotel prefers to receive my _____ by fax. (confirm)

5) Please tell me your _____ date before you _____ so that I can meet you at the airport. (arrive)

6) If a guest has to cancel a group reservation, he has to _____ the hotel a month earlier. The _____ may either be made by phoning or writing. (notify)

7) Facilities for the disabled are _____ at any hotel, but you have to confirm the _____ with the registration center before you get there. (available)

8) The school principal _____ about a month ago whether David would care to take the physics teacher's position in his school, but he hasn't received an answer to his _____ yet. (inquire)

6 **Put the sentences into English, using the words or expressions given in the brackets.**

1) 如果她能及时赶到这里的话，她可以和我们一起去。(provided that)
2) 儿童和父母同住一室可以免费。(stay free)
3) 取消预订房间必须提前30天通知。(prior to)
4) 团体预订房间要求提前交付押金。(advance payment)
5) 客人用信用卡担保的话，房间可以整夜保留。(hold)

SECTION II

Trying Your Hand

Write More by Yourself

A. Applied Writing: Hotel Reservation Card
Sample 1

Guest's name: Lennox Dan
Check in: 12 / 28   **Check out:** 1 / 2
Room type: Double
Room rate: US$125.00 per night
Payment: Success Card 934 243 132342
Travel agent: Jane Williams
Agent's fax number: (914) 997-8115

Sample 2

Marshall Hotel Price List (All prices include breakfast and VAT.)				
	Single room without bath	Single room with bath	Double room without bath	Double room with bath
Price per night	£ 49	£ 59	£ 78	£ 89
Price per week	£ 144	£ 162	£ 196	£ 210

Expression Tips

Words related to hotels:	
hotel	旅店，酒店
motel	汽车旅馆
airtel	机场旅馆
boatel	水上旅馆
hostel	招待所
inn	小旅馆，客栈
lodge	小旅馆
single room	单人房间
twin room / twin-bedded room	放两张床的房间
double room	双人房间
family suite with three bedrooms	三卧室家庭套房
suite	套房
president suite	总统套房
mini suite	小型套房
executive suite	经理套房
kitchen / kitchenette	厨房/小厨房
lounge	休息处
cocktail lounge	酒吧间
lobby	大厅
entrance hall	门厅
meeting room	会议室
fitness center	健身中心
multi-purpose rooms	多功能房间
single bed	单人床
double bed	双人床

twin bed	对床，（成对的）单人床
king size bed	大号床
crib	儿童床
receptionist / desk clerk	接待员
switchboard operator	电话接线员
room service waiter	客房服务员
maid	清扫房间的女服务员
bell-man / bell-boy	侍应生，行李员
doorman	门厅接应员

1 **Translate the following advertisement into Chinese. Refer to the samples and the Expression Tips for reference.**

On-Campus Housing
University Residence Halls

The University provides limited housing for undergraduate and graduate students who are registered for an approved program of academic work as determined by the school in which the student is enrolled.

University Residence Halls for students include traditional dormitory-style facilities with single/double rooms, suites with shared common areas, and apartments. Assignments are made for the academic year (250 days). The average room rate for 250 days is $3 975, and for 359 days, $5 153. All residence halls spaces are furnished, and utilities, such as gas, water and electricity (excluding telephone service) are included in the room charge.

2 **Translate the following sentences into Chinese.**

1) When returning to your hotel or motel late in the evening, use the main entrance of the hotel.

2) Place all the valuables in the hotel's safe deposit box.

3) Bed sheets are washed daily in thousands of hotels in the world.

4) If your plans change, please cancel your reservation by calling the same number used to make the reservation.

5) Some hotels require advance deposits to secure rooms in resort areas during high season.

B. **Sentences Writing: Relative Clause 定语从句**

在句中用作定语的从句称为定语从句。定语从句通常位于它所修饰的名词或代词之后，这种名词或代词称为先行词。引导定语从句的关联词为关系代词和关系副词。关系代词在定语从句中可用作主语、宾语、表语、介词宾语和定语等；关系副词在定语从句中只用作状语。

1. 由关系代词 who、whom、whose、which、that 引导的定语从句

1) Who代替人，在从句中作主语。

A man **who does not try to learn from others** cannot hope to achieve much.

一个不努力向别人学习的人是不能指望有多大成就的。

2) Whom代替人，在从句中作宾语，通常可省略。

The engineers **whom we met yesterday** have worked out a new automatic device.
我们昨天碰到的那些工程师设计出了一种新的自动化装置。

3) Whose代替人或物，在从句中作定语。

Madame Curie is a great scientist **whose name is known all over the world**.
居里夫人是一位全世界闻名的伟大科学家。(指人)

They live in the house **whose door and windows are all broken**.
他们居住的房子门窗都坏了。(指物)

4) Which 代替物，在从句中作主语、宾语或介词宾语。作宾语时，通常可省略。

A direct current is a current **which flows in one direction only**.
直流电是沿着一个方向流动的电流。

The music **to which we listened last night** was written by my father.
我们昨晚听的那首曲子是我父亲写的。

5) That代替人或物，在从句中作主语或宾语，但不能作介词宾语。作宾语时通常可省略。

He is the only one among us **that knows English**.
他是我们当中唯一懂英语的人。(指人)

The car **that almost crashed into me** belonged to Brown.
差点撞上我的那辆车是布朗先生的。(指物)

She talked about the professors and colleges **that she had visited**.
她谈到了她所访问过的教授和大学。（指人和物）

注意：

关系代词 **that** 和 **which** 的区别如下：

1) 先行词为 **all**、**anything**、**something**、**nothing**、**everything**、**little**、**much** 等不定代词时，只能用 that。

Matter is anything **that has weight and takes up space**.
任何具有重量并占有空间的东西都是物质。

2) 先行词前有最高级形容词以及 **first**、**last**、**every**、**some**、**any**、**very**、**next**、**only** 等修饰词时，只能用 **that**。

The first thing **that they should do** is to work out their plan.
他们应该做的第一件事就是制定个计划。

3) **Which** 引导的定语从句前可使用逗号，表示这是非限定性定语从句；that 从句则不能。

His speech, **which bored everyone**, went on and on.
他的演讲不断持续着，令每一个人都心烦。

I never met Judy again, **which was a pity**.
我再也没见到朱迪，十分遗憾。

---

2. **由关系副词when、where、why所引导的定语从句**

1) When作状语，其先行词多为表示时间概念的名词。

We can never forget the **day when Hong Kong returned to our homeland**.

我们永远不会忘记香港回归祖国的那一天。

2) Where作状语，其先行词多为表示地点概念的名词。

The **building where you used to live** has been pulled down.

你过去曾住过的那栋大厦已经被拆除了。

3) Why作状语，其先行词多为表示原因概念的名词。

We know the **reason why he was very angry**.

我们知道他为什么非常生气。

3. 限定性定语从句与非限定性定语从句

1) 限定性定语从句

通常限定性定语从句与先行词关系密切，因此不能缺少，否则会影响全句的意义；从句前不用逗号。

You can't answer the question **which he put forward**.

你们回答不了他所提出的问题。

2) 非限定性定语从句

非限定性定语从句与先行词只是一种松散的修饰关系，一般只是补充其意思，即使省略了也不会影响主句意义的完整性；从句前常用逗号分开，从句中的关系代词不能省略。

Helen was much kinder to her youngest child than she was to the others, **which**, of course, **made others jealous**.

海伦对最小的孩子比对别的孩子体贴得多，这当然使别的孩子妒忌。

3 Complete the following sentences by using the appropriate connective words to introduce the relative clauses given in the brackets.

1) Nothing in the world is difficult for one (who, whom) sets his mind to it.

2) The course normally attracts 35 students per year, (of whom, of which) up to half will be from abroad.

3) The students will put off the outing until next week, (when, while) they won't be so busy.

4) The next thing (that, what) you should do is to buy a computer.

5) The car (whose, which) engine broke down was bought last year.

6) Substances (which, who) allow electricity to flow through freely are called conductors.

7) Government reports, examination compositions, legal documents and most business letters are the main types of writings (in which, on which) formal language is used.

8) I don't know the reason (which, why) he came.

9) A desert is a great plain (which, where) nothing will grow.

10) Professor Martin, (who, whose) was always early, was in the office already.

4 Correct the errors in each of the following sentences.

1) All which you have to do is to press the button.

2) The ambassador, which had long been interested in African affairs, was frightened, too.

3) This is the way which she does her hair.

4) Who was the lady which he danced with in the auditorium?

5) His son, to that he had been devoted, was living abroad.

6) The river broadens at its mouth which it meets the sea.

7) I was in the same class with Judy, that I liked a lot.

8) Science plays an important role in the society which we live.

9) This is the pen with that I wrote the letter.

10) Peter, which bicycle you borrowed, is their monitor.

5 **Translate the following sentences into English, paying attention to the use of appropriate relative clauses.**

1) 他是我一生中所见到的最聪明的人。

2) 我总渴望有一天自己能够独立。

3) 我把情况告诉了约翰，他后来又告诉了他的兄弟。

4) 来中国我要参观的第一个地方是北京。

5) 我们把所有的书都还给了图书馆，它们全是用英语写的。

6) 商业广告是我们在看电视时不得不忍受的东西之一。

SECTION III

Data Bank

Here is the Data Bank. Practice the patterns and expressions for making reservations.

Questions	Responses
What can I do for you?	I'd like to make a reservation, please.
May I help you?	I'd like to reserve a single room for one night.
What kind of room do you want / like?	I would like a single room with bath (a balcony, a good view etc.).
How long do you intend / want to stay here?	
May I book a single room in your hotel?	I would like to stay here for two nights.
Could we book two double rooms for this weekend?	We have a double room with bath available.
	We have a single room with a good view for you.
May I reserve a suite on the third floor till Friday?	Sorry, we don't have such a room with a balcony / bath ...
Are there any rooms available tonight?	
Have you got any vacant rooms?	The bellboy will show you to the room.
May I go to my room now?	You may pay by check or in cash.

What is the price of the single room?

What is the room rate per night?

What is the daily price here?

Do I need to send you the deposit?

How would you like to pay, in cash or by credit card?

Would you please fill out this registration form?

Is breakfast included?

Does the charge include everything?

Can I have supper here?

When shall I check out?

What is the check-out time?

Of course we accept traveler's checks.

We would like to pay by credit card.

You must leave a deposit of $30.

I am sorry, sir. All our rooms are fully engaged / occupied.

Fifty dollars a night, including breakfast.

The charge includes only the bed and breakfast.

You can have supper here. The dining room is open until midnight.

You may check out before 2:00 p.m.

Unit 2   At a Restaurant

Unit Goals

❖ What You Should Learn to Know About

1. Western and Chinese food
2. The way to make a toast speech at a wedding
3. Adverbial clause

SECTION I

Maintaining a Sharp Eye

Read More by Yourself

Eating Out

外出吃饭

It would be interesting to know what Americans eat at home, but the information probably would not tell us very much. The **population** of the country is so **varied** and there are such different **traditions** in different parts of the world that we would probably find in the country a mixture of diets found everywhere else in the world. Where U.S. eating **habits** have changed, however, and where they have become very similar, is in what happens when people go outside their homes to eat. A recent **survey** tells us a lot about the restaurant eating habits of Americans.

人口

多样的；传统

习惯

调查

The people of the United States eat out often. In an average month, 98 **percent** of U.S. families eat at least one meal in some kind of restaurant, and most families eat out over nine times a week. Although not all of the meals they eat out are **regular meals**—breakfast, lunch, or dinner—that means that people eat over one-third of their meals in restaurants. Can you guess which meal they eat out most often? Not

百分比

正餐

surprisingly, it is lunch. The following list shows how often different meals are eaten in a restaurant:

Lunch	38%
Dinner	30%
Snacks	20%
Breakfast	12%

Where Americans eat is a second interesting question. A real symbol of modern life in the United States is the **fast-food restaurant**—that is, a restaurant where there is usually no service at the table; where you **pick up** your food yourself, sometimes in a car from an outside window; and where the food is often already prepared before you get there. The most popular kind of fast food is the hamburger, and the most popular type of restaurant is the fast-food hamburger restaurant.

A third question is why Americans go out to eat. The answers to this question **depend on** what kind of restaurant they choose. The fast-food restaurant seems to have replaced a lot of home meals, and people eat at them for **convenience**. Most Americans say that they eat out in fast-food restaurants in order to avoid having to cook. Another reason is that they can eat quickly. Although there are still a lot of full-service restaurants, people go to them mostly to **celebrate** special **occasions**, such as birthdays and **anniversaries**, and simply to relax. The relaxing experience makes full-service restaurants very different from fast-food restaurants, where eating fast food is just that—fast.

The United States is certainly a restaurant society, but we may ask whether the restaurants are actually that good or whether eating in them is healthy. They must be good because they are very popular, but a look at the food that people order shows that fried foods and soft drinks are their greatest **preference**. Since we know that too much fat and sugar is not healthy, it appears that Americans would rather eat their fast food than be healthy.

令人吃惊地

小吃

快餐店
拿走

依靠

方便

庆祝；场合
周年纪念

偏爱

1 **Read the passage and check your understanding by doing the multiple choice exercises.**

1) People in the United States _____.
   a. have different traditions   b. have similar eating habits
   c. always eat at home   d. always eat in restaurants

2) Nearly all the people of the United States eat out _____.
   a. once a week   b. once a month
   c. nine times a week   d. nine times a month

3) In a fast-food restaurant you can _____.
    a. call for a waiter to serve you   b. buy your food from an outside window
    c. make a reservation one day earlier   d. enjoy service at any time

4) What's the main reason for Americans to go out to eat?
    a. They can meet with many friends.   b. They can have cheaper food there.
    c. They can save time by not cooking.   d. They can avoid washing dishes after the meal.

5) Which of the following statements is True?
    a. Americans like to eat healthy food in a restaurant.
    b. Americans find fast food more delicious.
    c. Fried foods and soft drinks are Americans' favorite foods.
    d. Fast food is both healthy and convenient.

2 Choose the proper word or phrase in the box to fill in the blank in each of the following sentences, changing the form if necessary.

habit	surprisingly	at least	celebrate	similar
percent	pick up	appear	regular	convenience

1) The four restaurants are all serving _____ food at the similar prices.
2) They have a(n) _____ of having lunch together twice a week.
3) He is a heavy drunker and drinks _____ half a bottle of whisky a day.
4) You need to take _____ exercises to keep fit.
5) Not _____, the suggestion has been accepted by the teacher.
6) Now only ten _____ of their salary is spent on food and clothes.
7) I might get my brother to come and _____ my son.
8) The company _____ its fiftieth anniversary now.
9) Americans eat in a fast food restaurant mainly for their _____.
10) Currently he often _____ in the TV series "Funny Man".

3 Put the following sentences into English, using the words and expressions given in the brackets.

1) 他们的胜利是用音乐和舞蹈来庆贺的。(celebrate)
2) 住在这座楼里真是太方便了。(convenience)
3) 我使用自己的符号来表示练习中的"正误"。(symbol)
4) 会议成功与否主要取决于主席工作效率的高低。(depend on)
5) 被损坏的书将被更换。(replace)
6) 我们每个人都有各自对于某种娱乐形式的偏爱。(preference)

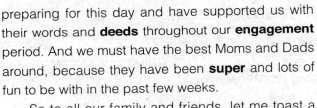

Toasts at Parties

1) A Bride's Sincere Thanks to Her Friends at the Wedding Party

My friends,

There are really no words to **adequately express** my appreciation for all that has been said and done here today, and over the many years I've known most of you. So let me just say "Thank you".

I see so many good friends here today. It is so special for you to be here with Peter and me on our wedding day. It makes this day more meaningful to see ones who have helped us along the way in our growing-up years. There have been so many times when a word of **encouragement** was spoken, a hand offered, a bit of advice given when it was most needed. There is no way to repay this kindness. We can only offer our love back to you as freely as it was given to us.

Peter's and my families have been the best source of help in preparing for this day and have supported us with their words and **deeds** throughout our **engagement** period. And we must have the best Moms and Dads around, because they have been **super** and lots of fun to be with in the past few weeks.

So to all our family and friends, let me toast a sincere and loving gratitude.

2) Toast at a Business Party

Ladies and gentlemen,

We have asked you to come to our "Thank-you" party today to show our gratitude to all of you for being our **reliable** business **partners**.

As you all know, doing business is not an easy thing. There may be different ways of doing business: some do it for an endless **pursuit** of profit, and others, for the well-being of society. One thing, however, that we should not forget in doing business is to have a sense of appreciation. A sense of **regret** or **resentment** will not help us in any way. Having a sense of appreciation for all the people will keep us going on well in business.

That is why we have asked you to come tonight. We really appreciate your being our partners. And I hope you have a good time tonight.

Let me **propose** a toast to a **prosperous** business.

充分地；表达

鼓励

行为；订婚

极好的

可靠的；伙伴

追求

遗憾；怨恨

提议；繁荣的

4 **Are the following statements true or false according to the passage? Write T or F accordingly.**

☞ 1) Most of the people at the wedding party know the bride well.

☞ 2) The bride doesn't know what to say to express adequately her gratitude to the guests.

☞ 3) Peter is a friend of the bride's.

☞ 4) Both families have given the couple strong support for the marriage.

☞ 5) The business party is given to celebrate the company's successful operation.

☞ 6) Everybody can be successful in doing business.

☞ 7) The purpose for doing business is not only to make profit.

☞ 8) The speaker thinks having a sense of appreciation is very important in doing business.

5 **Fill in the blank with the right form of the word provided at the end of each sentence.**

1) Because there is _____ rainfall in that area, the trees there are growing well. (adequately)

2) He phoned his wife to remind her of their lunch _____. (engage)

3) We are _____ informed that her new record will be released in the autumn. (reliable)

4) I should say I _____ your service very much. (appreciation)

5) During that period they devoted themselves to an _____ search for new supplies. (end)

6) These rules were _____ designed to protect travelers. (special)

7) Tom's father always _____ him to make new progress in his study. (encouragement)

8) He is a good boss and treats his workers with _____ and understanding. (kind)

9) Nobody has ever explained electricity to me in a _____ way. (meaning)

10) Since my sister has been studying French for 3 years, she can now _____ herself quite clearly in French. (expression)

6 **Translate the following sentences into Chinese.**

1) There are really no words to adequately express my appreciation for all that has been said and done here today.

2) It makes this day more meaningful to see ones who have helped us along the way in our growing up years.

3) There have been so many times when a word of encouragement was spoken, a hand offered, a bit of advice given when it was most needed.

4) And we must have the best Moms and Dads around, because they have been super and lots of fun to be with in the past few weeks.

5) We have asked you to come to our "Thank-you" party today to show our gratitude to all of you for being our reliable business partners.

6) One thing, however, that we should not forget in doing business is to have a sense of appreciation.

7) Having a sense of appreciation for all the people will keep us going on well in business.

8) Let me propose a toast to a prosperous business.

SECTION II

Trying Your Hand

Write More by Yourself

A. **Applied Writing: Menu**
    Sample 1

Abernethy's

1246 W. Davenport

Dinner time: 5:30-10:30, Tuesday-Saturday

245-2886 for reservation

Soup

Homemade, piping hot & delicious

Cup .... $ 1.50   Bowl .... $ 2.00

Salads

Chef's Salad $ 3.95

Tossed green salad with slices of Cheddar and

Swiss cheese, thinly sliced turkey and ham

House Salad $ 2.25

Sliced tomato and alfalfa sprouts top this salad

Choice of dressing

Wines

We are proud of our fine selection of distinctive domestic and imported wines. Please consult

our wine list.

Dinners

Served with salad, vegetables, and a variety of breads from our kitchen.

Chicken Teriyaki $ 5.59

Maintained in a mild sauce and char-broiled.

Filet of Fish $ 5.59

Halibut seasoned with garlic and herbs and Served with our own sauce.

Top Sirloin and Shrimp	$ 10.59
The best of both worlds.	
Prime Rib	$ 12.59
Our famous prime rib, tender and juicy.	

Desserts

Lemon cheesecake	$ 1.75
Buttermilk chocolate Pie	$ 1.50

Sample 2

Breakfast

3-pancakes .... $ 1.40	hot cereal ...... $ 0.85	toast .... $ 0.15
1-egg .... $ 0.50	yogurt .... $ 0.35	muffin .... $ 0.65
2-eggs .... $ 0.80	fruit salad ...... $ 0.60	sweet breads ..... $ 0.60
3-bacon strips .... $ 1.30		

Hours

Mon. — Fri. 6:30 a.m. to 9 p.m.   Saturday: 7 a.m. to 9 p.m.

(Breakfast until 10:30 a.m.)   (Breakfast until noon)

Expression Tips

Words and expressions used in restaurants	
Kinds of food	
main dish 主菜	dessert 甜点
soups 汤类	Chef's special 大厨特色菜
salad 色拉	cold dishes 冷盘
Drinks and beverages	
soft drinks 饮料	Martini 马提尼
soda water 汽水	Whisky 威士忌
mineral water 矿泉水	Sherry 雪莉
orange juice 橘汁	brandy 白兰地
soy milk 豆奶	champagne 香槟

light drinks 低度酒

strong drinks 高度酒

black beer 黑啤酒

draft beer 生啤酒

red wine 红葡萄酒

gin 杜松子酒

cocktail 鸡尾酒

About cooking

tender 嫩的

rare 三分熟的

medium rare 七分熟的

well-done 熟透的

soft-boiled 煮得半熟的

underdone 不熟的

overcooked 烹煮过头的

About taste

sour 酸的

sweet 甜的

bitter 苦的

spicy / hot 辣的

salty 咸的

weak 淡的

light 清淡的

fragrant 香的

delicious 可口的

fishy 腥的

rich 油腻的

tasty 味道好的

tasteless 没味道的

crisp 脆的

Kinds of eating places

café 咖啡店

snack bar 小吃店

fast-food restaurant 快餐店

bakery 面包店

tavern 酒店

ice cream parlor 冰淇淋店

pizzeria 比萨饼店

drive-through restaurant 免下车餐厅

Table-ware

knife 餐刀

fork 叉子

table spoon 汤匙

tea spoon 茶匙

cup / glass / bowl 杯 / 玻璃杯 / 碗

chopsticks 筷子

napkin 餐巾

tooth pick 牙签

plate 盘子

1 **Translate the following menu into Chinese. Refer to the samples and the Expression Tips for reference.**

Golden Dragon Restaurant

- Famed for its Chinese food with special strong drinks.
- All the dishes served to everyone's taste.

● Free salad or desserts after 4 main dishes.

       Open: 11:30 a. m. to 11:00 p. m.

       Orders go to: 233-9768

       Address: 325 Cart Avenue

2 **Translate the following sentences into Chinese.**

1) Which do you prefer, coffee or milk?
2) Could I offer you another help of roast duck?
3) Some Chinese people like to start their meal with soup.
4) You have to serve yourself in a fast-food restaurant.
5) That restaurant will prepare special orders for customers on request.

B. **Sentence Writing: Adverbial Clause 状语从句**

    用作状语的从句称为状语从句；它在句中的位置比较灵活，可以放在主句之前或之后，偶尔也可插在主句之中。状语从句由从属连词引导，不同的连词引出不同的状语从句。

状语从句的分类及形式

	用法	常用连词	例句
1	表示时间	when (当…时候) while (当…时候) as (当…时候) till (until) (一直到…为止) whenever (无论何时) since (自从…以来) after (…之后) before (…之前) by the time that (到了…时候…) not ... long before (…不久，就…)	She began to watch TV *after she had finished her homework.* 她做完作业后，才开始看电视。 *When it rains*, I usually go to school by bus. 天下雨时，我通常乘公共汽车上学。 Don't go *before I come back.* 别在我回来之前走掉。 Let's wait *until (till) the rain stops.* 我们等到雨停了再说。
		hardly / scarcely / barely ... when (before) / no sooner ... than (一…就) as soon as / directly (when) / immediately (when/ after) / the moment (that) / the instant (that) / the minute (that) (一…就) every time（每次）	*No sooner had they reached the top of the hill than* they all sat down to rest. 他们刚一到山顶就都坐下来休息。 *The moment you hear the news*, give me a call. 你一听到消息就给我打电话。 *Every time she came to the city* she would visit her old friends. 她每次来到城里都要去看看她那些老朋友。

2	表示地点	where (在…地方) whenever (无论哪里) everywhere (that) (无论…地方) anywhere (that) (无论…地方)	I'm finding oil for my motherland. ***Where there is oil***, my home is there. 我为祖国献（找）石油，哪里有石油，哪里就是我的家。 ***Wherever I am***, I will be thinking of you. 无论我在哪里，我都会想着你。
3	表示条件	if (如果，假如) unless (除非，如果不) as (so) long as (只要) in case (假如，一旦) if only (只要) on condition that (只要，假如) suppose (that) / supposing (that) / provided (that) / providing (that) （假如）	***If you are going to visit any foreign country***, you will need a passport. 如果你要到任何一个外国去旅行,都需要一本护照。 You can't learn English well ***unless you work hard.*** 除非你努力学习，否则是学不好英语的。
4	表示原因	because (因为) as (因为) for (因为，既然) since (因为，既然) now that (既然) considering that (既然) seeing that (鉴于) in that (因为)	***As they live in the countryside***, they can enjoy fresh air. 因为他们住在乡下，便可享受新鲜的空气。 ***Seeing that you are inexperienced***, you are not fit for the work. 鉴于你没有经验,你不适合干这份工作。
5	表示原因	so that (因而，因此，所以，结果) so ... that (这样…以致，因而，因此) such ... that (这样…以致，如此…以致) that (因而，因此)	You went early, ***so that you finished your work on time.*** 你们去得早，因此按时完成了工作。 The chief executive gave us such an excellent lecture ***that we'll never forget it.*** 总裁给我们做了一次非常精彩的演讲，我们永远也不会忘记。
6	表示比较	The ... the ... (越…越，愈…愈…) than (比…) as ... as (和…一样，像…一样) not so (as) ... as (不及…，不如…，不像)	***The greater*** the degree of industrialization in a country, ***the higher*** the standard of living. 一个国家工业化程度愈高，生活水平则愈高。 This work is ***more*** difficult ***than*** we thought. 这项工作比我们想的还要艰巨。

7	表示方式	as (像，照，如) just as ... so (正像，正如，犹如) as if (as though) (好像，仿佛，犹如，像…一样) according as (依照)	Air is to man *as water is to fish.* 空气之于人，犹水之于鱼。 I remember the whole thing *as if it happened yesterday.* 整个事情我都记得，就像昨天发生的一样。
8	表示目的	1. 表示"肯定目的" that (so that, in order that) ... may (might) (为了…，以便…)	They should do their utmost *in order that they may be able to over-fulfill the task.* 为了超额完成任务，他们应该全力以赴。
		2. 表示"否定目的" lest (for fear that, in case that) ... should (以免，唯恐，为了不)	Batteries must be kept in dry places *lest electricity should leak away.* 电池应放在干燥的地方，以免漏电。
9	表示让步	although (though) (虽然) as (尽管，虽然) even if (even though) (即使) however (尽管) whatever (不管) no matter (how, what, where, when) (不管怎样，什么，哪里，何时) whether ... or (不管)	We need to check the information, *though we think it is correct.* 我们需要核对这条信息,尽管我们相信它是正确的。 *However hard she tried*, she never seems able to do the work satisfactorily. 尽管她做出了努力，但她似乎从来未能够令人满意地完成任务。

3 **Complete the following sentences by choosing the appropriate conjunction for each of the adverbial clauses given in the brackets.**

1) The old gentleman was run down by a taxi (where, while) he was crossing the street.
2) These two areas are similar (in that, as long as) they both have a high rainfall during this season.
3) We'll visit Western Europe next year (so that, provided that) we have enough money.
4) Please take an umbrella with you (now that, lest) you should be caught in the rain.
5) The book disappointed me. It was not half so good (as, than) I had expected.
6) (Wherever, However) the criminal may hide, the police will seek him out.
7) (Although, When) I find the problems very difficult, I don't think they can't be solved.
8) I'm sure he is up to the job (if only, in case) he would pay attention to it.
9) (As soon as, So long as) he works hard, I don't mind when he finishes the experiment.
10) Recently, more schools have been set up (so that, even since) more children will be able to go to school.

4 **Correct the errors in the following sentences.**

1) As young she is, it is natural for her to commit such a mistake.
2) It won't be long after we work out a plan to promote our sales.

3) Where we do a job, we should see it through to the end.

4) Since your body temperature has risen to 40 degrees now, nothing is more essential as lying quietly in bed.

5) All kinds of technical training courses are offered in order to the workers can attend them during their spare time.

6) Nowadays, young people prefer to study more than one foreign language so that they should need them after graduation.

7) "What a beautiful day!"— "Yes, it's such a nice day so that I'd like to take a walk."

8) He makes a note of the assignment so he forgets it.

5 **Translate the following sentences into English, paying attention to the adverbial clauses.**

1) 由于所有的座位都占了，他只好站着。

2) 人们直到失去健康的时候，才意识到健康的可贵。

3) 我与其同意被调动，不如放弃我的工作。

4) 因为钱不够，所以我们什么东西也没买。

5) 一旦机器发生故障，就把开关关上。

6) 他们上个月来看我们，可是在我们见面之前已经有两年没见面了。

SECTION III

Data Bank

Here is the Data Bank. Practice the patterns and expressions for eating out at a restaurant.

Making reservations

I want to make a reservation for six people at 7 o'clock this evening.
我想订一桌今晚7点6个人的晚餐。

I'd like to reserve a table for Friday, Sep. 6 at noon.
我想订一桌9月6日周五的午餐。

I wish to book a table for tomorrow evening at 8 o'clock.
我想订一桌明晚8点的晚餐。

I'd like to reserve a table for tonight. Will you put me as close as possible to the stage, please?
我想订一桌今天的晚餐。你能给我留一张靠近舞台的桌子吗？

We'd like a table, please. 我们要订一桌酒席。

I haven't made any reservation, but do you have a table for me? 我没有预定，还有空桌吗？

We have reservations under the name of Mike. 我们以麦克的名义订了一桌酒席。

I would prefer a table near the window. 我想要一张靠窗的桌子。

Do you have a table for three? 还有三人吃饭的桌子吗?

Is this table available? 这张桌子空着吗?

Taking order

What will you have? 您要点儿什么?

May I take your order? 您现在要点菜吗?

Are you ready to order now, sir? 您现在可以点菜了吗?

What are you going to have? 您要点什么?

What would you like for lunch? 您午餐吃什么?

What would you like for your main dish? 您主菜吃什么?

How would you like your steak? 牛排怎么做,嫩点儿还是老点儿?

Do you want to order your dessert now? 您现在就点甜点吗?

Anything for dessert now, sir? 现在要甜点吗,先生?

Would you like your coffee now? 现在要咖啡吗?

Anything to drink? 您喝点儿什么?

Can I bring you anything else? 再给您来点儿什么?

Would you like something to drink? 您喝点儿什么?

Anything else? 还要其他的吗?

Which do you prefer, meat or fish? 您喜欢什么,肉还是鱼?

Ordering food

May I have the menu, please? 给我看一下菜单,好吗?

Take our order, please. 我们要点菜。

Is there a menu? 有菜单吗?

I'd like to see the menu, please. 我想看一下菜单。

What do you recommend? 您推荐什么菜?

What do you suggest? 您推荐什么菜?

What's your special today? 你们今天的特色菜是什么?

I don't know anything about American food. Would you give me a suggestion? 我对美国菜一无所知。给我推荐一下好吗?

I'll have green salad and fried chicken. 我点蔬菜色拉和炸鸡。

I'd rather have beef. 我要牛肉。

Do you have any Chinese food? 你这有中餐吗?

A well-done beefsteak, please. 一份全烂的牛排。

I'd like to try some Shanghai food. What's your recommendation? 我想尝一尝上海菜。你推荐点什么?

I want coffee with dessert. 我要咖啡和甜点。

I'd like the vegetable soup, please. 我要蔬菜汤。

What kind of pie do you have? 你们有什么饼？

I'll have a soup later. 我一会再要汤。

I'd like to change the soup you recommended me. 请把你推荐的汤换一下。

Make me a chocolate milk shake. 我来一份巧克力牛奶饮料。

I'd like some fried sausages if you have any. 我要一份炸香肠，有吗？

I think I'll start with soup. 我先来点儿汤。

Making recommendation

Will you try sea-food? 您来点儿海鲜吗？

How about the Chef's Steak Special? 来点主厨的牛排特色菜怎么样？

Fried shrimps and roast beef are the specialty of the house. 炸虾和烤牛肉是本店的特色菜。

I'd like to suggest your trying some sea-food. 我建议您来点儿海鲜。

Would you like to try some Chinese food? 您要尝一尝中餐吗？

Have you ever tried Beijing Roast Duck? 您吃过北京烤鸭吗？

Would you care for some wine with your dinner? 您晚餐来点酒吗？

I would recommend chicken soup with vegetables and mushrooms. 我向您推荐蔬菜香菇鸡汤。

Unit 3 Shopping and Sightseeing

Unit Goals

❖ **What You Should Learn to Know About**

1. Shopping online
2. Tourist attractions
3. Present participle and past participle as att-ributive

SECTION I

Maintaining a Sharp Eye

Read More by Yourself

Home Shopping TV Networks: the Wave of the Future?

Have you ever watched a home shopping program on TV? Can you **describe** what it's like to shop at home by television? Have you ever had to decide whether to go shopping or stay home and watch TV on a weekend? Now you can do both at the same time. Home shopping television networks have become a way for many people to shop without ever having to leave their homes.

Some shoppers are tired of department stores and shopping malls— fighting the crowds, waiting in long lines, and sometimes not even finding anything they want to buy. They'd rather sit quietly at home in front of the TV set and watch a friendly **announcer** describe an **item** while a model **displays** it. And they can shop **around the clock, purchasing** an item simply by making a phone call and charging it to a credit card. Home shopping networks understand

描述

解说员；产品
展示；昼夜不
停；购买

the power of an enthusiastic host, the **glamour** of **celebrity** guests **endorsing** their products, and the emotional pull of a bargain.

魅力；名人；认可

Major fashion designers, department stores, and even mail-order catalogue companies are eager to join in the success of home shopping. Large department stores are experimenting with their own TV channels, and some **retailers** are planning to introduce **interactive** TV shopping in the future. Then, viewers will be able to communicate with their own personal shoppers, asking questions about products and placing orders, all through their TV sets.

零售商；互动的

Will shopping by television replace shopping in stores? Some industry executives claim that home shopping networks represent the "electronic shopping mall of the future." Yet for many people, going out and shopping at a real store is a way to relax and even be **entertained**. And for many shoppers, it is still important to touch or try on items they want to buy. That's why experts say that in the future, home shopping will exist alongside store shopping but will never entirely replace it.

款待

1 **Read the passage carefully and complete the outline of the passage.**

  I. Advantages and disadvantages of store shopping
  Advantages:
  a. a way to _____ and to _____
  b. _____ and try on items
  Disadvantages:
  a. _____ the crowd
  b. waiting _____
  c. _____ nothing to buy

  II. Advantages and disadvantages of home shopping TV Networks
  Advantages:
  a. _____ at home and _____ in front of the TV set instead of going to stores
  b. watch the product _____ by an announcer and _____ by a model
  c. shop around the clock by making a _____ and charging it to a _____
  Disadvantages:
  a. unable to _____ and try on items
  b. have no _____ to relax and to _____ in store shopping

  III. The future of home shopping TV Networks
    a. offer _____ between customers and their own shoppers through TV _____
    b. will represent _____ in the future
    c. will never entirely replace _____

2 Choose the proper word or phrase in the box to fill in the blank in each of the following sentences, making changes if necessary.

around the clock	in line	shop	bargain	place an order
experiment with	network	go out	alongside	credit card

1) Many computer applications rely on the _____ of computers.

2) The children stood _____ until the teacher said they could move.

3) People with very important jobs sometimes have to work _____.

4) Mrs. May is out _____, so we can be left alone for some time.

5) He made a _____ with his wife: "You cook and I'll wash up".

6) Over 75 million Americans use _____ to pay for everything from tickets on American Airlines to AAA car rental.

7) Please _____ and tell the children to make less noise.

8) That man _____ dyes to get the color he wants .

9) "Mariculture" — farming the ocean's food resources — will take its place _____ "Agriculture".

10) This country _____ $2 billion _____ with the Boeing Company for 40 new medium-sized airliners.

3 Translate the following sentences into English.

1) 整天坐办公室，我早就厌倦了。

2) 对消费者来说，信用卡允许他们即使存款很少，仍可以购买商品及享受服务。

3) 如果"信用卡付款"这几个字听着耳熟，那不足为怪。

4) 要是她参加进来，这场辩论就更热闹了。

5) 我渴望去贵校深造。

Summer in London

When most people think of London, they think of Big Ben, Westminster Abbey and Trafalgar Square. But there is much, much more to London than these tourist **landmarks**. This is especially true during the summer months, when the usual "menu" of museums and theatres is **enriched** by a number of special events and exhibitions.

著名景物
使丰富

One place literature lovers should not miss is Charles Dickens' House in Doughty Street, a short walk away from the British Museum. You can wander through Dickens dining room, bedroom and **drawing-room** to the small study where the great English writer wrote *Pickwick Papers* and *Oliver Twist*, two of his most famous novels. The house also has a collection

客厅

of Dickens' **manuscripts** and letters. | 手稿

Another interesting spot for culture hunters is Shakespeare's Globe Theatre Exhibition on the south bank of the Thames. Visitors can **explore** the **fascinating** world of 17th-century theater, through manuscripts, drawings and **costumes** dating back to the Elizabethan period. | 探求 迷人的 服饰

If you're a lover of British beer, make sure that you're in Olympia, West London, from 1 to 5 August, for the "Great British Beer Festival", when more than 300 traditional British beers, also called "**real ales**", will be poured into thousands of **pint** glasses. But be careful, one visit might not be enough! According to Stephen Cox, one of the organizers, "Real ales need to be tasted on different days to be appreciated. The quality, the color, and even the taste of the beer can change from day to day. They are a bit like race horses: performance on the day is **crucial**. " | 正宗麦啤酒 品脱

极重要的

For two days, during the last weekend of August, Notting Hill becomes the scene of one of London's most exciting events — the Notting Hill **Carnival**. The whole area is taken over by this Caribbean carnival in which over 100 **bands** with people in **elaborate** and colorful costumes take to the streets, and thousands of people dance to the sounds of **reggae**, jazz, **hip hop** and house music. | 狂欢节 乐队 精致的

雷盖乐；摇摆乐

If your musical taste is rather more traditional than reggae or hip hop, you shouldn't miss the season of the world-famous BBC **Promenade** Concerts at the Royal Albert Hall. Commonly known as the "Proms", these classical music concerts are performed seven nights a week from the end of July until the middle of September. | 漫步音乐会

If, after literature, beer, carnivals, and classical music, you still want to experience something out of the ordinary, your best bet is to go looking for it yourself. London has thousands of places and events to suit all tastes, just waiting to be discovered. Whoever you are, and whatever you want, you've got a pretty good chance of finding it in London.

☞ **Notes**

1. Big Ben 大本钟（英国议会大厦上的大钟）
2. Westminster Abbey （伦敦）威斯敏斯特教堂（举行国葬之处）
3. Trafalgar Square 特拉法尔加广场（位于英国伦敦威斯敏斯特）
4. Charles Dickens 查尔斯·狄更斯（1812–1870，英国小说家）
5. *Pickwick Papers* 狄更斯的作品《匹克威克外传》
6. *Oliver Twist* 狄更斯的作品《雾都孤儿》

4 **Read the passage carefully and check your understanding by doing the multiple choice exercises.**

1) According to the passage, visitors will have more activities to enjoy _____.
    a. during the summer months
    b. during the golden autumn
    c. during the carnival season
    d. during the musical festivals

2) From Shakespeare's Globe Theatre Exhibition, you can learn about _____.
    a. the costumes in their best forms
    b. the 17th century theatre.
    c. Queen Elizabeth's life
    d. Shakespeare's manuscripts and letters

3) If you're a lover of British beer you must _____.
    a. drink British beer from a pint glass
    b. buy a bottle of real ale
    c. taste the traditional British beers
    d. go to the "Great British Beer Festival"

4) Classical music lovers shouldn't miss _____.
    a. the dances to country music
    b. the exciting events on Notting Hill
    c. the world-famous BBC Promenade Concerts
    d. the Caribbean carnivals

5) What is the passage mainly about?
    a. British Museum and Shakespeare's Globe Theatre Exhibition.
    b. Works written by Charles Dickens.
    c. The entertainments visitors to London may have during the summer.
    d. Big Ben and Trafalgar Square often related to London.

5 **Choose the proper word or phrase in the box to fill in the blank in each of the following sentences, changing the form if necessary.**

miss	study	wander	taste	date back
suit	enrich	from day to day	take over	make sure

1) Peter will _____ my job while I'm on holiday.
2) The weather is unpredictable; it changes _____.
3) John _____ what the professor said about the test because he wasn't listening.
4) My friend Mary has a _____ for music.
5) Many foreign words and phrases have_____ the English language.
6) Last Sunday I ___ through the stores, hoping to get some idea for Julia's birthday present.

7) The painting sent by Mr. Smith now hangs in my _____.

8) He said he knew of a hotel which might _____ our needs.

9) If you are speaking in a business setting, _____ that you organize your thoughts in logical order.

10) This manuscript _____ to the 19th century.

6 **Translate the following sentences into English.**

1) 下星期有一个代表团来考察本市的环境状况。(explore)

2) 那天至少有两千人观看了演出。(at least)

3) 珍妮收集了许多外国硬币。(a collection of)

4) 现在是足球赛季，下个月开始篮球赛季。(season)

5) 这就是昨晚发生事故的现场。(scene)

SECTION II

Trying Your Hand

Write More by Yourself

A. Applied Writing: Shopping and Travel Ads

Sample 1

Minolta AF-E Camera

On your next trip, take along a Minolta AF-E. Auto film loading, auto rewinding and compact design make it the lightweight auto-focus 35mm camera that lets you take high quality pictures with snapshot simplicity.

Sample 2

STUDENT TRAVEL
It's **YOUR** trip
TAKE IT

London .... $ 242

Paris... $ 239

Frankfurt...................................... $ 286

Amsterdam .... $ 258

Madrid .... $ 294

San Jose C. R. .... $ 370

Fares are round-trip.

FIVE-STAR TRAVEL

10 Downing St. 212-325-3411

2381 Broadway, 223-345-1256

30 Third Ave., 212-346-6100

www.statravel.com

Expression Tips

Some expressions and patterns related to CD players and cameras	
CD OPEN	CD门开关
MODE	功能键
PROGRAM	编序键
BASS-BOOST	重低音
SKIP / SEARCH ▐▐/▐▐	快进键/快退键
BATTERY COMPARTMENT	电池盒
STOP ■	停止播放
PHONE	耳机插座
LINE OUT	线路输出
DC 4.5V ⊙--⊙-- ⊙	直流电源插孔
PLAY ▐▶ +	放音键
PAUSE ▐▐	暂停键
VIEWFINDER WINDOW	取景孔
BACK DOOR	后盖
TRIPOD SOCKET	三脚架插口
LENS COVER SWITCH	镜头盖开关
FILM COUNTOR	胶片计数器
FLASH READY INDICATOR	闪光灯就绪指示灯
AUTO FILM REWIND BUTTON	自动回卷键
FLASH	闪光灯
SHUTTER BUTTON	快门键
GLASS LENS	镜头
AUTO FOCUS	自动聚焦
Facilities and services in hotels	
restaurant / café	餐厅/咖啡厅

conference room	会议室
gift shop	礼品店
game room	游戏室
guest lounge	酒廊
business center	商务中心
outdoor swimming pool	室外游泳池
check-in	办理入住登记
check-out	办理离店手续
reservation service	预订服务
free breakfast	免费早餐
wake-up call	叫醒服务
fax service	代客传真
laundry service	代客洗衣
car rentals	租车服务
free shuttle service	免费机场接送

1 Translate the following advertisement into Chinese, using the samples and the expressions in the Expression Tips for reference.

CANON ESO Camera

The latest ESO-IN RS camera enables professional photographers to precisely catch the significant moment, with a constantly visible viewfinder image and an ultra-fast continuous shooting speed of up to 10 pictures per second.

2 Translate the captions of the following famous landmarks into Chinese.

1) The Great Wall of China was constructed in 214 B.C. It's the longest structure ever built in the world.

2) The Taj Mahal (泰姬陵) in India was built between 1630 and 1652. It's a tomb for the wife of an Indian Prince.

3) The Eiffel Tower in Paris was completed in 1889. It was built for the 100th anniversary of the French Revolution.

B. Sentence Writing: Present Participle and Past Participle as Attributives 分词作定语

分词是一种非限定动词。分词分为现在分词 (V-ing) 和过去分词 (V-ed) 。现在分词作定语表示主动和未完成含意，而过去分词则表示被动和完成含意。

1. 分词作定语时，可以置于所修饰的名词之前，表示此名词具有某种特性，此时分词的作用更像形容词。如：

a freezing wind 刺骨寒风   frozen food 冷冻食品

a recorded talk 谈话录音   a recording machine (正在) 录音的机器

the spoken English 英语口语   a singing bird 唱歌的小鸟

a lost career 失败的事业   a losing battle 打不赢的战斗

2. 当分词处于所修饰的名词之后作其定语时，则更强调分词的行为动作含意，而不是属性含意。如：

the only ticket left 剩下的最后一张票

the high score just obtained 刚刚获得的高分

the people singing 在唱歌的人

the people questioned 被询问的人

3 Complete the following sentences using the correct forms of the words given in the brackets.

1) Could you see the flowers _____ (nod) gently in the wind?

2) Her job was to take care of the _____ (wound) soldier.

3) The performance they saw last night was an _____ (excite) one.

4) Having heard the news she had a _____ (please) look on her face.

5) Mr. Smith asked Peter to present his _____ (write) report soon.

6) Professor Green wonders if there is anything _____ (plan) for tonight.

7) Here is a TV Guide _____ (give) you all the programs for the next week.

8) There are more than ten thousand students _____ (study) in this university.

9) The bookstore will deliver the books _____ (order) by Mr. Black tomorrow.

10) Mr. Knight gave a _____ (satisfy) smile when he received my term paper.

4 Correct the errors in the following sentences.

1) The government plans to build a highway led into the mountains.

2) She didn't notice the surprising look on his face when he arrived here.

3) The experience gaining will be of great value to us.

4) All students concerning are asked to be present at the meeting.

5) This is a market where only using cars are sold.

6) All the textbooks using at this university are the latest editions.

7) He is a historian (历史学家) studied the history of Ming Dynasty.

8) The children played outside made so much noise.

9) The boy didn't like his room painting light blue.

10) There is a bus run between our school and the railway station.

5 **Translate the following sentences into English, paying attention to the difference between the present participle and the past participle.**

1) 她不喜欢这位年轻作者的新著作。
2) 坐在我父母中间的那个年轻人是一位画家。
3) 他注意到母亲眼中流露出的关切的神情。
4) 使用前请阅读盒子上的说明。
5) 所有与此事有牵连的人都受到了询问。
6) 我看到她脖子上带了一串珍珠。

SECTION III

Data Bank

Here is the Data Bank. Practice the patterns and expressions for talking about invitations.

What can I do for you? 您想买点什么？

I need a handbag. 我要买一只手提包。

Can I help you? 您要买点什么？

I'd like to buy some real Chinese souvenirs for my relatives and friends. 我想为我的亲戚和朋友买一些真正的中国纪念品。

We deal in TV sets, radios and the like. 我们经营电视机、收音机以及诸如此类的商品。

Shall we look round first? 我们先四处看看好吗？

How much is it? 要多少钱？

It would only cost you five yuan. 只要五块钱。

May I have a look at that set of china cups? 我可以看看那套瓷杯吗？

Can you come down a bit? 你能便宜一点吗？

That's our rock bottom price. 这是我们的最低价。

You can't be wrong on that. 这个价你不会吃亏的。

That's rather more than I was thinking of giving. 这可比我想出的价高得多。

OK. Let't call it a deal. 好吧，成交了。

Good! I'll take this one. 好的，这一个我买下了。

Here is your receipt. 给您收据。

Do you need anything else? 您还想买点什么吗？

Good-bye. Please drop in again. 再见！下次请再光临。

What's the city famous for? 这座城市有什么东西出名？

Can you show me some of the attractions here? 你能带我们游览这里的旅游景点吗？

I've never seen a garden/waterfall/mountain like that before. 我从未见过这么美丽的花园/瀑布/大山。

The Great Wall is a truly man-made wonder. 万里长城真是人造奇迹。

What a vast lake. The water extends as far as the eye can reach. 多大的湖啊，一望无际。

Unit 4

Keeping Healthy and Seeing a Doctor

Unit Goals

❖ What You Should Learn to Know About

1. Medical advances — body organ implantation
2. Traditional Chinese Medicine
3. Use of conjunctions

SECTION I

Maintaining a Sharp Eye

Read More by Yourself

PASSAGE I

Who Could We Turn to for Help?

I have been living in the past 7 years with a son that is not the son he once was. He survived a skull **injury** and was in a **coma.** He has his **intelligence** that still exists, but he is **limited** physically as to what he can do. He can no longer talk, and he uses a computer with a voice **attachment** to get his ideas across. He can no longer eat anything by mouth; he has a feeding **tube** placed in his **stomach.** He can no longer walk and is in a wheelchair for most of the day.

We are supposed to have **caregivers** to help us look after him, but that is a laugh. No one is ever **committed** to coming on a regular **basis.** We have them for a while, and then they "burn out." His care is constant; he needs someone with him 24 hours

受伤；昏迷；智力

受限制的

附件

管子；胃

护理员

承担义务的
基础

a day. He tells me **via** his computer that the food I am cooking smells so good, he wishes he could eat. He also longs to be able to talk and tells me he misses being able to be in a conversation with people. None of his "friends" come over; they cannot "handle" how he is. They say "it makes me feel so bad to see him like that."

通过

I have been advised to find a support group where I can air my **emotional** needs, but I have searched and there are none out there. None of the groups have anyone that is of my son's kind. Most of the people with brain injuries have made gains and are able to talk or eat, even if they are in a wheelchair. My son is not of that kind. It breaks my heart to see him day after day struggling to do things that most people take for granted. All of the family have hoped and prayed for the past years. Who could we turn to for help?

感情的

1 **Read the passage carefully and check your understanding by making the correct choices.**

1) Now the writer's son is able to _____.
   a. talk through an artificial mouth   b. walk slowly around the house
   c. eat with his father's help   d. communicate by using a computer

2) What did the writer say about the caregivers?
   a. Their patience soon got exhausted.   b. The food they cook smelled delicious.
   c. They felt so bad to see the son like that.   d. They didn't know how to handle the son.

3) What was the family advised to do?
   a. To check the Internet for relevant cases.   b. To turn to a support group for emotional needs.
   c. To consult other patients for useful advice.   d. To talk with other patient who made gains.

4) What is the tone of the writer ?
   a. Impatient.   b. Optimistic.
   c. Helpless.   d. Angry.

2 **Choose the proper word or phrase in the table to fill in the blank in each of the following sentences, making changes when necessary.**

burn out	commit to	even if	for a while	gains	get ... across	limit to
no longer	on the basis of	once	pray for	turn to	take for granted	via

1) Most of his time _____ his experiments on drugs to cure AIDS.
2) The most important thing in communication is to _____ your ideas clearly.
3) She'd keep her promise _____ it's very hard for her to do so.
4) The heads of the two countries exchanged their views _____ mutual understanding.
5) Chinese medicine is no longer as difficult to prepare as it _____ was.

6) Now I still keep in touch with my friends in Australia _____ e-mail.

7) You have to wait _____ for the tea to brew before you drink it.

8) To seize the good luck, you should do something instead of simply _____ it.

9) He _____ depends upon his parents for every decision.

10) Some patients may _____ superstition (迷信) for help when they feel hopeless.

11) One can not enjoy the true value of life if he takes everything _____.

12) Does the proverb "No sweat, no sweet" mean "No pains, no _____"?

13) The speed of cars _____ 60 kilometers per hour.

14) The soil may _____ under constant heavy cropping.

3 Fill in the blanks with the right form of the word provided at the end of each sentence.

1) Thank you for being so _____. I do appreciate all the _____ you've given to me. (help)

2) The mother selects _____ carefully to _____ her baby. (food)

3) Don't _____ the poor girl. Your _____ may hurt her. (laugh)

4) Bob does everything with _____ while his _____ brother never does anything _____. (care)

5) She is fond of _____. And everything _____ by her is enjoyed heartily by her friends. (cook)

6) When I smelt something _____, the cake had already been _____ black. (burn)

7) Human beings are _____ creatures. That's why _____ quotient (情商) is believed to be very important. (emotion)

PASSAGE II

His Life Continued

February 28, 1999 marks the day that an **organ transplant** from a legally **brain-dead donor** was **performed** for the first time in Japan. After two rounds of **legal** tests by **licensed** doctors under the Organ Transplant Law, a patient from Kochi was **diagnosed** as brain dead.

But although this case was a first for Japan, it was not the first **involving** a Japanese person. For Taigen Chiba, 64, a **jewelry dealer** in Tokyo, the Kochi organ transplant case brings back **vivid** memories of his eldest son. In March 1987, his son Genzan, 23, lost **consciousness** after breaking his **skull** in an **accidental** fall from a **dormitory** window while studying in the United States. When he failed to recover, doctors **declared** him brain dead five days after the accident. They gave his father a 20-minute explanation of brain death.

Chiba knew nothing about brain death or transplants at the time, but offered to donate his son's organs. His wife agreed with the decision. As a result, his son's heart, **liver**, **kidneys** and eyes were given to six seriously ill patients **respectively**.

器官移植
脑死亡捐献者；
进行；法律的；
有执照的；诊断

涉及；珠宝商
人；栩栩如生
意识
头颅；意外的；
宿舍
宣布

肝脏；肾脏
分别地

After returning home, Chiba received a letter from a U.S. transplant officer, who said that his son's gift had saved six persons — Genzan, the young man, actually continued his life in other people's lives. Although Genzan had never spoken about organ donation, Chiba is certain that his son would have been happy to help others.

Chiba said the family of the brain-dead patient in Kochi must be **overcome** with sadness, just as he was. He also **applauded** the deep love and courage of the family, who respected the patient's wishes of donating his organs to those who need them. He went on to say that the **media** should be **considerate** of the family's feelings and should be **extra sensitive** in **covering** the case because of the terrible **pressure** on the family.

Concerned that people are looking at the **issue** only from the view of those in need of organs, Chiba thinks that brain death should not be declared **solely** for the purpose of transplantation. Under the **current system**, brain death is considered a special type of death, rather than simply the end of life. Viewed in this way, few people, he fears, will offer to donate their organs.

击垮；赞颂

媒体；考虑周全
的；额外的；敏感
的；掩盖；压力
担心；事件

单纯地；目前的；
制度

4   **Are the following statements true or false according to the passage? Write T or F accordingly.**

☞ 1) The brain dead young man from Kochi was the first Japanese who donated his organs to others.

☞ 2) Organ transplant from a brain dead person demands extremely strict legal tests.

☞ 3) The organ donation case reminded Chiba of his son who died in 1987 in America.

☞ 4) Chiba's son, Genzan, died immediately after he accidentally broke his skull.

☞ 5) Chiba got to know something about brain-death only after Genzan's accident.

☞ 6) Chiba offered to donate his son's organs because that was Genzan's own will.

☞ 7) In a sense, Genzan's life continued as his donated organs have saved six persons.

☞ 8) Chiba could understand the feelings and emotions of the family of the brain-dead patient in Kochi.

☞ 9) Chiba suggested that the media be thoughtful of the family's feelings and the big pressure they were experiencing.

☞ 10) Currently, brain death is considered simply the end of life by law.

5   **Rewrite the story about the case of Genzan in about 150 words as if told by his father. You can begin the passage like this: "An organ transplant from a legally brain-dead donor was performed for the first time in Japan. It reminded me vividly of my eldest son."**

6 **Translate the following sentences into Chinese.**

1) The passenger lost his consciousness because he had lost too much blood in the car accident.

2) He wrote in his will that he would be happy to donate his organs to those who need them after his death.

3) This patient's life was saved after a donor's kidney had been successfully transplanted into his body.

4) The hearty talk will help relieve your worries and sadness.

5) The patient still has to stay in bed for a few days after leaving the hospital.

6) The doctor will write a prescription for you after the diagnosis.

SECTION II

Trying Your Hand

Write More by Yourself

A. Applied Writing: Medicine Instruction

Sample 1

Fenbid Capsule（芬必得）

Indications:	For the relief of severe pain and inflammation due to various causes.
Administration:	Take one capsule twice daily, morning and evening.
Caution:	Before giving to children under 12, consult a doctor. Overdose may cause headache and sickness.
Duration:	Three years.
Manufacturer:	Tianjin SmithKline & French Laboratories Ltd.

Sample 2

Cinnamon Leaf Oil（红花油）

Ingredients:	Cinnamon leaf oil and other inflammation reducers.
Function:	For bone & muscular aches, fracture swelling, sprains.
Administration:	External use only. Apply and rub over affected part frequently.
Warnings:	Avoid direct contact with eyes.
Validity term:	Two years.
Storage:	Keep tightly sealed in cool place.

Expression Tips

This medicine is in the form of syrup/spray/capsule/lotion/ointment/powder/injection

It is made up of .../consists of .../is composed of ...

The medicine can help ... /relieve .../enhance .../soothe .../cure ...

Take 3 tablets/1 pill .../4 capsules .../3 spoonfuls ... /10 cc once

It should be applied three/four/several times a day before/after meals/on empty stomach.

Keep/Store in a cool/dry/dark place.

Do not apply/use on/spray it to eyes and mouth.

Avoid it before driving/swimming/drinking.

Shake/Warm well before use.

May cause drowsiness/thirstiness/dizziness/nausea.

Here are some more sentences often used in a medicine instruction.

1. The usual dose is 1-2 tablets twice daily, taken night and morning.
   常用量为每次一至两片，每日两次，早晚各服用一次。

2. Indications: This drug is indicated for the relief of pain in various conditions.
   适应症：此药用于各种病因引起的疼痛。

3. Deleterious effects: light nausea, dizziness, or rash.
   不良反应：轻度恶心，眩晕或皮疹。

4. Form: The drug is in pale-yellow powder.
   性状：本品为淡黄色粉末状。

5. This disinfectant is a colorless solution.
   本消毒液为无色溶液。

6. For children, the dosage should be decreased according to the prescription of a physician.
   儿童用量遵医嘱酌减。

7. Composition: multiple kinds of vitamins and amino acids.
   本药品成分：多种维生素及氨基酸。

8. Storage: Tightly sealed and kept in refrigerator.
   储藏：密封保存于冰箱内。

9. This eye drop is clinically applied for dry eyes.
   此种滴眼液临床上用于眼干燥症。

10. Oral: 20-30 ml each time, 3-4 times a day before meals.
    口服：每次20至30毫升，每日3到4次，饭前服用。

11. Manufacturer: Xi'an-Janssen Pharmaceutical Ltd.
    制造商：西安杨森制药有限公司

12. 30 tablets/packet, 10 mg/tablet.
    30片/盒，10毫克/片

1 Translate the following medicine instruction into Chinese. Use the samples and the Expression Tips for reference.

> ### Yunnan Baiyao
>
> **Indications:** For women's diseases and various wounds.
>
> **Function:** Arresting bleeding and curing wounds, activating blood circulation and dispersing blood clot, eliminating inflammation and swelling.
>
> **Administration:** Oral for women's diseases, taken with warm water. External for wounds, evenly mixing the powder in wine and put over affected part.
>
> **Dosage:** 2 capsules each time, 4 times a day for adults. For children, the dosage should be decreased by half.
>
> **Warnings:** No fish or cold food within the day.
>
> **Storage:** Kept in dry place.
>
> **Manufacturer:** Yunnan Baiyao Pharmaceutical Group Co., Ltd.

2 Translate the following sentences into English.

1) 常用量为每次2至4片，每日3次，饭后服用。
2) 适应症：此药用于各种病因引起的疲倦无力。
3) 性状：本品为白色溶液。
4) 孕妇用量遵医嘱。
5) 储藏：保存于冰箱内，谨防儿童动用。
6) 此药临床上用于缓解头痛及退烧。

B. Sentence Writing: Conjunctions

漏用与错用连词是写作中常见的错误之一，这种错误往往是受中文的影响，学习中要特别注意。

错误用法	正确用法	译文
The machines are humming, the workers are busy working.	The machines are humming, and the workers are busy working.	机器轰鸣，工人们繁忙地工作着。
Practice makes perfect is believable.	*That* practice makes *perfect* is believable.	熟能生巧是可信的。
If Jane is happy doesn't concern me.	*Whether* Jane is happy doesn't concern me.	珍妮是否高兴跟我没关系。
What had the boy done really annoyed his parents.	*What* the boy had done really annoyed his parents.	男孩所做的事着实惹火了他的父母。
No matter who does wrong is punished in the end.	*Whoever* does wrong is punished in the end.	恶有恶报。

The reason for his hesitancy was *because* he did not like to blame anyone without sufficient proof.	The reason for his hesitancy was *that* he did not like to blame anyone without sufficient proof.	他犹豫的原因是他不喜欢在没有足够证据的时候责备任何人。
It seems of little consequence *you appear in the court or you do not.*	It seems of little consequence *whether or not* you appear in the court.	你出不出庭似乎意义不大。
It is generally accepted *silence is agreement.*	*It* is generally accepted *that* silence is agreement.	人们通常认为，沉默就是同意。
Those write about science are careful in checking the accuracy of their reports.	*Those who* write about science are careful in checking the accuracy of their reports.	科学论文的撰写者都会精心检查其报告的精确性。
Because of the traffic jam *which we were* caught, we were late. The students all show concern to the boy whom *the teacher says is an orphan.*	Because of the traffic jam *in which* we were caught, we were late. The students all show concern to the boy *who* the teacher says is an orphan.	由于遇到了交通阻塞，我们迟到了。 学生们都很关心那位据老师说是个孤儿的男孩。
Many Welsh people are going to settle in North Carolina, *which land is cheap.*	Many Welsh people are going to settle in North Carolina, *where land* is cheap.	我们很多威尔士人要到北卡罗来纳州定居，那里的土地便宜。
Whoever *has read Mark Twain* will forget his humor?	Whoever *that* has read Mark Twain will forget his humor?	读过马克·吐温作品的人有谁能忘掉他的幽默？
When was graduating from college, my generation also found the world in a mess.	When *I* was graduating from college, my generation also found the world in a mess.	当我大学即将毕业时，我那一代人也觉得世界被搞得一团糟。
He dislikes the environment more than *John.*	He dislikes the environment more than *John does.*	他比约翰更厌恶这个环境。
Mr. Thompson showed less interest in Beijing Opera than *the actors and actresses.*	Mr. Thompson showed less interest in Beijing Opera than *in* the actors and actresses.	与其说汤普森先生对京剧感兴趣，还不如说他对演员感兴趣。
Although he is in his seventies, *but he* is still learning English very hard.	*Although* he is in his seventies, *(yet)* he is still learning English very hard.	尽管已经70多岁了，他仍努力学习英语。

3 **Select the best conjunctions to translate the following sentences.**

1) 尽管医生很和蔼，但患者还是很紧张。

2) 中秋节是家人一起赏月的日子。

3) 谁来都欢迎。

4) 失败的原因之一是他的粗心大意。

5) 雨停之后我们去散个步。

6) 实验是否成功还是个谜。

7) 她比她妈妈更喜欢吃甜食。

8) 那位中国球员即使不比那位外国球员表现得更为出色，起码也同他一样好。

9) 人们普遍认为熟能生巧。

10) 他们在展销会上推出的新产品仍需改进。

4 **Correct the errors in each of the following sentences.**

1) Some say the doctor is merciful, others say he is killing people.

2) "In Rome do as the Romans do" works for every overseas students.

3) I said hurt her so deeply.

4) He comes or not makes no difference.

5) Who laughs last laughs best.

6) We went to the museum, which it was very crowded.

7) Jimmy is not better at skating than his brother.

8) He'll answer her letter once he will receive it.

9) The presents will be given to those whoever come early.

10) The day will come that peace-loving people enjoy a world without war.

SECTION III

Data Bank

Here is the Data Bank. Practice the patterns and expressions for giving and receiving concerns and medical advice.

Showing Concern to a Friend	A Patient's Complaints
What's the matter/trouble with you?	I'm feeling awful/weak now.
Can you tell me what the problem is?	I've got a bad headache and a fever/ a bad cold.
What has happened to you?	The toothache is killing me.
What's wrong?	I'm having more stomach trouble.
What seems to be the trouble?	I'm feeling so sick/I hurt all over.

Is there anything wrong?

Are you all right?

Are you sure you are OK?

You look pale.

You look feverish.

I keep putting on weight.

Your arm/foot/leg/nose is bleeding.

Have you had/taken any medicine?

Have you seen a doctor?

Do you need any help?

Shall I go with you to the hospital?

You'd better go to see a doctor immediately.

You'd better lie down.

You should have a good rest.

You must take some medicine.

That's too bad.

I'm sorry to hear that.

What can I do for you?

I'm feeling dizzy and tired.

My whole body feels weak.

I'm not feeling quite myself.

I couldn't sleep well.

A Doctor's Advice and Instruction

Open your mouth and say "Ahhhh".

Come here for the injection.

Lie on the couch and breathe deeply.

Did you have a temperature?

I'll write out a prescription for you.

You've got the flu.

You need a minor operation.

You can try some Chinese therapies.

Let's make an appointment for next week.

Don't worry. You will feel better soon.

Come for a follow-up treatment.

Take this pain-killer three times a day after meals.

Unit 5   Farewell

Unit Goals

❖ What You Should Learn to Know About

1. The way an English farewell speech and farewell letter are written
2. Emphasis, ellipsis and inversion

SECTION I

Maintaining a Sharp Eye

Read More by Yourself

Farewell to Our Chinese Friends

Ladies and gentlemen,

    We are very happy to be here tonight when we can have the opportunity to express our thanks and to bid farewell to our Chinese friends.

    We have just **concluded** a journey through your remarkable country and we were deeply impressed. **Traditionally**, Americans **admire** progress and the People's Republic of China is an outstanding example of **progress**. You have experienced an **amazing** 52 years of national achievements.

    During our stay here we traveled more than 8 000 kilometers in your great country under the **expert guidance** of the **capable** people with China International Service. In traveling through China we were impressed by the determination and confidence of the Chinese people and by the site of **construction** everywhere, which show that you are pressing ahead with your national programs under the economic development plan.

结束
传统地；钦佩

进步；惊人的

专家；引导；
有能力的

建设

The Chinese people are modest and **prudent**, hardworking and brave, clever and **resourceful**. I've recorded, with my pen and my camera, the most exciting scenes I **witnessed** on the visit. I shall make them known to my people when I get home. I am sure that will give **tremendous** encouragement to them.

谨慎的
足智多谋的
目击
巨大的

Of my many visits to various areas of the world, the visit to your country was the most culturally **rewarding**. The **friendliness**, hospitality, **superb** food, comfortable accommodations and beautiful **scenery** combined to make this journey a memorable **sojourn** for all of us.

有收藏的；友好；精美的；景色；逗留

We are all leaving tomorrow. You can be sure that we shall always **cherish** the happy memories of your country and your **delightful** people. Yes, China is one place we would like to return to — there is a lot one can learn here. In the **meantime**, we look forward to the opportunity of receiving you, our Chinese friends, in our country so that we can return some of your kindness and hospitality.

珍惜
可爱的

其间

Thank you and goodbye.

1 **Read the passage carefully and check your understanding by doing the multiple choice exercises.**

1) The speaker made a warm-hearted speech to _____.
   a. evaluate the great achievements made by the Chinese people
   b. demonstrate the fast economic development in China
   c. express his thanks and bid farewell to his Chinese friends
   d. tell what he saw of China during his visit

2) During his stay in China, what most impressed him was _____.
   a. the superb food and local delicacies he enjoyed in China
   b. China's national programs pressing ahead
   c. China's rapid progress in the past 52 years
   d. the national economic development plan of China

3) During his stay in China, the speaker traveled more than 8 000 kilometers guided by _____?
   a. an experienced old traveler
   b. one of his close friends
   c. a friendly Chinese expert
   d. excellent travel agents

4) According to the speaker, what would give tremendous encouragement to his people?
   a. The exciting record of what he saw on his visit.
   b. The happy experiences he had gained during his visit.
   c. The 8 000-kilometer journey he made in China.
   d. The unique sceneries he saw in different places.

5) From the speech we can infer that the speaker was _____.
   a. satisfied with the visit
   b. amazed by the Chinese culture
   c. proud of the visit
   d. regretful of the visit

2 **Choose the proper word or phrase in the box to fill in the blank in each of the following sentences.**

farewell	in the meantime	brave	prudent	return one's kindness
make a journey	friendliness	encouragement	sure	scene

1) _____, his case won't come to court for several reasons, and more than half of the people think him guilty.
2) She is going to _____ across the world this year.
3) The flowers were looking up through the green grass and laughing. It was a lovely _____.
4) We shall give a _____ party before we leave the country.
5) It's _____ to wear a thick coat when the weather is cold.
6) For over four hundred years they have conducted a _____ struggle for independence.
7) The teacher must make an effort to maintain a classroom atmosphere charged with _____ and acceptance.
8) My wife hoped to have the pleasure of _____ at our own house one day.
9) A little _____ is all people need to keep doing a good job.
10) I am not _____ whether the article you mentioned is still in print.

3 **Put the sentences into English, using the words and expressions given in the brackets.**

1) 时钟敲了9下；她悄悄地向母亲道别。(bid farewell to)
2) 我们期待贵公司在未来的岁月里会有振奋人心的发展。(look forward to)
3) 这次参观中的所见所闻使我感受颇深。(impress)
4) 我们正在目睹一种更为有效的使用计算机的新方法的诞生。(witness)
5) 研究生学业完成后，我将返回中国，在企业谋职。(return to)

PASSAGE II

My First Time in China

I can still remember quite clearly the day I arrived in Beijing. It was a sunny autumn day, and a bit cold for us who are used to the weather back home. Some **Filipino** friends met us at the airport, for we really did not know our way around. We did not speak any Chinese at that time. I was quite impressed by how fast we were able to get our luggage. **In no time** we were proceeding to Beijing Language & Culture University, our

菲律宾人

马上

school and home for the next eleven months. Beijing was everything that I dreamed it would be, and more.

My stay here in Beijing has been one of the most enjoyable experiences in my life. How can I describe it? It's one of the few places I have been to that really felt like home. I have been to Singapore, Thailand, **Brunei**, **Indonesia** and **Malaysia**. Those are really beautiful places, but after a few weeks at those places I was **itching** to go back home. Unlike there — I've been three months here and it seems just like yesterday.

文莱；印度尼西亚；马来西亚

渴望

Beijing for me is a very **exotic** place. It's a mixture of the modern and the traditional worlds. I can definitely say it's a modern city by any standard. We can see very well the high rise buildings **towering** over the city, the **massive** road system where hundreds of cars pass every day, the amazing ongoing **infrastructure** preparation for the 2008 Olympics, the huge **recreational** facilities like parks, museums, zoos etc. There are also the convenient **subway** and **transportation** systems to take you around.

奇异的

高耸
大规模的
基础设施
娱乐的
地铁；交通

Going to the countryside, on the other hand, you'll see a lot of old brick houses and **farmlands**. You can also notice old people **gathering** in parks in the mornings and evenings to get their regular exercise and chat with each other. Sometimes when I look at them I can't help but appreciate the **contentment** and joy they take in the simple **routines** of life. In spite of the progress of time, some things really don't change and you can still see a lot of **traces** of the past.

农田；聚集

满足；常规

痕迹

My impression of the **general** population is that most of the people here are **warm-hearted**. The old people are still very much respected by the younger generation, and they also actively participate in the society. However, to be **frank**, Chinese people are still a mystery to me **at present**. For example, there is the combination of conservatism and the sometimes **liberal** attitude of the youth. People here are **fascinated** by the West, but at the same time they **hold on to** the traditional ways of doing things. I think it would take me years before I could really understand Chinese culture and society. I believe the first step to have a better understanding is to learn how to speak the **native** language.

普通的
热心的

坦诚
现在
不拘泥的；迷住
坚守

本地的

4 Are the following statements true or false according to the passage? Write T or F accordingly.

☞ 1)　The author is probably an overseas student who came from Singapore.

☞ 2)　The author is going to study at Beijing Language & Culture University for eleven months.

☞ 3)　The author has been to some other countries, but Beijing is more homelike.

☞ 4) Beijing is a big city with modern and traditional cultures combined.

☞ 5) Beijing is busy preparing for the 2008 Olympic Games.

☞ 6) The transportation system in Beijing is convenient to take people around.

☞ 7) Old people in Beijing are content with their simple routines of life.

☞ 8) Respect shown for old people in Beijing has left a deep impression on the author.

☞ 9) What makes the author feel puzzled about Beijing is the liberal lifestyle of the youth.

☞ 10) The author thinks that the mastery of Chinese is the first thing to do in order to understand China.

5 Rewrite the story in the third person in less than 200 words. You may begin your passage with "The author could still remember quite clearly the day he arrived in Beijing."

6 Translate the following sentences into Chinese.

1) It was a sunny autumn day, and a bit cold for us who are used to the weather back home.

2) My stay here in Beijing has been one of the most enjoyable experiences in my life.

3) Beijing for me is a very exotic place. It's a mixture of the modern and the traditional worlds.

4) In spite of the progress of time, some things really don't change and you can still see a lot of traces of the past.

5) The old people are still very much respected by the younger generation, and they are also actively participating in the society. However, to be frank, Chinese people are still a mystery to me at present.

6) People here are fascinated by the West, but at the same time they hold on to their traditional ways of doing things.

SECTION II

Trying Your Hand

Write More by Yourself

A. Applied Writing: A Farewell Letter
Sample 1

April 6, 2010

Dear Mr. Johnson,

Much to my regret I was unable to see you off at the airport yesterday. I honestly feel you've done your best on your part. Our business would not be so fruitful without your cooperation.

I hope we'll keep in touch with each other and cooperate closely in the future.

Yours sincerely,
Zhang Lin

Sample 2

March 18, 2010

Dear Mr. Town,

It is over one week since you saw me off. I can still vividly recall the impressive scenes I saw at the airport. You were among the friends who accompanied me from my home to the airport and the affectionate care you showed for me I could never forget.

I plan to return one day in the near future. When I come back, I will call on you.

Thank you again.

Yours truly,
Xiao Ping

Expression Tips

Patterns related to writing a farewell letter:

Our visit to China is drawing to a close and we are leaving for Canada shortly.
我们对中国的访问即将结束，很快就要回加拿大。

On the eve of our departure, it gives me a great deal of pleasure to write to you to express our appreciation of the hospitality you showed to us and the time you spent with us during my stay at your university.
在离别的前夕，我怀着十分愉快的心情给您写信，对您的热情友好及在访问贵校期间的接待表示感谢。

Much to my regret I was unable to see you off at the airport yesterday.
昨天没能去机场为您送行，十分遗憾。

Excuse my being unable to see you and your wife off.
请原谅我未能为您和您的夫人送行。

Every time I recollect our close friendship over the last few years, I am personally very sad to see you leave China.
每次回忆起近几年我们结下的亲密友情，我就会因为你们要离开中国而感到难过。

We really don't know how to thank you. You have been very considerate and helpful.
我们真的不知道该如何感谢你们。你们真是热情周到。

Before leaving, I'd like to say thank you for all the assistance you gave me during my stay here.
在离开之前，对您为我在此期间所给予的一切帮助表示感谢。

Thank you for your warm reception and hospitality.

感谢您热情友好的接待。

Thank you again for all the trouble you've taken to make my visit a success. I hope we'll meet again sometime.

再次感谢您为我这次成功的访问所做的一切。希望以后能再见面。

I hope we will keep in touch as you resume your work at your new post.

希望在您就任新职以后我们会继续保持联系。

I hope we'll keep in touch with each other and cooperate closely in the future.

希望我们保持联系，并在将来更加密切地合作。

With very good wishes for the future and thanks for what you have done for us.

祝愿你们未来一切都好，非常感谢您为我们所做的一切。

Please say thank you to your parents for me.

请代我向你父母问好。

Remember me to John.

请代我向约翰问好。

By the way, say hello to your children, please.

顺便向你的孩子们问好。

Please give my best regards to your family.

请代我问候您的全家。

It's a pity that you're leaving us tomorrow.

真遗憾，你明天就要离开我们了。

I'm sorry to leave you too.

要离开你们我也感到非常遗憾。

I wish you a pleasant journey. And don't forget to keep in touch.

希望你旅途愉快。别忘了保持联系。

Farewell, dear friend. May we meet again someday!

再见吧，亲爱的朋友。但愿我们后会有期。

1 **Translate the following farewell note into English. Use the samples and the Expression Tips for reference.**

亲爱的王芳：

　　我在这里的事情已经全部办好了。这次没少麻烦您，我万分感激。我定于今天下午两点乘飞机回家，特此辞行，并请代向您的妻子问好。

挚友

怀特

2010年8月20日

2 Translate the following sentences into Chinese.

1) Thank you for your nice welcome (and reception). Let's hope we'll meet again sometime in the future.

2) Finally, we want to take this opportunity to ask David to convey our profound friendship.

3) I wish you a pleasant journey, and I hope you'll have a good time!

4) It's very kind of you to come and see me off.

5) Ladies and gentlemen, CAAC announces the departure of Flight No.127 to London.

6) As we see you off, we feel deep regret at your leaving and wish you a pleasant journey home. We hope you will come and join us again next year.

B. Sentence Writing: Emphasis, Ellipsis and Inversion 强调、省略与倒装

I. Emphasis 强调

英语中常用的强调结构是：**It is (was)** +被强调部分（主语、宾语和状语）+ **that (who)** …
被强调部分用**that**引出，指人时也可用**who**强调句中的时态应与原句时态一致。如原句为：
Professor Smith made a wonderful speech at the meeting last week.
我们可以用强调句型来分别强调句子中的主语、宾语和状语：

It was Professor Smith that / who made a wonderful speech at the meeting last week.
（强调主语）

It was a wonderful speech that Professor Smith made at the meeting last week.（强调宾语）

It was at the meeting that Professor Smith made a wonderful speech last week.（强调状语）

It was last week that Professor Smith made a wonderful speech at the meeting.（强调状语）

强调结构也常用于强调状语从句。例如：
It is because English is very useful that we study it so hard.
It is only when you nearly lose something that you can realize how much you value it.

否定词也可以用于强调结构中。例如：
It was not I who am late.
It's not you who are responsible for the accident.

强调结构*It was not until … that …*的意思是"直到…才…"。例如：
It was not until the chief engineer came that they began the test.
It was not until last year that the economic situation of this plant became better.

*强调谓语动词则需用其助动词，一般式需在其前面加助动词**do**，其他时态则只能通过重读谓语动词前的助动词来强调。例如：
I *do know* what he is doing now, but I don't want to tell you.

She **did see** you going into that room yesterday.

He **does show** us his new book.

He **is** coming tomorrow.

We **have** finished the job as scheduled.

II. Ellipsis 省略

为了避免重复，句子中某些部分可以省略。常被省略的部分有以下几种：

1. **省略主语。祈使句和表示祝愿的句子可省略主语。例如：**

Open the door, please. (省略主语you)

Wish you a wonderful weekend. (省略主语I)

某些惯用的说法：

Thank you for coming to see me. (省略主语 I)

See you later. (省略主语I和助动词will)

2. **并列句中的后一子句可省略与前一子句相同的谓语动词、系动词或表语。例如：**

Some of the students study Japanese, others English. (others后省略了study)

Jim is in the classroom and Tom in his bedroom. (Tom后省略了is)

*状语从句中与主句相同的部分有时也可省略。例如：

I love rock music as much as classical music. (as后面省略了I love)

3. **省略状语从句中的主语和谓语。例如：**

When heated, water will change into vapor. (when后面省略了water is)

Please change the form of the verbs if necessary. (if后面省略了it is)

He often comes to help me, though very busy. (though后省略了he is)

In winter it's much warmer in Shanghai than in Shenyang. (than后省略了it is)

4. **在对疑问句的简略回答中常用省略句。例如：**

When did you go to Canada?

— Long ago. (long 之前省略了 I went to Canada)

Will you be able to come to our party?

— I'd love to. But I'm busy. (to 后省略了come to your party)

Have you passed the final exam?

— Yes, I have. (have 后省略了passed the exam)

Would you mind my smoking here?

— No, I don't. (don't 后省略了mind your smoking here)

III. Inversion 倒装

将句子的谓语动词或其助动词放在主语之前称为倒装。如果将谓语全部移到主语之前，叫全部倒装；如果只将助动词放在主语之前，则叫部分倒装。例如：

Then **came the teacher**. (全部倒装)

Have you ever **been** to that museum? (部分倒装)

倒装常用于下列两种情况：

1. 用于句子结构的需要

1) 在疑问句中。例如：

How often **do you go** swimming?

Is your brother still **working** in that company?

2) 在**there be**句型中。例如：

There **are different forms of energy**.

Is there anyone in the office now?

3) 在以**so**、**neither**、**nor**等词表示"也一样"、"也不"等的结构中。例如：

I have finished writing my paper.

— So **has he**.

He didn't go to the meeting last night.

— Neither **did I**.

4) 在某些表达祝愿的结构中。例如：

Long **live the people**!

May you succeed!

5) 在虚拟条件从句中。例如：

Were you in my position, you would help him, too.

Had I had the time, I would have gone with him.

2. 用于强调

1) 在以否定词**not**、**neither**、**never**、**hardly**、**scarcely**、**rarely**、**seldom**、**little**、**no sooner ... than ...** 等开头的句子中。例如：

Never has any **country made** so much progress in such a short time.

Barely did he catch the early bus.

2) 在某些副词，如 **only**、**here**、**there** 等开头的句子中。例如：

Only then **did he understand** why she couldn't come.

Only when she met her son **did she learn** the news.

Here comes our **bus**.

* 注意：若主语为人称代词，则主谓不倒装。试比较：

Here comes the bus.

Here it **comes**.

3) 为了强调表语，将表语放在句首，此时主谓语倒装。例如：

Among them was a **student** whose arms were hurt badly.

Gone forever **are** the **days** when the workers had to work for 12 hours a day.

3 Rewrite the following sentences to emphasize the underlined parts.

1) <u>The well-known Chinese cuisine</u> has a long history.

_____

2) This food manufacturer has supplied the market with sugar-free food.

    a. _____

    b. _____

3) A thank-you letter must include proper praise of the hostess.

    a. _____

    b. _____

4) She didn't finish the course at college because of her illness.

    a. _____

    b. _____

    c. _____

4 Correct the errors in the following sentences.

1) Never before I have seen such a beautiful park.

2) There Professor Black came.

3) Hardly he had passed the interview.

4) Only in this way they can carry out their plan successfully.

5) There were no electricity, there would be no modern industry.

6) No sooner they had got to the plant than they started to work.

7) Scarcely he spoke about the difficulties in his work.

8) Not only he is a scientist but a great artist.

9) It had not been for your help, we couldn't have finished the experiment on time.

10) Only after they had performed hundreds of experiments they succeeded in solving the problem.

5 Leave out the words that can be omitted in the following sentences.

1) Wood gives off much smoke while it is burning.

2) When I was in trouble, I always turned to her for help.

3) He speaks English much better than he speaks French.

4) You read the text again, please.

5) I'll see you next week.

6) Can you do this work?

    — I'm afraid I cannot do it.

7) They came from America and we came from England.

8) She is as tall as I am.

9) Have you ever been to Xinjiang?

    — I have never been there.

10) When did you meet him?

    — I met him two days ago.

6 Translate the following sentences into English.

1) 他在寻找的是他的汽车钥匙。
2) 他们选择的是红色。
3) 正是由于他在面试中表现不错，他才获得了这项工作。
4) 上学期是彼得教我们英语的。
5) 只有当他到家时才明白发生了什么事。
6) 如果他能做，你也能做。

SECTION III

Data Bank

Here is the Data Bank. Practice the expressions and patterns related to farewell.

I've come to say goodbye, as I'm leaving for Canada tomorrow.
明天我要去加拿大，来向您辞行。

Really? Couldn't I persuade you to stay a couple of days more?
真的吗？能否请您再多留些日子？

Much as I wish to, I really can't.
我也很想再多住些日子，但确实不行。

We'll be very sorry to see you go.
看到您要走了，我们十分难过。

Could you stay a little longer?
您不能再多留几天吗？

I really wish I could stay here a few days longer.
我真的很想再多待几天。

By the way, what time are you setting off?
顺便问一下，您什么时候动身？

I'm catching the 9:30 plane.
我乘9:30的飞机。

Then please have your luggage ready.
请把行李准备好。

Our car will take you to the airport at 7:30.
我们7:30开车送您去机场。

Thank you. See you then.
谢谢！到时候见。

It's very kind of you to come and see me off.
您来送我，真是太好了。

Thank you very much for coming to see me off.

十分感谢您来送我！

Not at all, it's the least we could do.

别客气，这是我们应该做的。

Have you checked in yet?

您检票了吗？

Please convey our best regards to our old friends there.

请转达我们对老朋友的问候。

Sure. I hope we may welcome you in our country some day in the future.

一定。希望将来有一天在我们国家能迎接您。

Thank you for all the trouble you've taken.

谢谢您，费心了。

My pleasure.

别客气。

Don't forget to write to / phone / e-mail me.

请别忘了给我写信/打电话/发电子邮件。

No, I won't. Goodbye.

不会忘记的，再见！

Good-bye, Ann, and do keep in touch.

再见，安，一定保持联系呀。

Yes, I will, Mary. Good-bye.

一定, 玛丽，再见！

Goodbye and good luck!

再见了，祝您好运。

Hope you'll have a pleasant trip!

祝您旅途愉快!

I wish you a very pleasant journey home.

祝您回国一路顺风。

Wish you a pleasant journey.

祝您旅途愉快!

Wish you a safe trip home.

祝您安全抵达家乡!

Have a nice trip.

旅途愉快!

Take care!

一路保重!

Unit 6 Applying for a Job

❖ **What You Should Learn to Know About**

1. The way successful people start and run a business
2. How to apply for the right job
3. Topic, supporting and concluding sentences

SECTION I

Maintaining a Sharp Eye

Read More by Yourself

My First Job

My first job was at a local **diner** called the Buttercup Bakery. I worked there for seven years and learned so many lessons, especially from a fellow waitress.

Helen was in her 60s and had red hair and incredible self-respect, something I was lacking. I **looked up to** Helen because she was doing what she loved — serving people — and nobody did it better. She made everyone smile and feel good, customers and **co-workers alike**.

I also learned how important it is to **take pride in** life's little **accomplishments**. When I helped out in the kitchen, nothing made me feel better than putting two eggs on the grill, **flipping** them over easy, and serving them just the way the customer wanted.

Being a waitress changed my life. One of my regular customers was Fred Hasbrook, an electronic salesman. He always ate a Mexican **omelet**, and when I saw him walking toward the diner, I tried to have it on his table as soon as he sat down.

廉价餐馆

尊重

同事；同样的

为…而自豪；
成就
翻转

煎蛋饼

Thanks to the newfound **confidence** I picked up from Helen, I dreamed of having my own restaurant. But when I called my parents to ask for a **loan**, they said, "We just don't have the money." The next day, Fred saw me and asked, "What's wrong, sunshine? You're not smiling today." I shared my dream with him and said, "Fred, I know I can do more if somebody would just **have faith in** me."

信心

贷款

相信

He walked over to some of the other diner regulars and the next day handed me checks totaling $50 000 — along with a note that I have to this day. It reads, "The only **collateral** on this loan is my trust in your honesty as a person. Good people with a dream should have the opportunity to make that dream come true."

担保品

I took the checks to Merril Lynch — the first time I had ever entered a **brokerage** house — where the money was invested for me. I continued working at the Buttercup, making plans for the restaurant I would open. My investments **soured**, though, and I lost the money.

经纪业

变坏

I found myself thinking about what it would be like to be a **stockbroker**. After great **deliberation** I decided to apply for a job at Merril Lynch. Even though I had no experience, I was **hired** and ended up becoming a pretty good **broker**. Eventually I paid back Fred and my customers the $50 000, **plus** 14-percent annual interest. Five years later, I was able to open my own firm.

股票经纪人；
考虑
雇佣
经纪人

加上

I got a thank-you note from Fred, which will be **imprinted** on my heart forever. He had been sick and wrote that my check had helped cover his **mounting** medical bills. His letter read, "That loan may have been one of the best investments that I will ever make. Who else could have invested in a counter 'girl' with a **million**-dollar personality and watch that investment **mature** into a very successful career woman. How few 'investors' have that opportunity?"

铭刻

增加

百万
成熟

1 **Read the passage carefully and check your understanding by doing the multiple choice exercises.**

1) From the passage we know that Helen _____.
   a. had been working in Buttercy Bakery for 5 years
   b. was a good waitress in Buttercy Bakery
   c. had learnt a lot from a fellow waitress
   d. wanted to open her own business

2) Fred Hasbrook always ate _____.
   a. at the same table

  b. at the same time

  c. the same food

  d. the same dessert

3) The author wanted to borrow money from her parents because she wanted to _____.

  a. buy the restaurant she was working in

  b. invest in the stock market

  c. return the money she had borrowed

  d. open her own business

4) What did the author do with the first 50 000 dollars she borrowed?

  a. She bought stocks at a brokerage house.

  b. She invested it in a restaurant.

  c. She deposited it in a bank.

  d. She used it to buy a restaurant.

5) Which of the following statements is true?

  a. The author spent her money buying a restaurant.

  b. The author paid the money back to Fred with interest.

  c. The author paid the medical bills for Fred.

  d. The author told Fred that she wanted to be a broker.

2 **Choose the proper word or phrase in the box to fill in the blank in each of the following sentences, changing the form if necessary.**

take pride in	invest	annual	mature	look up to
regular	personally	alike	have faith in	hire

1) Because he always helps the people around, he is _____ by others.

2) All the children, poor or rich, are treated _____ in that school.

3) He _____ great _____ the success of his son.

4) It's easy to draw because it's such a _____ shape.

5) I _____ Alan — I knew he could take care of me.

6) If you _____ your money in the company, you will become one of the owners of the company.

7) We _____ a car and drove across the island.

8) The average _____ income of teachers in that country is about 40 000 dollars.

9) Since then I have undertaken all the responsibilities _____.

10) She _____ into a self-possessed and successful career woman.

3 **Put the following sentences into English, using the words and expressions given in the brackets.**

1) 由于他的缘故，我开始喜爱我的事业。(thanks to)

2) 他对自己的想法是如此兴奋，觉得一定得跟别人说一说。(share ... with)

3) 晚会是以玛丽的舞蹈结束的。(end up)

4) 我将给你一张支票来付你的旅费。(cover)

5) 他是这个乡村酒吧的常客之一。(regular)

6) 买股票可能是较好的投资。(investment)

PASSAGE II

Are You Having Fun at Work?

The lack of humor in workplace is a real shame, according to experts. Studies have shown that happy workers are **productive** workers, which **enhances** profitability.

多产的
提高

The **stress** that is **endemic** in today's workplace is no joke. If you can learn to laugh, you and everyone around you will better **weather** the stress storms.

压力；特有的
经受

Experts say that a good sense of humor will **contribute to** your success in these ways:

有助于

1. Coping with change. Roles and **responsibilities** are changing rapidly in today's workplace. Your sense of humor provides the **resilience** needed to cope with change.

责任
恢复力

2. Building up leadership skills. As your career progresses, you'll probably be asked to lead more and make more decisions in your organization. Building your humor skills will **boost** your ability to lead effectively.

提高

3. Managing increased stress. As already mentioned, stress is a factor in all jobs. The more responsibility you **assume**, the more stress you experience. Humor is one of the most powerful stress-**management** tools around. **Laughter** helps you reduce **muscle tension**, release anger, improve your ability to overcome panic and bring **anxiety** under control, as well as keep a more positive **frame** of mind.

承担

管理；笑声
肌肉紧张

忧虑
框架
创造性；创新

4. Developing **creativity** and **innovation**. A better sense of humor will enhance your creative thinking abilities.

5. Enhancing communication skills. Everyone in your organization needs these skills, and humor can be a wonderful way both to boost interest in what you have to say and help become an accepted team member.

Okay, are you ready to **laugh** it **up** and encourage your **colleagues** to do the same? Here are several helpful suggestions to get you started using humor.

谈笑；同事

Step 1. Surround yourself with humor and determine the nature of your sense of humor. How can you do this? Watch more **comedy** movies; look

喜剧

for cartoons in newspapers; spend more time with your funniest friends and colleagues.

Step 2. Become more playful and overcome seriousness. Spend more time playing with your kids; make a list of things you find fun and do one of them every day.

Step 3. Laugh more heartily and start telling jokes.

Step 4. Enjoy language games, **puns**, and other **verbal** games.

Step 5. Find humor in everyday life. Look for the unexpected, **incongruous**, **bizarre**, and **ridiculous** aspects of life.

Step 6. **Take yourself lightly**; laugh at your own mistakes.

Step 7. Find humor in the **midst** of stress.

双关语；口头的
不协调的；古
怪的；可笑的
别太看重自己
中间

4 **Are the following statements true or false according to the passage? Write T or F accordingly.**

☞ 1) If workers feel happy, the productivity will increase.

☞ 2) A sense of humor is very helpful for one's success.

☞ 3) Humorous people often change their workplaces.

☞ 4) If you become a leader, it's unnecessary for you to have humor skills.

☞ 5) People in all kinds of jobs may feel stressed.

☞ 6) If you want to become a better team member, you should have a sense of humor.

☞ 7) A sense of humor is good for one's thinking abilities.

☞ 8) After you have seen some comedy movies, you can become a humorous person.

☞ 9) Telling jokes is one of the best ways to learn to be humorous.

☞10) It's hard for a person to laugh at his own mistakes.

5 **Fill in the blanks with the right form of the verb provided at the end of each sentence.**

1) The children were _____ for cleaning their own rooms. (responsibility)

2) Being creative and productive is seen as a _____ value. (positively)

3) People outside the door could hear the burst of _____. (laugh)

4) I wish you could _____ the time to come and talk to us. (management)

5) He has a month to _____ whether he is going to stay. (decision)

6) She couldn't appreciate the _____ of the remark. (humorous)

7) It would be _____ to pretend that there were no difficulties. (ridiculously)

8) She is always sending _____ letters to the newspapers. (anger)

9) It was becoming _____ difficult to find jobs in those days. (increasing)

10) People think that the laws have given the president too much _____. (powerful)

6 **Translate the following sentences into Chinese.**

1) The lack of humor in workplace is a real shame, according to experts.

2) If you can learn to laugh, you and everyone around you will better weather the stress storms.

3) Roles and responsibilities are changing rapidly in today's workplace. Your sense of humor provides the resilience needed to cope with change.

4) Laughter helps you reduce muscle tension, release anger, improve your ability to overcome panic and bring anxiety under control, as well as keep a more positive frame of mind.

5) Everyone in your organization needs these skills, and humor can be a wonderful way both to boost interest in what you have to say and help become an accepted team member.

6) Surround yourself with humor and determine the nature of your sense of humor.

7) Look for the unexpected, incongruous, bizarre, and ridiculous aspects of life.

SECTION II

Trying Your Hand

Write More by Yourself

A. **Applied Writing: Application Form and Resume**
Sample 1

Application for Employment
(Pre-employment questionnaire) (An equal opportunity employment)

Date: <u>July 20 2011</u>

Name (Last Name First): <u>Johnson, Michael</u>   Soc. Sec. <u>No. 621-01-8866</u>

Address: <u>423 Asbory Dr. Los Angeles, CA 90043</u>   Telephone: <u>555-6432</u>

What kind of job are you applying for? <u>Advertising designer</u>

What special qualifications do you have? <u>Certified programer</u>

What office machines can you operate? <u>Computer</u>

Are you 18 years or older? Yes: <u>√</u>   No: __

Education

School	Period of Years	Name of School	City	Course	Did You Graduate?
High	4	L. A. High School	Los Angeles		Yes
College	4	San Diego College	San Diego	Vocational	Yes
Other					

Experience						
Name and Address of Company	Date		List Your Duties	Starting Salary	Final Salary	Reason for Leaving
	From	To				
Lynn's Apparel	2005	2011	Helping design advertisements	$2 500	$4 000	Need full-time job

Business References		
Name	Address	Occupation
Ted Anderson	Lynn's Apparel, 14923 Commons Pl.	Manager

Sample 2

Resume

Wang Wei-li

No. 235 Nujiang Street Hongyuan City

Telephone: 8687×××

E-mail: wlwrd@hotmail.com

Employment Objective:

Employment as Secretary / Receptionist / Administrative Assistant

Education

2007　Graduated from Hongyuan Applied Technology College, majoring in business management

2008　Received a Secretarial Certificate from Hongyuan School of Business

2009　Took up courses in computer training — DOS, dBase IV, WordPerfect, Windows, Excel

Employment History

Sep. 2009 – present　Administrative Assistant (full time position)

New Computer Park Co.

Duties: Ensuring smooth running of the office; ensuring standards and deadlines are met; setting up meetings; ordering supplies; orientating and training of new clerical staff; troubleshooting office equipment.

Software used: Microsoft Office, Excel, and WordPefert.

Sep. 2007 – July 2009
Secretary / Receptionist (half-time position)
Taiheng Road High School

Duties: Typed reports, exams, lesson plans and routine correspondence; attended meetings and took minutes; ensured smooth running of the office; set up meetings; set and maintained a filing system of students records.

Software used: Microsoft Word, Microsoft Outlook, DOS, Windows.

Interests

Music, novels, swimming

References

1. Fang Ming, Director of personnel department, New Computer Park Company
   Telephone: 86493×××
2. Dr. Li Dajun, Principal of Taiheng Road High School
   Telephone: 28281×××

Expression Tips

Items on resume	履历表上的项目
1. full name	全名
2. address and telephone number	地址和电话号码
3. date of birth	出生日期
4. place of birth	出生地点
5. nationality	国籍
6. marital status	婚姻状况
7. sex	性别
8. personal information / data	个人情况
9. health	健康状况
10. work experience (employment highlights)	工作经历
11. personal interests (miscellaneous)	个人爱好（其他）
12. educational background (education)	受教育情况
13. college activities	大学参加的活动
14. job / career objective	求职目标
15. training	培训情况
16. awards and honors	获奖情况
17. references	证明人

1 **Translate the following into English. Refer to the samples and the Expression Tips for reference.**

个人履历

马洪光

滨海市黄河大街135号

电话：86856793

电子邮件：mhg88@sohu.com

工作意向：

与农业机械有关的工作

学历和培训情况：

2009　毕业于滨海农业技术学院

2010　在滨海农业大学培训6个月，学习农业机械课程

工作经历：

2011.8～现在　　东方农业机械研究所助理工程师

2009.9～2010.7　滨海农业技术学院实验员

个人情况：

出生年月：1986 年5月12日

性　　别：男性

婚姻状况：未婚

健康情况；良好

个人爱好：运动、音乐、读书

2 **Translate the following sentences into Chinese.**

1) When you write a resume, you should supply key information about yourself.

2) I'm now seeking employment where I can fully use my knowledge of electronics.

3) The following persons have agreed to provide references regarding my qualifications and work capabilities.

4) In a traditional resume, each employer's name is listed first, underlined, and followed by the city and province.

5) Employers are particularly interested in an applicant's activities and interests outside normal work.

B. Sentence Writing: Topic, Supporting and Concluding Sentences 主题句、展开句和结论句

句子是构成段落的基础。写得较为成功的段落一般包含有三种句子，即主题句、展开句和结论句。

主题句是在一段文章中用来揭示或说明主题内容的句子。主题句的特点是句式简洁、中心

突出、具有概括性，且一次只能涵盖一个议题。

比较下列主题句：

1. In the United States, the system of forced labor, which was known as slavery, lasted almost 250 years.

2. In the United States, the system of forced labor lasted almost 250 years.

3. Slavery lasted almost 250 years in the United States.

上述三个句子中，第一句累赘；第二句比第一句简单，但第三句的措词更简洁、清晰，而且一目了然。

展开句是用来支持主题句所阐述的思想或观点的句子。这类句子用各种细节或例证来阐明主题的各个方面。

例1

An educated man is a tolerant man. He respects the opinions of his friends. For example, Dr. Reynolds likes old things. He likes old paintings. He enjoys old books. He owns old furniture. Some people don't like any old things. They don't like old paintings; they don't enjoy old books. They always buy modern furniture. Dr. Reynolds never criticizes them. He respects people's differences. He understands human nature. He is a wise and kind man.

主题句 "An educated man is a tolerant man." 说明本段的中心思想 —— "有教养的人是心地宽广的人。" 后面的句子（除最后一句外）通过举例和论证来阐明主题句，以便较好地展开主题。

例2

My father is very strict with his children, especially me. He never allows me to go out of the house unless I have done all my homework. Frankly, <u>I do not care whether I go to school or not. School is such a waste of time. There are not any good jobs, anyway. My mother does not agree with my father. They quarrel a lot. Sometimes I wish they would get a divorce, but then who would I live with?</u>

本例中的画线部分没有围绕主题展开，内容由一个主题跳到另一个主题，既讲到父亲，又讲到学校和母亲，不能围绕一个中心思想，这样的展开句违背了一致性原则。

结论句用来表示对前面内容的概括和总结。这种句子常由副词、动词、介词或名词短语以及固定句型来引导，相当于汉语的 "总的来说"、"总之"、"大体上"、"所以"、"毫无疑问"、"显然" 等。

1. 由副词引导的结论句

常用的副词有：**obviously** (显然)、**clearly** (显然)、**overall** (大体上)、**so** (所以)、**therefore** (所以)、**then** (那么)

He gave me a phone call as soon as he got home, ***so*** I knew he was safe and sound.

Overall, the children have done a good job.

All right ***then***, it's time for you to begin your work.

Obviously, the situation of higher education in China is changing greatly.

2. 由动词不定式引导的结论句

常用的动词不定式有：**to sum up** (总之)、**to summarize** (简言之)、**to conclude** (总之)。

To sum up, this experiment has been the most successful one in the past five years.

The Whites now have two cars and a large house. ***To conclude***, they are living a better life now.

3. 由介词或名词短语引导的结论句

常用的介词和名词短语有：**in short** (简言之)、**in brief** (简言之)、**in conclusion** (总之)、**in summary** (总之)、**in a word** (总之)、**all in all** (总的来说)、**no doubt** (毫无疑问)。

In a word, health is more important than wealth.

In conclusion, I would like to say that change is a problem confronting most of us today.

No doubt, unless the teacher changes his attitude, any efforts are likely to be useless.

His father is ill in hospital, and his mother has lost her job. *All in all*, they are having a hard time now.

4. 由固定句型引导的结论句

常用的固定句型有：

1) From what has been discussed above, we may come to the conclusion that ... (综上所述，其结论是…)，

2) The conclusion we can draw / arrive at / come to is that ... (我们得出的结论是…)

From what has been discussed above, we may come to the conclusion that honesty is the best policy for whatever we do.

The conclusion we can arrive at is that the explosion of population is a matter of life and death—a matter no country can afford to ignore.

3 **Read each of the following paragraphs carefully and select the best topic sentence from the four possible answers that follow the paragraph.**

1) Topic sentence: _____

The first is the sort of brain he is born with. Human brains differ considerably, some being more capable than others. But no matter how good a brain he has to begin with, an individual will have a low order of intelligence unless he has opportunities to learn. So the second factor is what happens to the individual — the sort of environment in which he is reared. If an individual is handicapped environmentally, it is likely that this brain will fail to develop and he will never attain the level of intelligence of which he is capable.

a. There are two major factors.

b. Two major factors are considered important.

c. Intelligence and human beings.

d. There are two major factors which determine an individual's intelligence.

2) Topic Sentence: _____

First, he is able to express his thoughts and desires very precisely. This ability greatly helps him in business operation. When other people become annoyed because they cannot find the right words to express their thoughts, Peter can make everyone comfortable by helping them to do so. Peter's second characteristic is his ability to get work done on time. He has always been a devoted employee and his working style has earned him the respect of his superiors. He can also make plans which get work done efficiently.

a. Peter was made president of his company last week.

b. Peter was a very capable person.

c. There are two reasons why Peter was made president of his company last week.

d. There are two reasons why Peter can make everyone comfortable.

4 **Complete the passage by making proper supporting sentences according to the topic sentences given in the following form. You are required to give at least two supporting examples or reasons in each paragraph.**

English Study

Topic Sentence 1: English is a popular language in the world.

Supporting Examples:

1. _____

2. _____

Topic Sentence 2:   As we know, language is one of the most useful communication tools. English, as an international language, is especially so.

Supporting Examples:

1. _____

2. _____

Topic Sentence 3: What shall we do in order to study English well?

Supporting Examples:

1. _____

2. _____

Concluding Sentence: Based on your perseverance and diligent practice, plus proper study methods, you can surely grasp this very useful language.

5 **Translate the following sentences into English.**

1) 演讲者对他演讲的题目不熟悉，讲得也不好。简而言之，他令人失望。

2) 根据我的观察，我可以得出的结论是：他适合作这项工作。

3) 显然，没有必要再次说明这项工作有多么重要。

4) 我哥哥原以为他的课后作业太多，不能去参加晚会。但是，他毕竟还是去了。

5) 毫无疑问，如果约翰到城里来，他会给我们打电话的。

SECTION III

Data Bank

Here is the Data Bank. Practice the patterns and expressions often used in a job interview.

The questions asked by interviewers:（面试者询问的问题）

Why don't you begin by telling me something about yourself?

先讲一下你的个人情况，好吗？

Would you tell me about your studies?

讲一下你的学历。

Why do you want to leave your present job?

你为什么要放弃现有的工作？

Why do you want this job?

你为什么申请这份工作？

May I ask why you are interested in this particular job?

请问你为什么对这份工作有兴趣？

What are your special interests?

你有什么特殊兴趣？

Do you think you can handle both a job and school?

你认为你能同时既工作又学习吗？

Have you got any experience in this field?

你有这方面的经验吗？

How soon can you start if we offer you a job?

如果我们给你这份工作，你什么时候可以上班？

We'd like you to explain your views on the use of computers in our business.

我们想听听你对计算机在我们公司的用途有什么看法。

Do you have the confidence to do your work well?

你有信心做好这项工作吗？

Why do you want to join our organization?

你为什么想加入我们的机构？

How do you think you can contribute to our company?

你认为你能对我们公司做出什么贡献？

What do you expect to be doing in five years? Ten years?

你在 5 年或 10 年内有什么打算？

What salary do you expect?

你期望的工资是多少？

The responses given by interviewees:（应试者的回答）

I'd like to work in a larger company that offers more opportunities for growth.

我想在一个有更多发展机会的大公司工作。

I think this job is a challenge for me.

我认为这项工作对我具有挑战性。

I know your company is famous in China and I'd like to be its member.

我知道贵公司在中国很有名气，我愿意成为它的一员。

I've been long enough in this job and I'm going to shift to a new job.

我这项工作做得太久了，我准备换一个新工作。

I don't think there is any problem for me to work on computers.

我想在计算机方面我没有问题。

I have a lot of experience in marketing.

我在营销方面有丰富的经验。

I don't have any experience, but I can learn quickly and I'll try my best.

我没有任何经验，但我会学得很快，并会竭尽全力。

I want to apply for the position of sales manager.

我想申请销售经理的职务。

My previous experience will be very valuable to me in this new job.

我早先的工作经历对这份新工作会很有益处。

I have confidence that I will be able to handle the job.

我有信心做好这项工作。

If you give me the opportunity, I think I can meet your requirement.

如果给我机会，我想我能满足你们的要求。

I am a person who plans things well.

我是一个做事很有计划的人。

The questions interviewees may ask:（应试者可能提问的问题）

May I ask about the salary?

我可以了解一下工资情况吗？

Could you tell me about the work hours?

您能说说工作时间吗？

How about the vacations and sick leave?

休假和病假有什么规定？

Can you tell me about the company benefits?

您能告诉我关于公司的福利情况吗？

Is there any opportunity to advance?

有晋升的机会吗？

Unit 7 Promoting Activities

Unit Goals

❖ What You Should Learn to Know About

1. Key to producing bestsellers
2. Preparation for the business negotiations is needed not only in the business sense but in a cultural sense as well
3. Product prospectuses

SECTION I

Maintaining a Sharp Eye

Read More by Yourself

Marketing: Key to Producing Bestsellers

Kunming was full of the **fragrance** of paper and printing ink during last month's sunshine. From September 15 to 25, when the 12th National Book Trade Fair was held in this remote but **picturesque** city, book publishers from all over the country have **flocked** with their books of more than 100 000 titles to set up more than 1 300 book-trade **stalls** at the exhibition site.

Of the more than 100 000 titles of books that were brought to exhibition and sale, bestsellers stole almost all of the **limelight**. Among them, Economic Books, Educational Books and Internet Books were the most popular. This grand **feast** of books not only raised a large profit — more than 670 million *yuan* was made in the first four days only — it also revealed the newest advertising of publication in China.

A long queue of enthusiastic fans **zigzagged** in front of the desks where the best-sellers were sold. It was rare to see any clear space in

芬芳，香味

风景如画的
聚集
货摊，出售摊

聚光，引人注目
的中心
盛宴，宴会

成 "Z" 字形，
曲折前进

front of the stands holding these books, and the staff were always busy carrying new copies of them to the shelves. The book fair will please publishers, who already have a keen and **optimistic** awareness of marketing strategies.

乐观的

Books are often made popular by how well they are promoted, rather than how well they are written. At least this is true of some novels. Behind every bestseller, there is a successful **marketing campaign**, a huge investment would have gone into the **promotional campaign**. Take *Rich Dad, Poor Dad* for example. Before it was printed in China, the World Book Publishing Company had it promoted in more than 40 advertisements in newspapers and magazines and over 600 websites in just one month. They invested a considerable sum of money into it. "It's a business secret how much they've spent or earned, but I can tell you the income is worth the investment."

促销活动
销售活动

The difference between books and other **commodities** is that they are cultural products. But just like any other commodity, books have to be advertised in order to become known by the public.

日用品，商品

However, this was not known to the Chinese publishing industry until it was pushed into the market in the 1990s. There are so many books competing in the market. If you don't promote them and just rely on **word of mouth**, you're **doomed** to fail. To promote a book, a publishing house first decides on a good topic and invites a writer to write on it. If you find the right topic, the topic readers are interested in, you find the market, and you have done half the job of making your book succeed. Publishers also choose books from the yearly publishing schedule that are likely to be popular and to launch campaigns for these books.

口头宣传
注定

After deciding which books to promote, publishers work out the selling points of the books, design a promotion plan for them and then organize the promotion campaign. **Commercials** in newspapers and magazines are always the first step. Readers have also become familiar with the activity of authors' signing names while selling books.

商业广告

Now various activities are held to attract readers. But readers must be cautious not to be led **blindly** by the promotional activities. People have gradually realized that they shouldn't pay too much attention to what the commercials say. Some believe in the reputation, but some others don't. As a result, people should take a careful look at them first.

盲目地

1 Read the passage carefully and check your understanding by doing the multiple choice exercises.

1) It can be seen from the passage that the weather was _____ when the book fair was

going on.

a. windy   b. rainy   c. humid   d. fine

2) Of all those attending the book fair, the _____ were the happiest.

a. book buyers   b. publishers   c. readers   d. fair organizers

3) The success of a bestseller depends very much on its _____ according to the passage.

a. appealing content   b. huge investment

c. beautiful print   d. promoting campaign

4) It wasn't until the 1990s that Chinese publishers realized the importance of _____ in marketing books.

a. advertising   b. good writers   c. good topics   d. readers' interest

5) The author's advice is to buy a book based on _____.

a. the book commercials   b. the author's reputation

c. the author's signature   d. the reader's judgement

2 **Choose the proper word or phrase in the box to fill in the blank in each of the following sentences, making changes when necessary.**

optimism	invest	flock	commodity
sign	reveal	blind	publish

1) Visitors came in _____ to see the old residence of Luxun.

2) An entire week has passed before the new book about the general's sudden death _____.

3) The journalist refused _____ the source of her information.

4) Mary can't give up, for she _____ a lot of time and money in getting a good education.

5) Color TV sets are one of the best selling _____ of China in the overseas market.

6) The CEO has expressed _____ about the company's bright future.

7) My eyes were momentarily _____ by flash bulbs.

8) Many booksellers invite writers to _____ their names on the books for promotion.

3 **Put the following sentences into English, using the words or phrases given in the brackets.**

1) 专家们聚集在一起商讨新产品的销售策略。(strategy)

2) 强有力的投放市场活动使该款新空调的销售额大增。(launch)

3) 有关国家都必须在这个问题上表明立场。(take a stand)

4) 相信金钱万能是非常错误的。(believe in)

5) 米勒先生是一位好教授，很受学生欢迎。(popular)

6) 千万别指望顾客会相信嘴上说的那些好话，他们相信的只是你到底在做什么和能为他们提供什么。(word of mouth)

Business Is Business Around the World, or Is It?

Mr. Smith, the head of a U.S. **beverage** firm, is involved in negotiations with a Japanese food company to export beer to Japan. **Exploratory** discussions have already been held with the U.S. representative for the Japanese company. Now Mr. Smith is flying to Japan to discuss details and, preferably, secure an agreement that can be drawn up for signature.

In the United States, he has usually **finalized** similar deals successfully in a day or two. His habit is to **get down to business** as soon as possible and not spend a lot of time on **preliminaries**. He would like to adopt the same approach in Tokyo, so he has allowed only three days for his stay. "Business is business," he says, and, he has been **briefed**, his Japanese partners are just as interested in the planned cooperation as he is.

Once in Tokyo, Mr. Smith takes the opportunity to begin discussions on the main points of the projected transaction over dinner the first night of his stay. However, instead of definite statements, Mr. Smith hears nothing but friendly and **noncommittal** conversation. The following day, at his first meeting with the heads of the Japanese company, the situation remains unchanged. In spite of several attempts by Mr. Smith to begin discussions, his **counterparts** say nothing about the project but instead concentrate on talking about the history, traditions, and **ethos** of their company. He is also frustrated that only one member of the Japanese group speaks English.

Mr. Smith is irritated. After all, the principle that "time is money" surely must apply everywhere. He finally loses patience when he learns that the afternoon is not devoted to business discussions but has instead been reserved for sightseeing. In **despair**, he turns to the Japanese with a **stern** request that they get down to business. After a brief **consultation** among themselves, the Japanese finally agree to his request. However, **contrary to** his expectations, the negotiations do not progress as **anticipated**. They proceed without any definite statements, **let alone** promises, and no conclusions are reached. The fact that he puts forward specific proposals makes no difference. After three days of frustration and little progress, Mr. Smith flies home without having achieved anything, or so he feels. He feels he was well prepared to discuss any aspect of the business deal, and yet nothing happened.

Preparation, however, is needed not only in the business sense but in a cultural sense as well. Just a few of the potential areas in which Mr. Smith was not prepared include: (1) **insufficient** understanding of different ways of thinking; (2) insufficient attention to the necessity to save face; (3) insuf-

饮料
探索的

把…定下来
着手干正事
准备

简要说明

不明朗的

对方
精神

绝望；严厉的
磋商，商榷
与…相反
预期，期望
更不用说…了

不充分的

ficient knowledge and **appreciation** of the host country — history, culture, government, and image of foreigners; (4) insufficient recognition of the decision-making process and the role of personal relations and personalities; and (5) insufficient **allocation** of time for negotiations.

欣赏

分配

4 **Are the following statements true or false according to the passage? Write T (for True) or F (for False) accordingly.**

☞ 1) Mr. Smith is familiar with Japanese culture.

☞ 2) He hates to waste time and is usually quick in handling business matters.

☞ 3) His Japanese partners are as eager to discuss business as he is.

☞ 4) The Japanese company doesn't want to cooperate with Mr. Smith.

☞ 5) Despite the great effort Mr. Smith has made, his Japanese partners won't hasten the business negotiation.

☞ 6) Mr. Smith loses his patience because he doesn't have time to go sightseeing.

☞ 7) Mr. Smith leaves Japan without reaching an agreement, as he expected.

☞ 8) Mr. Smith made no preparations for the business negotiation.

5 **Give brief answers to the following questions according to the passage.**

1) What does Mr. Smith's company specialize in?

2) What habit does Mr. Smith have when doing business?

3) How long does Mr. Smith expect to stay in Japan for the business negotiations?

4) What do you guess is the Japanese who can speak English?

5) Despite his efforts, why isn't Mr. Smith's trip fruitful?

6) What preparations has Mr. Smith failed to make for doing business in Japan?

6 **Fill in the blanks with the appropriate form of the word given in the brackets.**

1) His attempts to improve the Post Office's _____ were successful. (imagine)

2) The captured soldier _____ to die rather than surrender. (preferably)

3) A good story-teller often makes the _____ of the story very exciting. (end)

4) The young man has been suffering from a serious _____ problem since childhood. (converse)

5) All her life, the late school teacher _____ to raising money for charity. (devote)

6) Tom Keller is _____ to know whether he has passed the final examinations or not. (patience)

7) This is a very _____ firm that uses the most modern techniques. (progress)

8) The police _____ the robbers' attempt to rob the bank. (frustration)

SECTION II

Trying Your Hand

Write More by Yourself

A. **Applied Writing: Promoting a Product**

Sample 1

> *Cooler King* is a new product of Toto Electrical Appliances Company. Made of imported-rubber, it's better than a fan and is safer, too. This air cooler has a water evaporating (蒸发) cooling system that blows out refreshingly cool air. It works anywhere: on a desk, kitchen table, nightstand (床头柜) and even in your car or boat. Simply fill it with water and turn it on! No installation is required! It can cool the air around you for up to 5 continuous hours per water change. Light weight, portable and low power consumption: the cooler uses only 4 C batteries or an AC adapter.
>
> For more information, please call 1-402-464-0044.

Sample 2

> *Solar Curtain* is a new product of Solar Household Co. Ltd. Made of specially treated material: polyethylene (聚乙烯), the curtain will keep sunrays out in summer and prevent heat loss in winter. Just hang it on a curtain rod between your curtain and the window. It protects your furniture from sun fade and increases your privacy — you can see out, but no one can see in.
>
> Available colors are: purple, green, red, blue and silver.
>
> Available sizes are: # 29017 Solar Curtain 30x63
>
> # 29033 Solar Curtain 30x81
>
> # 29041 Solar Curtain 36x63
>
> # 29058 Solar Curtain 36x81

Expression Tips

1. Made of imported rubber, our radio-controlled toy car is extremely durable.
    我们生产的无线电遥控玩具车采用进口橡胶精制而成，特别耐用。
2. This new type of toy car is safe for kids to play with.
    该新款玩具车在孩童玩耍时很安全。

3. *Chunlan Air Cooler* is portable, easy to operate and can work anywhere.
春兰空气冷却机轻巧、易操作，到处都能用。

4. Haier mini-fans are quite simple to operate and no installation is required.
海尔袖珍型电风扇操作简单，无需安装。

5. Our refrigerator is light in weight, portable in size and low in power consumption.
我们生产的冰箱重量轻、体积小、耗电低。

6. Made of special formula, *Liangli Pearl Cream* may erase the wrinkles from your face and keep your skin looking youthful.
靓丽珍珠霜采用独特配方精制而成，能除去您脸上的皱纹，使您的皮肤永葆青春光彩。

7. *Sunlight Curtain* will keep sunrays out in summer and prevent heat loss in winter.
阳光窗帘夏天能挡光，冬天能保暖。

8. This curtain allows your furniture to be safe from sun fade and increase your privacy.
这种窗帘能保护您的家具不受阳光照射而褪色，还能增加私密感。

9. We have various types and sizes available. Delivery can be made right from stock.
我们可提供各种型号和尺寸的产品，且是现货供应。

10. This type of eye-protecting lamp is made especially for young kids.
该款护眼灯是专为孩子们制作的。

11. This sweater is made of specially treated pure wool and is worm-proof.
该款毛衣采用特殊处理过的羊毛编织而成，能防虫蛀。

12. Try your luck with these exciting electronic hand-held casino games.
来碰碰运气吧，玩玩这些有趣的手握式电子纸牌游戏。

13. This portable phone amplifier (扩音器) easily slips over any phone handsets and makes conversations loud and clear.
该款轻便电话扩音器可以很容易地装入你的电话听筒，使你的谈话声更大、更清晰。

14. These inexpensive furniture covers have a stylish dragon print that gives your furniture a custom-decorated look.
这些便宜的家具套子上印有一种漂亮的龙的图案，这种图案使你的家具带有一种传统的装饰风格。

1 **Translate the following product-introducing advertisement into Chinese. Use the samples and the Expression Tips for reference.**

Slim Shorts are new products of Carson's Clothing Company. Made of 70% of treated rubber and 30% nylon, these specially-designed shorts use natural body heat to increase perspiration (排汗) around the waist, stomach, buttocks and thighs. They help reduce the extra water weight so you quickly lose unwanted inches. Washable. Great for men and women.

Sizes available: From 24 inches to 44 inches.

Colors available: Black, blue and gray.

2 **Complete the following product-introducing advertisement by filling in the blanks with the information given in Chinese.**

　　Nature Curtain is a new product of Nature Household Co., Ltd. Made of specially 1) (处理) _____ rubber, the curtain will 2) (遮挡太阳光线) _____ in summer and 3) (保暖) _____ in winter. All you have to do is hang it on a 4) (窗帘架) _____ between your curtain and the window. It also protects 5) (你的家具) _____ from fading and increases your 6) (私密感) _____ — you can 7) (看到外面) _____, but no one can 8) (看到里面) _____. Great for 9) (家庭和旅馆) _____.

　　Available colors are: White, blue, pink, green and silver.

　　For 10) (详情) _____, please call 1-435-876-6116.

B.　General Writing

3 **Complete the following sentences, using the appropriate form of the words given in the brackets.**

1) This new type of washing machine _____ (design) with advanced technology.

2) This fashionable ring-watch with up-to-the-minute design _____ (feature) an easy-to-read, built-in digital watch that can keep its time accurate.

3) It wasn't until three years later that they _____ (adapt) to the food and life of this country.

4) This classic no-ironing cotton dress is very _____ (style) today.

5) It is essential that medical companies _____ (warn) their customers of the possible side effects a certain medicine may bring them.

6) This high-tech, easy-to-use safety system with a wireless motion detector (探测器) will warn you when someone _____ (approach) your home.

7) Made of specially-treated cotton, this curtain is easy _____ (take care of).

4 **Correct the errors in the following sentences.**

1) Styled for comfort and convenient, this pretty dress is ideal to wear while you work around the house.

2) These attractive and eye-catching pants are perfect for special occasions, or when you want to feel especially.

3) All you need to do is to splash the dirty-removing (去除) agent over and wash it off your pots and pans.

4) Please push the button on the handhold remote controller to reduce the noisy sound.

5) Try your luck with these excited electronic video games.

6) This book is breathtaken and everybody tries to get a quick glance at it.

7) This *Bacon Keeper* is a clear plastic container that neatly hold a full pound of bacon.

8) Made of importing material, this shirt is machine washable.

5 Translate the following sentences into English.

1) 穿上这些漂亮的服装，你的小狗会成为街上人们注意的焦点。

2) 这种女式肩包系真皮制作，携带方便，永不过时。

3) 这些短袜采用100％的纯棉制作，给你一种软如真丝的感觉。

4) 该大衣由经过特殊处理的面料做成，重量轻，可机洗。

5) 这种会说话的彩色鹦鹉装有一个隐藏的录音装置，使它能够重复你说的每一句话，而且用你自己的声音！

6) 这只漂亮的怀表有一个精确的石英运转装置。

SECTION III

Data Bank

Here is the Data Bank. Practice the patterns and expressions for talking about present situations and potentials of products.

1. What findings have you got from the market survey?
   你的市场调查有什么新发现？

2. Our new type of PC is well received by the customers.
   我们的新型PC机很受顾客／消费者的欢迎。

3. We should find the cause of the delay and deliver the goods to the customer immediately.
   我们应该找出耽误的原因，马上将货给顾客／消费者送去。

4. The patent office has turned down / approved our application.
   专利局已拒绝／接受我们提出的申请。

5. We should try to find a better way to handle this problem.
   我们应该找到一个更好的方法来处理这个问题。

6. An increasing number of people are interested in buying laptops instead of desktops.
   越来越多的人愿意买手提电脑，而不买台式电脑。

7. We should develop more models to meet the needs of the consumers.
   我们应开发出更多类型的产品以满足消费者的需求。

8. The present situation of our CD players is not pleasing.
   我们生产的CD机的现状不令人乐观。

9. This new type of air-conditioner will find a smooth way into the home market.
   该款新型空调机将在国内市场打开销路。

10. The sales figures have decreased this month.
    这个月的销售量下降了。

11. Competitively-priced quality products are the most desirable.

    价廉物美的商品最受人欢迎。

12. Our laptop computers enjoy a ready market both at home and abroad.

    我们生产的手提电脑在国内外都很畅销。

Unit 8   Company Profiles

Unit Goals

❖ **What You Should Learn to Know About**

1. A company's profiles
2. A company's prospectus

SECTION I

Maintaining a Sharp Eye

Read More by Yourself

A Perfectly Fair Business Deal

It was like a piece of **amber**. It was like a warm, wine-red jewel. As soon as I saw it, I knew it had to be mine.   琥珀

It was a Giordano, of course. I knew it was a Giordano the minute I saw it. There are very few Giordano **violins** left in the world. An expert in New York said that there were twelve. Now I knew that the expert was wrong. I had just found the thirteenth.   小提琴

Six months ago, I was in Italy. I had been invited to **attend** a festival of early music on the island of Ischia.   出席

The music festival was very boring. These things are usually nothing **remarkable**. They played pieces by Bach and Purcell which were nice enough, but nothing **special**.   不平常的 特殊的

It was when the next piece started that I saw it. I don't know how I had missed it before. Perhaps it was because the violin hadn't played very important parts until then.

As soon as the concert ended, I walked up to the stage and went up to the young violin player. I didn't look at the violinist; I looked at the violin.

"It's a beautiful violin, isn't it?" he said to me. I was surprised — he spoke English very well.

"How did you know I was English?" I asked him.

"You're Mr. Hobbes, aren't you?"

"Yes, I am." I'm quite famous, I thought to myself.

"My name is Franco."

"Pleased to meet you, Franco. Now tell me about your violin. Where did you get it?"

"Oh, I can't remember. It's my father's. He's got lots of old **instruments**. I think this violin is quite old, but I'm not sure. It's very special, isn't it?"   乐器

"Er, yes, yes. It is very special. Very special indeed."

I couldn't believe it! I was so lucky — the young man, whom I thought seemed quite stupid, had no idea that the violin he was playing was an **incredibly** rare, incredibly valuable **antique**!   不能相信地 古董

"May I have a look at it?" I asked him.

"Certainly." He gave the violin to me. On the back of the neck, in very very small writing, I found the **inscription** in Latin: Jordanus Neapolis Faciebat Annus, 1722. It was certain! I was so excited; I didn't know what to do. I tried to **control** myself, and asked Franco some more questions.   题字

控制

"Would it be possible to meet your father?"

"Certainly. Why don't you come to dinner with us?"

"That would be lovely, thank you."

Five minutes later, I was in Franco's car and together we were driving through the narrow, **winding** roads across the island to his father's house.   蜿蜒的

I know it's not right to tell lies. But sometimes you have to do everything you can to get ahead in this world.

"I'd like to buy that old violin from you!" I said to Franco's father, "Let me make you a **generous** offer."   慷慨的

"Well, Mr. Hobbes," replied the old man. "I am an **amateur** in this field. I'm not an **expert**. I don't really know a lot about antique musical instruments."   业余爱好者 专家

"I am an expert in this field," I told him, "and I think that this old violin is interesting, but perhaps not very valuable. Perhaps £200 would be a fair price."

The old man was shaking his head.

"My father doesn't want to seem **impolite**," said Franco, "but he thinks that £200 is perhaps not quite generous enough!"   无礼的

We all laughed.

"I can see that your father is a clever man, Franco," I said. "He knows how to do business! I'll offer £250, but no more!"

The old man and his son started talking again.

"It is a very generous offer, Mr. Hobbes," said the old man, "and I am happy to accept it!"

I couldn't believe how lucky I was! I was paying only £250 for a violin which I could sell for £25 000! I quickly wrote a **cheque**, took the violin and called a taxi to take me home before they changed their minds.

"Goodbye! Nice meeting you!"

"I hope to see you again," said Franco. I hope I never see you again, I thought.

(*To be continued*)

支票

1 **Answer the following questions according to what you have read.**

1) Where did Mr. Hobbs find this valuable violin?
2) Why did Mr. Hobbs think the young violinist was quite stupid?
3) When was the violin made?
4) Why did Mr. Hobbs say that sometimes one had to do everything he could to get ahead?
5) How much money did Mr. Hobbs pay for the violin?
6) Why did Mr. Hobbs hope he would never see Franco again?
7) Could you imagine what would happen to the violin later?

2 **Choose the proper word or phrase in the box to fill in the blank in each of the following sentences, changing the form when necessary.**

attend	expect	miss	polite	control
leave	rare	value	accept	cheque

1) He _____ to be here on the tenth of next month.
2) The book is _____ to a science student.
3) The production in this factory _____ by these computers.
4) These flowers are very _____ in this country.
5) Please be quiet; I don't want to _____ a word of the news on the radio.
6) We _____ the Chinese Export Commodities Fair and concluded enormous transactions.
7) He received a _____ from Mr. Wilkes for five thousand pounds.
8) It is _____ to turn your back to someone who is speaking to you.
9) If our price is _____, please let us have your order as soon as possible.
10) Your effective management _____ a deep impression on us.

3 Put the following sentences into English, using the words and expressions learned from the passage.

1) 他们主动提出在获取贷款方面给予我们帮助。(offer)
2) 他没有被邀请参加上周的聚会。(invite)
3) 他们因城市足球队取得的胜利而欢欣鼓舞。(excited)
4) 这只是许多可行的解决办法之一。(possible)
5) 对不起，我们占用了你很多宝贵的时间。(valuable)
6) 他以惊人的速度准备好了这份报告。(remarkable)

PASSAGE II

A Perfectly Fair Business Deal

(Continued)

The next morning I woke up early, packed my suitcases and went to the airport. I was extremely happy about the incredible bargain I had found, but at the same time I was a little worried. Let me **explain** why. Even though Europe is now a single market, there are some things that it is still not possible to take from one country to another. Anything that we call "artistic or cultural **heritage**" — works of art, or antiques, for example —

are **restricted**. That is why I was worried when I arrived at the airport. I **checked in** my suitcases, and took the violin as hand luggage. I didn't want to put the valuable violin through the X-ray machine at the **security** check. I had to open the case and show the instrument to the customs officers.

Three **customs** officers took the violin and looked at it very carefully. They were all talking very seriously. They called a more important officer. The important officer looked at the violin very carefully. Then he looked at my **passport**. Then he looked carefully at me. He talked a little more with the other customs officers. Finally he put the violin back in its case and told me to get on the plane. Again, I couldn't believe my luck. I **breathed a sigh of relief** and thought I was the luckiest person in the world. But it wasn't over yet! Now I had to go through British customs.

When I got off the plane my heart was already beating very quickly. It sounded so much like a drum to me — I thought that everybody must be able to hear it. I waited for my suitcases at the baggage **reclaim** area, thinking that police or customs officers would arrest me at any second. Because it was a European flight, I could decide if I wanted to

解释

遗产
受限制的
办理登机手续

安全

海关

护照

放心地松了一
口气

要求归还

declare anything I was bringing into the country. There were two **exits**. If I take the green exit, I thought to myself, I can leave the airport without saying anything — even though it is **illegal**! If I take the red exit, it will be necessary to show the violin, and I could be arrested!

申报应纳税的货物；出口 违法的

I took the green exit. I walked out of the airport without saying anything. I went to get a taxi. When I was getting into the taxi, I felt a hand on my shoulder.

"Excuse me, Sir," a voice said. It's over! I thought. I'm going to be arrested and put in prison!

"I think you've forgotten your suitcase." I turned round and saw that one of my suitcases was still on the ground.

"Thank you!" I said.

I was certainly the luckiest person in the world.

When I **finally** arrived home, I felt relieved. I took my key out of my pocket to open the door ... and found that the door was already open.

终于

"Oh no!" I said to myself. "Burglars!"

I walked into my flat slowly and carefully. I was worried that there was somebody still in the flat. I was right. There was somebody still in the flat. There were two people in the flat. The young violinist Franco and his old father were sitting in my living room.

"Hello again, Mr. Hobbes!" they said, "We were waiting for you."

I was **horrified**. It was **incredible**. How was it possible that they were already here? What did they want? How did they know where I lived?

震惊；难以置 信的

"We must say thank you again, Mr. Hobbes," said the old man, "but not for the £250! Did you really think I was so stupid?"

I didn't say anything. I couldn't speak.

"We already knew that you have a good business dealing in antique musical instruments. We knew that you were not always **completely** honest in your business dealings! We wanted to bring the Giordano violin into Britain. Here we can sell it to a rich collector. But we knew it was dangerous to take it through customs. Thank you again, Mr. Hobbes, for the favour you did for us. Don't worry! We won't tell anybody about what you did! Now we know how well you work, we can ask you to do more favours for us in the future."

完全

Perhaps I wasn't as lucky as I first thought!

4 **Are the following statements true or false according to the passage? Write T (for True) or F (for False) accordingly.**

☞ 1) Hobbes was a businessman dealing in antique musical instruments.

☞ 2) Franco knew Hobbes's name because Hobbes was a famous businessman.

☞ 3) Franco was quite stupid because he was not aware of the value of his violin.

☞ 4) Sometimes Hobbes was not quite honest in doing business.

☞ 5) The old man wanted to have someone take the violin to Britain for him.

☞ 6) Hobbes knew that it was not legal to bring the violin out of Italy.

☞ 7) It turned out that the old man and the young violinist were burglars.

☞ 8) Hobbes did exactly what the old man and Franco had expected.

5 **Fill in the blanks with the appropriate form of the word given in the brackets.**

1) I guess I don't have any _____ talent. (music)

2) Your idea _____ like a good one. (sound)

3) When he _____ the sun was shining into the room. (wake up)

4) Most trade barriers are designed to _____ imports. (restrict)

5) They _____ a sigh of relief when the expected disaster did not happen. (breathe)

6) He _____ to pay back the money he borrowed. (forget)

7) The company _____ in a variety of products from industrial machinery to consumer goods. (deal)

8) It is _____ to ride a bike with a put-up umbrella in a hand. (danger)

6 **Put the following sentences into English, using the words and expressions learned from the passage.**

1) 得知这一消息我吓坏了。

2) 我觉得带太多手提行李是不明智的。

3) 这家公司经营计算机硬件和软件。

4) 我对他们作出的决定感到特别高兴。

5) 她发现儿子安然无恙时舒了一口气。

6) 他什么也没说就走出了房间。

SECTION II

Trying Your Hand

Write More by Yourself

A. Applied Writing: Company Prospectus
Sample 1

> Geokon Incorporated is located in New Hampshire, USA and operates on a worldwide basis. The company was founded in 1979 and currently has over 60 employees. Over the years,

Geokon has emerged as one of the leading designers and manufacturers of a broad range of high quality industrial instruments. In particular, Geokon, through innovation and experience, has developed a line of sensors unsurpassed anywhere in the world. These highly reliable devices have contributed in no small way to the growing worldwide acceptance of sensing device technology.

Sample 2

C&A Tool Engineering, Inc. (Indiana, USA)

The C&A head office is located in Churubusco, a town with a population of around 1 800 people in northeast Indiana. When the company was founded in 1969, it started with only two people, but now employs approximately 230. Extremely rare for an American company, C&A has never laid off a single employee.

The company was founded as a tool and die company for the metal molding industry, but has since expanded its business in a wide range of parts and engineering projects. These parts and projects include parts for fuel injection systems for diesel engines, parts for medical devices, and automobile parts. C&A now holds contracts with approximately 300 client companies.

Expression Tips

1. The company is a small privately owned business.
   本公司是一家小型私人企业。
2. We are a small firm with 21 professionals.
   本公司是一家有21名专业人员的小企业。
3. The company is a manufacturer of electronic components.
   本公司生产电子元件。
4. Our sales are up 30 percent over last year.
   销售比去年增长了30%。
5. In the year 2007, annual sales amounted to $15 million.
   2007年的年销售额达到1 500万美元。
6. This year we expect to see a 12 percent growth in annual sales.
   今年的年销售额预计可增长12%。
7. The company provides electronic systems and services for worldwide markets.
   本公司为世界市场提供电子系统和服务。
8. We produce a variety of small-sized molds for the telecommunications and medical appliance industries.
   我们为通讯和医疗器械产业生产各种小型模具。
9. We produce different products according to the customers' specifications.
   我们按照客户要求的技术规格生产各种产品。

10. We have developed several new chemical products.
   我们已开发出了数种化学制品。

1 Translate the following sentences into English. Use the samples and the Expression Tips for reference.

1) 本公司成立于2010年。
2) 本公司是柴油机生产厂家。
3) 我们是一家有80多名员工的小公司。
4) 公司2010年的销售额为600万元。
5) 销售额比去年增长了10%。
6) 我们的总部设在北京。
7) 我们开发了数种新产品。
8) 我们可以按客户要求的规格进行生产。

2 Read the following passage and fill in the blanks with the correct form of the words given in the brackets.

Corning Precision Lens, Inc. is the largest worldwide 1) _____ (manufacture) of lens systems for projection television, and a specialist at making lenses from optical plastics. The headquarters and manufacturing plants 2) _____ (locate) on the eastern side of Cincinnati, Ohio.

The company 3) _____ (found) in 1930 and 4) _____ (become) the largest American maker of watch crystals in the 1930's. In the 1950's, it 5) _____ (begin) making plastic lenses and maintained a modest business throughout the 1950's and 1960's.

The modern growth of the company stems from the 1970's, when it relocated to its current site. The company 6) _____ (change) its name in 2006 to Corning Precision Lens Incorporated. In the 1980's, Corning Precision Lens expanded its technology and capacity for making plastic lenses, selling to such companies as General Electric, IBM, and Xerox. Our current customers 7) _____ (include) Hitachi, Mitsubishi, Philips, Sony, and Toshiba.

In 2003, Corning Precision Lens 8) _____ (receive) an Emmy Award from The National Academy of Television Arts and Sciences. In 2004, Corning Precision Lens successfully 9) _____ (pass) the ISO9001 Regulation Assessment. With more than 70 manufacturing locations, Corning 10) _____ (employ) approximately 22 000 employees worldwide. Revenues for 2007 were $3.2 billion.

B. General Writing

The following sentence patterns are useful for describing a company or an organization.

1. The company is a joint venture founded in October 2006.
   本公司是2006年10月成立的合资企业。

2. The headquarters of the Stream Company is located at 85 Dan Road.
公司总部位于Dan路85号。

3. We produce motorcycles and new parts for motorcycles.
我们生产摩托车和摩托车配件。

4. The company is a wholly owned subsidiary of Shal Housing Limited.
本公司是Shal住宅有限公司的全资子公司。

5. The National Cancer Center consists of a hospital and a research institute.
国际癌症中心包括一家医院和一个研究所。

6. The Visitors Bureau is a nonprofit organization that promotes regional tourism.
旅游局是促进地区旅游事业发展的非营利性机构。

7. Our mission is to promote the health of the general public through disease prevention.
我们的任务是通过预防疾病来提高人民群众的健康水平。

8. The Centre for Women's Development Studies was founded by a group of scholars and social activists.
妇女发展研究中心是由一部分学者和社会活动家发起建立的。

9. The Foundation was founded to assist teenagers in finding self-worth and confidence.
设立这项基金是为了帮助青少年发现自我价值和提高自信心。

10. The Railroad Warehouse is a manufacturer and distributor of top-quality railroad products and detail parts.
"铁路货栈" 是一家生产优质铁路产品和零配件的厂商和经销商。

3 **Complete the following sentences, using the correct form of the words given in the brackets.**

1) The company _____ (base) in Shenyang, Liaoning Province.

2) We were able _____ (record) a 38 percent increase in sales in 2007.

3) The Group's total annual sales _____ (expect) to exceed 200 million dollars in 2007.

4) Western Light is a private company that _____ (publish) a weekly magazine.

5) We are a small firm _____ (locate) in Zhengzhou, with approximately 100 employees.

6) The Institute is a nonprofit organization that _____ (provide) science education programs for students of all ages.

7) The company has an annual turnover of $160 million and our business _____ (grow) rapidly.

8) The National Consumer Law Center is an organization _____ (specialize) in consumer issues.

4 **Correct the errors in the following sentences.**

1) Our company established in Chengdu in 1998.

2) Thomson Company has more 44 000 employees in 53 countries.

3) When Texans was found in 1953, the average annual sales was $4 000.

4) Since 1982, Chase Management has focused on provide software products and relate services.

5) NEC Corporation is founded in 1899 and has its headquarter in Tokyo, Japan.

6) Alumina is a private company that manufacture aluminum window and door frames.

7) Our mission is provide the highest quality public transportation.

8) Lemra Products are a manufacturer and distributor of quality electrical products.

5 **Translate the following sentences into English.**

1) 我们是一家设在温州经营计算机的小公司。(locate)

2) 我们从1987年开始经营业务。(in business)

3) 现在我们在中国大连有200多名员工。(employee)

4) 本中心包括三个部门，其中研究开发部最大。(division)

5) 我们的任务是改善病人的健康状况。(mission)

6) "第三世界之友"是一个非营利性的志愿者团体。(volunteer)

SECTION III

Data Bank

Here is the Data Bank. Practice the patterns and expressions for talking about a company.

1. What do you mainly deal in?
   你们主要经营什么？

2. How many employees do you have?
   你们有多少名员工？

3. What are your main products?
   你们的主要产品是什么？

4. What's your annual production / output?
   你们的年产量是多少？

5. Are you developing any new products?
   你们在开发新产品吗？

6. We've been in business for five years.
   我们开展业务已经有5年了。

7. Our registered capital is 50 million *yuan*.
   我们的注册资金是5 000万元。

8. Last year our net profit was 2 million *yuan*.
   去年我们的纯利润是200万元。

9. Our company is based in Beijing.
   我们的总公司在北京。

10. The annual output is 50 000 tons.
    我们的年产量是5万吨。

Unit 9   Purchase and Payment

Unit Goals

❖ **What You Should Learn to Know About**

1. Online credit cards are not completely reliable in some way
2. How to take advantage of the Internet in business
3. Letter of Credit

SECTION I

Maintaining a Sharp Eye

Read More by Yourself

My Shopping Experiences

After my recent experiences with NEXT, I thought I'd better share them and so have written this opinion about them.

The story **initially** began when I went shopping with my wife to NEXT in Milton Keynes. I was shopping for new suits for work and managed to find 3 that I really liked. The one thing with me is that I'm a short man and it can be hard at times to find my size and fair enough, the Milton Keynes branch didn't have my size. So, after a consultation with the sales assistant, I eventually signed up for the NEXT **Directory** Catalogue — as the suits were in there and I could order my size direct.

When the Catalogue first arrived, I was surprised at how much nice **stuff** was in there — **menswear**, shoes, accessories, home furnishings etc. I was beginning to get a little worried that my wife would see it all and go mad with the credit card!

Anyway, back to the story. I placed the order for my 3 suits in the cor-

最初

姓名地址录

东西；男服

rect size, and the lady on the other end of the phone could not have been any more polite and friendly. I thought at this stage that I was on to something good. She told me that my sizes were readily available, and that they would be delivered within 7 days. This is where the problems begin ...

After 14 days and still no suits, I decided to contact NEXT to find out what had happened. They informed me that as a new customer, I had a credit limit of £250, and as my order totalled £450, they were unable to **dispatch** it. I couldn't have too many **qualms** about that, but I couldn't see why they couldn't have contacted me sooner or told me when I placed the initial order. Anyway, to get round this problem, the lady from customer services recommended I pay by credit card, which I did, so that the order could be dispatched. Again, I was told that the suits would arrive within 7 days.

发货；疑虑

A further 12 days later, the suits finally arrived. When I opened the package, I found that one of the suits was the wrong size, and the other 2 suits were different from the ones I had ordered. So after another telephone call to customer services, I was told to send them back and the order would be re-processed.

5 days later I finally received the 3 correct suits, all of the right size. Problems were over at last I thought to myself. Wrong.

1 week after the correct suits arrived, my credit card bill arrive too, with two **separate** charges of £450 for NEXT. It turned out that although I sent the **original** incorrect items back to NEXT, they had forgot to **reimburse** my credit card. So back on the phone I went to NEXT, and this time I found that Customer Services were not as friendly. After explaining the situation to 2 different **personnel**, I then had to repeat myself a 3rd time to a **supervisor** before they agreed they were in the wrong. I was told that it would take 7 working days for it to appear on my credit card. As I had to wait for my next bill in 3 weeks' time, I simply thought that it would **DEFINITELY** be paid by then. Wrong again.

单独的
最初的；偿还

人员
主管人

肯定

Eventually, it showed up on my credit card bill, and the date it was paid was over 5 weeks after I notified them.

So from my experience, my advice to all of you NEXT shoppers is do your best to get what you want from the shop and only use the catalogue as a last resort.

1 **Read the passage carefully and give short answers to the following questions.**

1) What was "NEXT" in the story?
2) What did the writer manage to find at the shop?
3) What was "the NEXT Directory Catalogue"?
4) Why was the writer a little worried when the Catalogue first arrived?
5) What is the probable meaning of the word "dispatch" in Paragraph 5?
6) How many phone calls did the writer make?
7) What did the writer think of the catalogue at last?

2 **Choose the proper word or phrase in the box to fill in the blank in each of the following sentences, changing the form when necessary.**

initial	eventual	definite	manage	deliver
charge	recent	consult	notify	resort

1) Hawaii is an all-the-year-round tourist _____.
2) The team will _____ lose if he doesn't play.
3) _____ she opposed the plan, but later she changed her mind.
4) As this is a valuable article, we have to _____ you for the sample.
5) You are probably aware of the _____ rise in price of the raw materials.
6) The goods will be _____ at noon tomorrow.
7) _____ he realized he was in the wrong and had to eat his words.
8) She _____ to write five orders and take six phone calls all in ten minutes.
9) After _____ with his military advisers, the President decided to declare war.
10) The seller should _____ the buyer of the date of shipment as soon as possible.

3 **Put the sentences into English, using the words and expressions learned from the passage.**

1) 我想我们大家和你一样关心此事。
2) 竞赛的详细说明本总部可以提供。
3) 这标志着因特网发展历史上的一个新阶段。
4) 司机闯红灯显然不对。
5) 我们等了两个小时，他还没有出现。

PASSAGE II

Convenience Is Most Important

便利

    Like most people in today's fast-paced world, I don't have much time to shop. If you waste my time, I'll hate you forever.

    Ask most retail salespeople what's most important to the customer and they'll tell you "low price". Ask any customer, and they'll tell you "convenience".

That's why I find myself shopping more and more online. I don't have time to go to the **mall**, and when I do, I'm forced to deal with **ignorant**, rude, **indifferent** salespeople. I don't have time for that. I'd rather **log on**, pay a little more, and get it done with. Let me share a recent shopping experience with you:

商业街；无知的；冷淡的
登录

Friday evening, I went to the mall. I hate going to the mall. It's crowded, noisy, too big, and they don't have nearly enough mall directories to help me find my way around.

Nonetheless, I had just moved into a bigger office and I needed some computer furniture and art for the walls. A friend recommended a quick-frame shop in the mall. She said they had a large selection and their prices were quite reasonable. Well, I like "quite reasonable" prices, and a large selection is always a **plus**.

有利因素

When I finally found the store, I was pleasantly surprised. They did have a large selection, and the prices were very reasonable. After a quick look around, I approached the counter, and (after waiting longer than I'd like for a clerk to appear), said, "I'll take that one and that one, framed just like they are on the wall there, and oh by the way do you have any Boris Vallejo?"

"Never heard of him."

"Oh. Well, do you have that print of an angel leaning over the bed of a sleeping child; I can't remember the name of the artist, but it's a classic. I think it's called 'The **Guardian** Angel'... or something like that."

护卫者

"I don't think I've ever seen it — try looking through our Classics bin over there." And she pointed her long red fingernail somewhere beyond my shoulder.

"Where? Over where? There?"

"No, no — over there."

Well, no Boris, and no Guardian Angel. So after asking around and going out and back a few times, she found the right **mat** and **frames** for the first two prints and **proceed**ed to write me up.

（画与镜框之间的）衬边；框架；继续下去

"And when would you like these?" she asked.

Oh, did I mention they have a huge sign behind the counter that reads: 'Framing While You Wait'?

"Well, I have to go and pick out some furniture, so maybe an hour or so," I told her.

"Oh no," she told me. "We can't possibly have that ready for you until tomorrow afternoon."

"But ... the sign says 'Framing While You Wait,'" I protested.

"Yes, but we've been very busy," she explained. "We have other customers ahead of you. Tomorrow afternoon."

"But the sign says ..."

"Any time after 2:00."

"Okay, look, I can't come back tomorrow ... or the next day ... or the next day. Just give me the ones off the wall, that will be fine."

"Oh, I'm sorry, I can't do that. That's against store policy."

"But the sign says ..."

"I'm sorry, Sir, but like I explained, we've been very busy," she repeated.

"Well, I'm very happy business is good," I told her. "How nice for you. I'll tell you what, let's just forget it."

"Forget ...? You mean you don't want all this?!"

She seemed angry that I had wasted HER time. And you know what — that's too bad! Because she wasted an hour of my life. And spare hours are very difficult for me to come by.

Before you think I'm a complete **jerk**, let me tell you a little about my life. Monday through Friday I get up at 5:00. I leave for the office at 6:30 and arrive at 8:00. I work until 4:30, then arrive back home at 6:00. I spend an hour with my family, then go back to work in my home office, usually until midnight. On weekends, I don't go to the office; I work from home, usually until about 3:00 or 4:00 in the morning.

性情古怪的人

I do NOT have an hour to be wasted by salespeople who lie (via the sign), don't know anything about what they're selling, and then quote "store POLICY" to me.

If, knowing they were busy, she would have explained to me the situation before I wasted my time, I would have understood — or if they'd have just had enough sense to take the sign down! And these were not high-school kids working part time; these were (**seemingly**) educated adults.

从表面上看来

I'll never go back to that store.

I later ordered one of the prints I had chosen online, and paid about $75 more for it than I would have at the mall.

4   **Are the following statements true or false according to the passage? Write T (for True) or F (for False) accordingly.**

☞ 1) The writer needed some pictures to decorate his new house.

☞ 2) The writer waited for a long time before a shop assistant came.

☞ 3) It can be judged that Boris Vallejo must have been a famous painter.

☞ 4) The clerk would not sell the pictures on the wall because they had been sold.

☞ 5) The writer expected the pictures would be framed while he was shopping in the mall.

☞ 6) The clerk told the writer that he had to wait until two o'clock that day.

☞ 7) The clerk was lying because there was not such store policy.

☞ 8) The writer would not go to the store again because of the ignorance and rudeness of the sales girl.

5 **Fill in the blanks with the appropriate form of the word given in the brackets.**

1) The immense _____ of these people was really surprising. (ignorant)

2) They invited him to visit their country at a _____ date. (convenience)

3) The old man can walk only at a very slow _____. (pace)

4) He _____ an appropriate birthday card for his mother. (selection)

5) Your proposal sounds _____, but we'll have to talk about it further. (reason)

6) As we _____ the house I saw a man coming towards us. (approach)

7) The necessary _____ have been begun for the combining of the two firms. (proceed)

8) Before closing I'd like to _____ all those who contributed so generously. (mention)

6 **Put the following sentences into English, using the words and expressions learned from the passage.**

1) 他解释说他是因为交通拥挤而迟到的。(explain)

2) 浪费时间去讨论这件事是没有用的。(no use)

3) 在这么多人失业的情况下很难找到工作。(come by)

4) 或许你能给我推荐另外一家旅馆。(recommend)

5) 在春天，可供选择的冬装很少。(selection)

6) 警方竖了一块告示牌说此路禁止通行。(sign)

SECTION II

Trying Your Hand

Write More by Yourself

A. Applied Writing: Letter of Credit
Sample 1

THE BANK OF CALIFORNIA

DOCUMENTARY CREDIT IRREVOCABLE

Documentary credit number: 99 / 80000

Date of issue: 06 / 20 / 07

Validity date and place: 08 / 15 / 07 in Shanghai

Applicant: The Angeles Importing Inc.

        3710 West 9th St. Los Angeles, CA 90019, USA

Beneficiary: Wantong Trading Co., Ltd.

        P.O. Box 1267 Shanghai, China

Currency code and amount: USD $950 000.00 only

Draft at ... drawn on ...: Draft at 60 days after sight

Partial shipment: Not allowed

Transhipment: Not allowed

Shipment from ... for transportation to ...: Shanghai to Los Angeles by 07 / 31 / 07

Shipment of goods: 500 refrigerators Model DRF-F600

Documents required:

    Commercial invoice in quintuplicate

    Full set of clean on board bill of lading made out to shipper's order marked freight prepaid

Charges: All banking charges outside USA are for the beneficiary's account

John F. William

Authorized Signature

THE BANK OF CALIFORNIA

Sample 2

THE COMMERCIAL BANK

88 Prosperity Street,

Wheaton, Illinois 60187-2553

USA

OUR ADVICE NO.   MB-5432

ISSUING BANK REF. NO. & DATE   SBRE-777   January 26, 2007

TO

Dupage Transportation Company

421 N. Country Farm Road

Wheaton, Illinois

USA

Dear Sirs:

    We have been requested by Bank of China, Guangzhou, China to advise that they have opened with us their irrevocable documentary credit number SB-87654 for account of Deyuan Imports Company, 7 Sunshine Street, Guangzhou, China in your favor for the amount of not exceeding Twenty Five Thousand U.S. Dollars (USD $25 000.00) available by your draft (s) drawn on us at sight for full invoice value accompanied by the following documents:

1. Signed commercial invoice in five (5) copies indicating the buyer's Purchase Order No. DEF-101 dated January 10, 2007.

2. Packing list in five (5) copies.

3. Full set clean on board ocean bill of lading issued to order of Bank of China, Guangzhou, China, marked "freight prepaid", dated latest March 19, 2007.

> Covering: 100 Sets 'ABC' Brand Pneumatic Tools, CIF Guangzhou
>
> Shipment from Wheaton, Illinois USA to Guangzhou, China
>
> Partial shipment prohibited
>
> Transhipment permitted

Documents must be presented for payment within 15 days after the date of shipment.

We confirm this credit and hereby undertake that all drafts drawn under and in conformity with the terms of this credit will be duly honored upon delivery of documents as specified, if presented at this office on or before March 26, 2007.

Very truly yours,

James Porter

Expression Tips

1. We have opened a confirmed and irrevocable credit in your favour.
   我行已开具以贵方为受益人的不可撤销保兑信用证。

2. This credit remains valid in China until 23rd May, 2010(inclusive).
   本证到2010年5月23日为止（包括当日在内）在中国有效。

3. We instructed our bank to open an L / C in your favor for this order.
   我方已通知银行为此批订货开具以贵方为受益人的信用证。

4. We have received with thanks your letter of May 1 enclosing your price list.
   我方已受到并感谢贵方5月1日的来函及所付价格表。

5. We ask you to extend the said credit till August 20.
   我方请求贵方将此信用证延期至8月20日。

6. The following merchandise you shipped on the m.s. "Erlang" on the June 20 arrived here yesterday.
   贵方于6月20日交由"二郎"轮运输的下述货物于昨日抵达本港。

7. Will you please tell us the earliest possible date you can make shipment?
   请贵方告知货物可能装运的最早日期。

8. Accompanied by the following documents marked (_) in duplicate.
   随附下列注有（_）的单据一式两份。

9. We undertake that drafts drawn and presented in conformity with the terms of this credit will be duly honoured.

开具并提交的汇票，如与本证的条款相符，我行保证按时付款。

10. Transhipments are permitted at any port against the through transport B / L.

凭联运提单允许在任何港口转运。

1 **Translate the following sentences into Chinese. Use the samples and the Expression Tips for reference.**

1) We have opened a confirmed credit in your favour.

2) This L / C is valid for negotiation in China until July 15th, 2010.

3) Documents are to be presented to the negotiating bank within 15 days after shipment.

4) Shipment must be effected not later than (or on) July 30, 2010.

5) They want you to extend the above credit for 10 days.

6) Bills of lading must be dated not later than August 15, 2010.

7) The letter of credit should be accompanied by the following documents.

8) We hereby undertake to honour all drafts drawn in accordance with the terms of this credit.

2 **Read the following passage and fill in the blanks with the right form of the words given in brackets.**

The stages in the use of a letter of credit are as follows:

1. The buyer and the seller 1) _____ (agree) on prices, terms of payment, delivery and insurance.

2. The buyer applies to the issuing bank for a letter of credit. From the bank's point of view the issue of a letter of credit is similar to 2) _____ (supply) short-term finance.

3. The issuing bank sends the letter of credit to a bank in the seller's country, the advising bank. This may be 3) _____ (do) by mail or cable.

4. The advising bank informs the beneficiary of the letter of credit. At this stage the beneficiary should check that the goods can be shipped before the 4) _____ (require) date, and the required documents can 5) _____ (obtain).

5. The seller ships the goods, and then 6) _____ (assemble) the required documentation, which will usually 7) _____ (include) a transport document such as a bill of lading.

6. The seller checks that all these 8) _____ (document) conform to all the terms and conditions laid down in the letter of credit.

7. The seller presents the documents to a local bank. The 9) _____ (common) arrangement is for this bank to check the documents and, if they are in order, pay the beneficiary immediately.

8. The documents are 10) _____ (send) back to the issuing bank. If they are in order, the issuing bank will charge the applicant, send by post the funds to the seller's bank, and pass the documents to the applicant so the goods can be claimed from the carrier.

B. General Writing

The following sentence patterns are useful for describing time, size or a distance:

1. Office hours are from 9 a.m. to 5 p.m.
   营业时间由上午9时至下午5时。

2. The company's fiscal year ends on October 15.
   公司的财务年度于10月15日止。

3. The speed increased to nearly sixty miles per hour.
   速度提高至接近每小时60英里。

4. We spent nearly ten years on this project.
   我们在这工程上花了近10年时间。

5. There isn't enough space on the hard disk.
   硬盘里没有足够的空间。

6. The development zone is 5 kilometers away from the station.
   开发区距火车站5公里远。

7. The distance from our school to the gym is about 2 kilometers.
   从我们学校到体育馆的距离是大约2公里。

8. The ship is too tall to go under the bridge.
   这条船太高，不能从桥下通过。

9. Most orders are delivered within 2-3 business days.
   多数订货可以在2至3个工作日内交货。

10. The room is 10 meters by 8.
    这个房间10米长8米宽。

3 **Complete the following sentences, using the appropriate form of the words given in the brackets.**

1) This time next year I _____ in an office. (work)

2) You have taken a long time _____ the letter. (write)

3) The time _____ for the meeting was 2 p.m. (appoint)

4) We measured the room and _____ it was 20 feet long and 15 feet wide. (find)

5) During the 3 years since 2004, he _____ great progress in his study. (make)

6) The hours I spent with you _____ the happiest of my life. (be)

7) This morning I met someone whom I had not _____ for years. (see)

8) His experience of teaching English _____ a period of over 30 years. (cover)

4 **Correct the errors in the following sentences.**

1) The island is only 0.4 square kilometers area.

2) He doesn't spend much time for his homework.

3) The playground measures 70 and 50 meters.

4) He spent a whole week read the book.

5) Since I was a child I lived in Changchun.

6) In ten-year time the children will all have grown up.

7) We've been friends ever since we meet at school.

8) The factory enlarged to make room for more machinery.

5 **Translate the following sentences into English.**

1) 这个房间有10米长。

2) 谈判将持续到下个月。

3) 从北京飞到广州需要多长时间？

4) 那家工厂距离火车站有半小时车程。

5) 从这里到加拿大的路程很远。

6) 这家商店的面积有3个足球场大。

SECTION III

Data Bank

Here is the Data Bank. Practice the patterns and expressions for purchase and payment.

1. I'm interested in your personal computers.
   我对你们的个人电脑感兴趣。

2. Can you show us your catalogue?
   我可以看一下你们的商品目录吗？

3. We have decided to place an order with you.
   我们已经决定向你方订货。

4. We are pleased to accept your order.
   我们很高兴接受你们的订货。

5. This is our latest catalog.
   这是我们最新的商品目录。

6. What are your terms of payment?
   你们的付款条件是什么？

7. Do you quote FOB or CIF?
   你们的报价是船上交货价还是到岸价？

8. We usually quote on a CIF basis.
   我们通常报到岸价。

9. Can you quote in HK dollars?
   你们可以用港元报价吗？

10. What is the deadline for submitting the quotation?

提交报价单的最后期限是什么时候？

11. We'll ship the goods as soon as we receive your L / C.

我们收到信用证后会立即装运。

12. May I have some samples?

可以送我一些样品吗？

Unit 10 Training Across Cultures

Unit Goals

❖ **What You Should Learn to Know About**

1. Culture differences would cause stereotypes and misunderstandings
2. Why you should keep changing in the IT age
3. Conference invitation

SECTION I
Maintaining a Sharp Eye

Read More by Yourself

My Study-Abroad Experience at Lancaster University

By Elizabeth Castellan

During my **sophomore** year in college, I learned about a variety of study-abroad opportunities from my **peers** in the studio art department who were beginning to apply for different art programs overseas. After much thought and discussion with my advisor and professors, I decided that study abroad would allow me to grow as an artist and as an individual, further developing my artistic skills and personal style.

（大学）二年级的；同学

Before I came to Lancaster University, I had requested that I be placed in a flat on the first floor near an exit for easy accessibility. This request was easily **granted**. However, the Residence Life Office failed to mention that the first floor of every building is the ground floor and no women live there because of safety concerns. As a result, I was surprised to find that my three flat-mates were male! At first this was ex-

允许

tremely awkward. Thankfully, I only had to share a kitchen and I had a private bath. Because of my unique situation, the Residence Life Office and the college porters took special security precautions.

Probably the most difficult cultural and academic **adjustments** for me were in my three studio art classes: printmaking, photography and studio practice. At first, the art department was a little uneasy about having a visually impaired student in its midst. As I have been in many other places, I was the Art Department's first visually **impaired** student.

Art students are required to do a tremendous amount of self-guided research in the library and the field. The professor may **recommend** certain artists to study, but students are expected to go beyond a professor's suggestions with their own independent research. Therefore, I spent a great deal of time in the Lancaster University library, researching artists who influenced my work prior to my arrival in England. In addition, I investigated the 20th century Latin American art, African art, Asian art and Indian art. I was also able to persuade many of my new friends to pose for my sketches and photography so I could work from life, and I visited different museums and **galleries** in my spare time.

It was hard to do all of this in my little flat, and so I was forced to orient myself to the studios. My professors assigned me to the art technician, Rob, who oriented me to the building and its facilities and provided me with assistance when necessary. Rob showed me how to work independently in the print shop and in the photography lab. I began to work in both facilities without any assistance. Gradually I got accustomed to my surroundings, and came and went as I pleased with great ease.

A study-abroad experience provides the individual with wonderful personal, academic and career benefits. I feel that my artwork and knowledge of art history developed a great deal because of my studies there. I learned **innovative** techniques in both photography and printmaking, and learned how to conduct self-directed research. In addition, I became independent in my artwork, orientation and mobility, daily living skills and ability to travel. I gained a great deal of confidence in my abilities to adapt and succeed on my own. This gave me a greater sense of my identity, purpose and spirituality. Furthermore, I obtained a tremendous amount of insight about the British culture and how to

调整

有障碍的

推荐

艺术馆

革新的

interact with all types of people. Finally, I made life-long friendships and wonderful memories to last a lifetime.My time at Lancaster University was an experience I will treasure always.

1 **Read the passage and check your understanding by doing the multiple choice exercises.**

1) The author learned about all kinds of study abroad opportunities from her peers when she was a _____ college student.
   a. first year   b. second year
   c. third year   d. fourth year

2) What does "the second floor" mean in British English?
   a. ground floor   b. first floor
   c. third floor   d. fourth floor

3) What does the author mean when she says: "I was forced to orient myself to the studios"?
   a. She liked to work in the studios.
   b. She didn't need to work in the studios
   c. She had to go to work in the studios.
   d. She didn't know how to work in the studios.

4) Which of the following is NOT true according to the passage?
   a. Art students are required to do more self-guided research.
   b. Art students are expected to do a lot of their own independent research.
   c. Professors in the Art Department often recommend certain artists for students to study.
   d. Art students always sit in the studios and rarely do any field work.

5) What can we learn from the last paragraph?
   a. The author benefited a lot from the study-abroad experience.
   b. The author became a creative painter.
   c. Friendship will last for ever.
   d. Confidence is essential for an artist.

2 **Choose the proper word or phrase in the box to fill in the blank in each of the following sentences, changing the form when necessary.**

assign	adjustment	share	conflict
insight	equivalent	provide	

1) What is $5 _____ to in Euro?
2) I've made a few minor _____ to the seating plan.
3) Your statement is in _____ with the rest of the evidence.
4) They obtained an _____ into Chinese literature during the training course.
5) She _____ my troubles as well as my joys.

6) The painting _____ us with one of the earliest examples of farming technology.

7) It is impossible to _____ an exact date to the building of this bridge.

3 **Put the following into English, using the words and expressions given in the brackets.**

1) 部长接受了记者的采访。(grant an interview)

2) 我可以把他作为一位极好的会计推荐给你。(recommend)

3) 我将永远珍惜我们的第一次会面。(treasure)

4) 学会一些顺口溜和歌谣可以帮助父母与婴儿交流。(interact with)

5) 尽管他父亲是公司经理，他还是靠自己的努力得到了这个职务。(on one's own)

PASSAGE II

Continuous Learning

In a **knowledge-based economy**, only continuous learning will equip us for tomorrow's world. The Singapore Learning Festival and Learning Expo, which is now into its 3rd year, is therefore a timely undertaking and a demonstration of commitment to prepare ourselves for the future. While continuing education and re-training is not an instant **panacea** to our unemployment problem, it lays the solid foundation for our future economic prosperity. It will be the key factor in getting our workforce to adjust to the realities of the changing world and stay competitive.

知识经济

灵丹妙药

I have a story of learning to share. I left school without completing my secondary education. With my limited education, I started work as an office boy. Then came the war. I had no work and was encouraged to learn Japanese to secure my livelihood. Through self-study, I became sufficiently proficient in Japanese to work as an interpreter. After the war, I decided to complete my secondary education through self-study, while still working. I then entered the University of Malaya in Singapore, graduating with a Diploma in Social Studies at the age of 30.

For me, learning did not stop at 30. Over the next 40 odd years of my working life, I worked through various positions, and held jobs ranging from a medical social worker, to working in the Labour Movement, to being a diplomat. I also had a **stint** in the private sector, as Executive Chairman of Straits Times Press, and in the aca-

任期

demia as I started up the Institute of Defence and Strategic Studies in Nanyang Technological University. In all my jobs, I could not afford to stop learning.

I listened to my inner feelings and took them seriously. But instead of becoming upset and **lamenting** about my situation in life, I became motivated to learn and acquire knowledge and skills to do better. I had to be knowledgeable and master the critical demands of the work that I was engaged in. I had to accept the reality that I cannot change the world and hope for a free lunch. I had to make every effort to equip myself to be able to discharge the responsibilities entrusted to me. I had to learn on the job and from others with every job that I took, even after I secured reasonable success in life. It has become a habit for me — a good habit which, even now, serves me well.

I have shared my own story to **reinforce** the message that everyone, no matter what the circumstances, no matter how old, no matter how educated or lacking in formal education, and no matter how busy you are, must continue to pick up new knowledge and new skills as you move on in life.

The world is changing rapidly. Individuals, companies and even nations all need to learn and re-learn in order to remain relevant. For Singapore to remain prosperous and thrive in a globally competitive marketplace, our people need to be knowledgeable, skilled and adaptable. We need people and a workforce willing and able to undertake continuous learning. This **realization** will be critical for all.

While the economic benefits of learning are more obvious, it is as important for us to look beyond learning just for **employability's** sake. In a rapidly changing and developing society, the willingness to learn has also everything to do with keeping up with life around us, with participating in society and with having a place in society. As we all enjoy longer life-spans thanks to advances in medical science, we must keep learning throughout our lifetime to stay in touch and connected with the younger generation.

痛惜

加强

真正认识

可雇用性

4 **Are the following statements true or false according to the passage? Write T (for True) or F (for False) accordingly.**

☞ 1) Continuous learning plays an important part in a knowledge-based economy.

☞ 2) Re-training is the only means to help people to learn to adapt to a new job.

☞ 3) People with limited education cannot stay competitive in society if they do not equip themselves through continuous education.

☞ 4) The author was out of work after the war.

☞ 5) Self-study can help a person become successful in career.

☞ 6) According to the author, if you are over 30 years old, you won't be able to undertake continuous education.

☞ 7) Through self-study, the author succeeded in learning Japanese and becoming an interpreter.

☞ 8) If you want to keep up with society, you must continue to secure new knowledge and new skills.

☞ 9) According to the passage, modern medical science is not yet as advanced as to help people live a longer life.

☞10) The message the author wants to share with us is that life-long learning is a good habit everybody must learn to build up.

5 **Fill in the blanks with the appropriate form of the word given in the brackets.**

1) The state of _____ in the world is worth worrying. (economic)
2) The country's _____ was due to its rich oil resources. (prosperous)
3) _____ between bidders for this valuable painting has been keen. (competitive)
4) She is very _____ about art and literature. (knowledge)
5) All the crew members on board a plane are _____ for the passengers' safety. (responsibility)
6) No country can afford to neglect the _____ of its young people. (educational)
7) She's been _____ as a taxi driver for more than 10 years. (employment)
8) His silence would be _____ as a refusal. (interpreter)

6 **Put the following sentences into English, using the words and expressions given in the brackets.**

1) 年轻一代的举止和他们的父辈和祖父辈有很大不同。(generation)
2) 新的规则将对我们大家都有很大好处。 (benefit)
3) 我们觉得我们似乎跟不上计算机技术的快速发展变化。(keep up with)
4) 他承担了整个计划的组织工作。(undertake)
5) 她去法国居住后很快就学会了法语。(pick up)
6) 他爱好广泛，从下棋到划划艇，什么都喜欢。(range from to)

SECTION II
Trying Your Hand

Write More by Yourself

A. Applied Writing: Academic Invitation
   Sample 1

School of Foreign Languages
Shenzhou University
May 10, 2010

Prof. Joseph Wood
Binhai University of International Studies
Binzhou City

Dear Prof. Wood,

   The English teachers of our university were deeply impressed by your new book *A Study of English Intonation* and were very much interested in hearing in person your view on this and other subjects. Would you please be so kind to come to my school at your convenience and meet with them?

   You would, of course, receive our standard honorarium to cover traveling and other expenses.

   Please let us know as soon as possible if you can come and tell us when you would be able to do so.

Sincerely yours,
Zhang Hong
College Office Secretary

Sample 2

Shanghai College of Traditional Chinese Medicine
March 17, 2010

Mr. Robert Hopkins
Medical College
Princeton University

Dear Prof. Hopkins,

　　The Academic Conference on Traditional Chinese Medical Therapeutics sponsored by Shanghai College of Traditional Chinese Medicine will be held in Shanghai on May 20, 2010. We take great pleasure in inviting you to attend the conference. Your hotel accommodation will be borne by us, but we will not pay for your air fare.

　　If you have any paper or topics on which you would like to give a talk, please inform us as soon as possible since the program is being finalized soon.

　　Please confirm your participation at your earliest convenience.

　　With kind regards.

Yours sincerely

Liu Feng

Secretary of the School Office

Expression Tips

1. May we invite you to our university?
   我们可以邀请您来我们学校吗？

2. Would you please be so kind as to come to our school and give a lecture?
   您可以到我们学校来做一个讲座吗？

3. We take great pleasure in inviting you to attend the conference.
   我们十分荣幸地邀请您出席本次学术会议。

4. Could we have the honour of your presence at this conference?
   不知能否有幸请到您来参加这次学术会议？

5. It is very kind of you to have invited me.
   非常感谢您的盛情相邀。

6. We'd like to invite some knowledgeable scholars like you to deliver a series of lectures.
   我们将邀请一些像您这样的知识渊博的学者做一系列的讲座。

7. If you could accept our invitation, an early confirmation will be greatly appreciated.
   如果您能接受我们的邀请，请尽早与我们确认，谢谢。

8. We shall be much obliged if you will confirm it as soon as possible.
   如果您能尽快确认，我们将不胜感激。

9. Nothing could give me greater pleasure than accepting your invitation.
   能接受你们的邀请，我感到荣幸之至。

10. Please accept my sincere regrets for not being able to come to your conference.
    我实在不能来参加会议，请接受我真诚的歉意。

11. All the travel fares and accommodation costs will be for our account.
    您的差旅和食宿费用均由我们承担。

1 **Translate the following invitation into Chinese. Use the sample and the Expression Tips for reference.**

Dear Prof. Krashen,

The *Symposium on English Teaching in China*, sponsored by Binhai University will be held in Binhai City on June 12, 2010.

You are one of the famous scholars in English Language Teaching. We take great pleasure in inviting you to come to the symposium. And we sincerely hope you will present some proposals for improving the quality of English Teaching in China.

We hope you will be able to accept this invitation, and if you would kindly indicate the time of your arrival, we will make arrangements to meet you at the airport.

Sincerely yours,

Xie Yi

Office Secretary

2 **Translate the following sentences into English.**

1) 能邀请您参加我们的学术研讨会是我们最大的荣幸。

2) 我们希望邀请一些像您这样的知名学者来参加会议并为这个项目提出建议。

3) 我们真诚希望您能光临这次大会。我们将承担您全部的差旅和食宿费用。

4) 真诚地邀请您参加本年度最重要的学术会议。

5) 因为那段时间我将在外地出差，所以无法接受您的盛情邀请。

B. General Writing: Expressing Function

Example

One way that the information from a voice analysis can be used is with electric locks. Some electric locks open by a signal from a person's voice, rather than with a key. Based on the voice analysis, the lock is programmed in a certain way. It is controlled by a computer. When, for example, someone wants to open a door, he says some words. Only a few words are necessary, and what is said isn't important because from only a few words the lock can compare the person's voice with the pre-programmed voice it knows. If the two voices are exactly the same, the door opens. This type of system has both advantages and disadvantages. It's very safe and easy to operate. One disadvantage is that most electric locks can only be used by one person since no two voices are alike.

3 **Translate the following sentences into English.**

1) 本机使用4节1号电池供电。

2) 本机右侧有两个旋钮，控制速度和容量。

3) 按下右边的旋钮，可以收听中波电台。

4) 复位按钮(Reset Button)用来调定日历和时间。

5) 秒表(stopwatch)的起始键可以使本机用作秒表，并控制计时的开始和停止。

6) 请勿把废电池(dead battery)保留在电池盒内，因为这样可能会引起故障。

7) 本机灵敏度极高，务必小心轻放。

8) 本机配有外接天线，以改善短波的收听效果。

4 **Correct the errors (italicized parts) in the following paragraphs.**

1) This product, made of choice materials to precise standards, *undergoing* (1) rigid quality check and *has found* (2) to *meeting* (3) all the requirements. It's fully *guarantee* (4) against defective materials and workmanship under normal use. In the guarantee period, repairs, adjustments for defects and replacement of parts *are done* (5) free of charge upon presentation of this guarantee card.

2) On a CD, the data *read off* (1) the disc using an infrared (红外线) laser; a DVD *working* (2) in the same way, but it uses a shorter wavelength (波长) laser so that it *could* (3) read smaller "pits" or little pockets in which data *stored* (4). Smaller pits mean more of them on a disc, hence more information is stored. DVDs also have not one but two layers per side that can store information, and they can carry information on both sides for a *total* (5) four data-holding layers.

SECTION III
Data Bank

Here is the Data Bank. Practice the patterns and expressions for talking about salary, giving people bonus and fringe benefits.

1. Nowadays many people consider bonus a form of salary.
   现在许多人把奖金看作工资的一种形式。

2. We always get quite a handsome bonus every month.
   每个月我们可以得到一笔数目可观的奖金。

3. I think the bonus is actually a salary extension nowadays.
   我认为奖金在今天实际上是工资的一种延伸。

4. That's amazing you got such a high bonus.
   你得到如此多的奖金真令人吃惊。

5. My boss says he will cut my bonus if I don't work harder.
   老板说,如果我不努力工作,就会扣我的奖金。

6. This job offers you 2 000 *yuan* a month plus housing.
   这份工作除了提供住房以外，还提供每月2 000元的收入。

7. I am hunting for a job with higher salary.
   我正在寻找一份工资更高的工作。

117

8. My professional experience qualifies for the well-paid job.

我的专业经验使我能胜任这项工作。

9. I've been offered a job with higher pay that also gives me the opportunity of moving up the ladder.

我找到了一份工资更高的工作，而且使我有机会得到提升。

10. If we offer the best rate of pay for the job, no one will turn around and say they're leaving because of money.

如果我们为这项工作支付最高的工资，没有人说因为嫌钱少而要辞职。

Test One

Part I   Listening Comprehension   (15 minutes)

Directions: *This part is to test your listening ability. It consists of 3 sections.*

Section A

Directions: *This section is to test your ability to give proper responses. There are 5 recorded questions in it. After each question, there is a pause. The questions will be spoken two times. When you hear a question, you should decide on the correct answer from the 4 choices marked A, B, C and D given in your test paper. Then you should mark the corresponding letter on the Answer Sheet with a single line through the center.*

Example: *You will hear:*

You will read: A. I'm not sure.

                   B. You're right.

                   C. Yes, certainly.

                   D. That's interesting.

From the question we learn that the speaker is asking the listener to leave a message. Therefore, **C. Yes, certainly** *is the correct answer. You should mark C on the Answer Sheet.*

[A] [B] ■ [D]

Now the test will begin.

1. A. Let's go now.   C. No, it isn't

     B. I have no idea yet.   D. Yes, I can do it.

2. A. You can go by bus.   C. It's across the street.

     B. Nothing, thank you.   D. It's very kind of you.

3. A. Sorry, you're wrong.   C. I hope so.

     B. What about today?   D. It's a good idea.

4. A. I know him.   C. Go head.

     B. He's all right.   D. I suppose so.

5. A. Just about six months.   C. Seven weeks ago.

     B. The weather is wonderful.   D. It's a nice place.

Section B

Directions: *This section is to test your ability to understand short dialogues. There are 5 recorded dialogues in it. After each dialogue, there is a recorded question. Both the dialogues and questions will be spoken two times. When you hear a question, you should decide on the correct answer from the 4 choices marked A, B, C and D given in your test paper. Then you should mark the corresponding letter on the Answer Sheet with a single line through the center.*

6. A. In a shop.   C. In a classroom.
   B. In a lab.   D. In an office.
7. A. Two.   C. Five.
   B. Three.   D. Seven.
8. A. She went to hospital.   C. She was ill.
   B. She came to classes.   D. She attended a meeting.
9. A. It's salty.   C. It's expensive.
   B. It's unhealthy.   D. It's delicious.
10. A. Do all his work on the computer.
    B. Go to work in a computer company.
    C. Ask someone to repair his computer.
    D. Stop working too long on the computer.

Section C

Directions: *In this section you will hear a recorded short passage. The passage is printed in the test paper, but with some words or phrases missing. The passage will be read three times. During the second reading, you are required to put the missing words or phrases on the Answer Sheet in order of the numbered blanks according to what you hear. The third reading is for you to check your writing. Now the passage will begin.*

Houses come in all shapes and _____11_____. They may be new or old. They may be large or small. Houses usually have two bedrooms or more. Larger houses often have _____12_____ one bathroom. Modern houses are often built with a garage. Many houses have no garage _____13_____. If people have cars, they will park them on the street.

Nowadays most people like central heating. This is heating through the _____14_____ house. It means that all the rooms can be heated at the same time. Modern houses are built with central heating. A lot of older houses have had it _____15_____ later.

Part II   Vocabulary & Structure   (15 minutes)

Directions: *This part is to test your ability to use words and phrases correctly to construct meaningful and grammatically correct sentences. It consists of 2 sections.*

Section A

Directions: *There are 10 incomplete statements here. You are required to complete each statement by choosing the appropriate answer from the 4 choices marked A, B, C and D. You should mark the corresponding letter on the Answer Sheet with a single line through the center.*

16. It's very kind _____ you to help us when we are in such a trouble.

    A. to   C. with

    B. of   D. by

17. It was wise of him to _____ your advice, or he might have lost the game.

    A. hear   C. follow

    B. make   D. carry

18. It's a waste of time _____ to make the old man give up his own idea.

    A. try   C. have tried

    B. trying   D. tried

19. I didn't go to his party because I had to attend an _____ lecture.

    A. important   C. immediate

    B. impatient   D. impossible

20. It was because of the heavy rain _____ he didn't go to the concert.

    A. that   C. why

    B. while   D. since

21. We all know that the front door is the main _____ to the house.

    A. input   C. entrance

    B. way   D. path

22. Robert is said _____ in a Japanese company as a salesman for many years.

    A. to have worked   C. be working

    B. to work   D. having worked

23. I strongly _____ the proposals they put forward at the meeting.

    A. adjust to   C. aim to

    B. point to   D. object to

24. If you _____ to see Bob, please tell him that I am looking for him.

    A. occur   C. appear

    B. happen   D. contact

25. He was looking forward to the time _____ he would have to attend the interview.

    A. where   C. why

    B. that   D. when

Section B

Directions: *There are also 10 incomplete statements here. You should fill in each blank with the proper form of the word given in brackets. Write the word or words in the corresponding space on the Answer Sheet.*

26. The medical team discussed the case of the wounded man again and made the final (decide) _____.

27. The weather was extremely bad, which prevented them from (go) _____ out.

28. Tom, along with his family, (be) _____ satisfied with the service of the hotel.

29. After meal you have to leave a tip on the table for the waiter for his (serve) _____.

30. Here are the books which must (return) _____ to the library next week.

31. The proposal made by the marketing manager seemed to be (reason) _____.

32. We desire that the tour leader (inform) _____ us of any change in the plan immediately.

33. When the plane was landing, the staff representatives (wait) _____ for the CEO inside the main building.

34. Dr. Green made a long and thorough examination of the patient, (particular) _____ of her eyes.

35. Linda was asked (speak) _____ at the New Year's party, which made her nervous.

Part III   Reading Comprehension   (40 minutes)

Directions: *This part is to test your reading ability. There are 5 tasks for you to fulfill. You should read the reading materials carefully and do the tasks as you are instructed.*

Task 1

Directions: *After reading the following passage, you will find 5 questions or unfinished statements, numbered 36 to 40. For each question or statement there are 4 choices marked A, B, C and D. You should make the correct choice and mark the corresponding letter on the Answer Sheet with a single line through the center.*

The Working Holiday Training Program is a good opportunity for you to learn to work in Japanese hotel service. This program uses the Working Holiday System to provide visas for you to go to Japan. The length of each training is 6 to 12 months, depending on your particular request.

The organizers have recognized that the cost of living in Japan might be too high for you to decide to participate in the Working Holiday System. Therefore, this is a paid training program, in which you can get paid for the service you offer during the training. If you can successfully complete the interview process, you will then be sent to Japan to begin your training.

There are no specific educational requirements; however you must have an interest in Japan and be willing to learn the Japanese language. The other requirement is that you must be qualified for the Working Holiday Visa. This means you must be an Australian Citizen (公民) 18 to 30 years old, not having a bad record in the past and having not taken a working holiday before.

36. The Working Holiday Program provides one with a chance to _____.

   A. learn to work in hotel service in Japan

   B. go and do business in Japan

   C. settle down in Japan

   D. have a holiday in Japan

37. People who participate in the program will _____.
    A. get paid for the service they offer
    B. work for the same length of time
    C. be required to stay in the hotel
    D. have to pay for the training

38. In order to participate in the program, one must _____.
    A. have taken a working holiday before
    B. be willing to learn Japanese
    C. have a university degree
    D. be a Japanese citizen

39. The program is specially designed to hire _____.
    A. hotel people
    B. university students
    C. Australian citizens
    D. Japanese citizens

40. This passage is probably taken from _____.
    A. an employment report in Australia
    B. an introduction to education in Australia
    C. an ad for a paid training program in Japan
    D. a job guide for foreigners to look for a job in Japan

Task 2

Directions: *This task is the same as Task 1. The 5 questions or unfinished statements are numbered 41 to 45.*

Vacation time is almost here! Many people are looking forward to a trip to Paris, Hawaii or Tokyo — any place far away from school or the office.

Unfortunately, vacationers sometimes think only about having fun and forget to be careful. Here are a few safety tips (提示).

Make a list of your credit card (信用卡) numbers and the phone numbers to call in case they are lost or stolen. Keep the list in a safe place — separate from your credit cards.

Keep a photocopy (复印件) of your passport in a safe place. In that way you can replace it more easily if it is lost or stolen.

When traveling by plane, pack all your valuables in your carry-on bag. Never put them in the luggage you will check in.

Before you take a walk through a strange city, find out which areas to avoid. Tell someone where you're going and when you plan to return.

Don't leave your cash or valuables in your hotel room. Use the hotel safe (保险箱). It's a free service most hotels offer.

41. The passage tells us that when preparing for a vacation trip, people tend to _____.
    A. bring the wrong things

    B. neglect safety problems

    C. travel to world famous cities

    D. learn about possible dangers

42. What is the safe way for you to protect your credit card?

    A. To write down the card number in a list.

    B. To call to the police when it is lost.

    C. To keep it in your carry-on bag.

    D. To make a copy of the card.

43. According to the author, before leaving, you'd better make a copy of your _____.

    A. air ticket

    B. passport

    C. credit card

    D. phone number

44. If you are going to travel by air you'd better pack your valuables in _____.

    A. a specially-prepared case

    B. a place close to your seat

    C. the luggage you will check in

    D. the handbag you are carrying

45. What is probably the best title for this passage?

    A. What to Do When Traveling

    B. How to Check in a Hotel

    C. Tourist Attractions

    D. Travel Tips

Task 3

Directions: *The following is an advertisement. After reading it, you should complete the information by filling in the blanks marked 46 through 50 in* **no more than 3 words** *in the table below.*

Entering the competition is easy. Simply send us a brief report (up to 500 words) on how you used a *Teachit* resource effectively in the classroom or IT room. It could be that you changed our resources to fit your pupils, you used some *Teachit* materials online with your class in the IT room or that you found one of the *Teachit* worksheets really made your pupils create some great work. Whatever your experience we'd like to hear from you. Please remember to include the following information as well:

    1. The resource or resources you used;

    2. The age and ability group you were teaching;

    3. Your full name and email address.

We look forward to hearing your stories. The entries will be judged by our team of editors and the winners will be announced in January. Remember to email us your story by the 24th December.

Entering *Teachit* Competition for Great Prizes

The way to enter the competition: by sending a brief _____46_____

Information to be Included:

1. your _____47_____ in using Teachit resources
2. the resource or resources you used
3. the age and _____48_____ groups of your pupils
4. your full name and email _____49_____

Deadline for Entering: the _____50_____

Task 4

Directions: *The following is a list of job titles. After reading it, you are required to find the items equivalent to (与···等同) those given in Chinese in the table below. Then you should put the corresponding letters in the brackets on the Answer Sheet, numbered 51 through 55.*

A — Acting Manager
B — Assistant Manager
C — Chief Engineer
D — Dean
E — Deputy Director
F — Designer
G — Economist
H — General Manager
I — Marketing Manager
J — Official
K — Personnel Manager
L — Programmer
M — Sales Manager
N — Secretary-general
O — Surveyor
P — Technical Director
Q — Technician

Examples: (E) 副主任　　　　　　　　　　　　　　　(O) 调研员

51. (　　)总工程师	(　　)技术员
52. (　　)总经理	(　　)代理经理
53. (　　)经理助理	(　　)技术主管
54. (　　)经济师	(　　)销售经理
55. (　　)营销经理	(　　)人事经理

Task 5

Directions: *After reading the following passages, you are required to complete the statements that follow the questions (No.56 to No.60). You should write your answers in **not more than 3 words** on the corresponding Answer Sheet .*

Here at School of Engineering in Nanyang Polytechnic (南洋工学院), you do not only "hit the books" in all your 3 years of study — you get to experience what working in the real world is like! As final year students, you will be attached to certain companies in the local industry for a 12-week period under the Industrial Attachment Program (IAP).

Such an opportunity will allow you to experience first-hand what it takes to work out there in the real world, and you will be able to put into practice all that you have learnt; you will experience for yourself the company culture, public relations and how you can make it all work for you, what it takes to succeed in the working world. In short, you are prepared to join the workforce immediately upon graduation!

56. What special program is offered by School of Engineering in Nanyang Polytechnic?
     The _____.

57. What is the purpose of the above program?
     To let the students experience working in _____.

58. How long will the program last?
     _____ weeks.

59. What is good of the program?
     It enables students to put into _____ what they have learnt.

60. What kind of culture can the students learn to experience while working in the companies?
     The _____.

Part IV   Translation — English into Chinese   (25 minutes)

Directions: *This part, numbered 61 to 65, is to test your ability to translate English into Chinese. Each of the four sentences (No.61 to No.64) is followed by four choices of suggested translation marked A, B, C and D. Make the best choice and write the corresponding letter on the Answer Sheet. Write your translation of the paragraph (No.65) in the corresponding space on the Translation/ Composition Sheet.*

61. An even better year is expected after three years of steady increase in annual output.
     A. 希望今年要比前3年的生产更好，有更好的年景。
     B. 年产量3年来已快速增加，希望今年也会好些。
     C. 在年产量3年稳步增长后，预计今年会更好。
     D. 人们期待3年产量快速提高后能稳步增长。

62. When busy at work, which he often was, he would forget all about eating and sleeping.
     A. 他忙起工作来，就会废寝忘食。
     B. 他工作忙，常常忘了吃饭和睡觉。

C. 他工作很忙，而且常常不吃不睡。

D. 他工作忙昏了头，而一睡过头就没有饭吃。

63. All necessary information about the meeting will be supplied to us by the organizer in advance.

    A. 全部所需的资料都会在会议之前组织我们提供。

    B. 有关会议的全部信息我们将提前提供给会议组织者。

    C. 会议组织者让我们事先把所有有关的信息都准备好上交。

    D. 有关会议所需的全部资料将由组织者提前提供给我们。

64. Computers are taking over some of the tasks once finished by our own brains, but they are not replacing us.

    A. 计算机承担了我们大脑的一些职责，但它们不会妨碍我们。

    B. 计算机正在接替本来由人脑完成的部分工作，但是它们并没有取代我们。

    C. 计算机正在做一些只有我们的大脑才能做的事情，然而它们没有取代我们。

    D. 计算机占领了我们的某些职位，完成了我们任务，但是我们的大脑不能因此空闲下来。

65. Good afternoon, ladies and gentlemen. Captain (机长) Johnson and his attendants (乘务员) welcome you abroad British Airways Flight 197 to New York. We are now flying at a height of 30 000 feet. Our speed is about 600 km/h. We'll land in New York in five and a half hours. The temperature in New York is now -3°C. Our attendants on the airplane will serve lunch in half an hour.

Thank you for your attention.

Part V   Writing   **(25 minutes)**

Directions: *This part is to test your ability to do practical writing. You are required to write a notice for an activity to be postponed according to the instructions given in Chinese below. Remember to write your notice on the Translation/Composition Sheet.*

说明：以学生会的名义写一份活动延期举行的启事。

内容：我们原定于6月20日晚上7点在报告厅举行讲座。讲座的题目是：大学毕业生如何正确择业。因报告人Brown Company的王先生突然生病，讲座推迟到6月22日晚上7点。

Words for reference:

启事	notice
原定的	originally-scheduled
报告厅	lecture hall
推迟	put off
题目	topic

Test Two

Part I   **Listening Comprehension**   **(15 minutes)**

Directions: *This part is to test your listening ability. It consists of 3 sections.*

Section A

Directions: *This section is to test your ability to give proper responses. There are 5 recorded questions in it. After each question, there is a pause. The questions will be spoken two times. When you hear a question, you should decide on the correct answer from the 4 choices marked A, B, C and D given in your test paper. Then you should mark the corresponding letter on the Answer Sheet with a single line through the center.*

Example: *You will hear:*

You will read: A. I'm not sure.

B. You're right.

C. Yes, certainly.

D. That's interesting.

From the question we learn that the speaker is asking the listener to leave a message. Therefore, **C Yes, certainly** *is the correct answer. You should mark C on the Answer Sheet.*

[A] [B] ■ [D]

Now the test will begin.

1. A. It's too short.
   B. It's too cold.
   C. Mary did.
   D. In Italy.

2. A. Yes, go straight on.
   B. Yes, please.
   C. No, it isn't.
   D. No, thanks.

3. A. That's too bad.
   B. It's a pleasure.
   C. That's right
   D. Here you are.

4. A. I want to be a teacher.
   B. Well, let me try.
   C. Thank you for your advice.
   D. Fine, thank you.

5. A. Well, let me see.
   B. Not at all.
   C. Thank you.
   D. That's important.

Section B

Directions: *This section is to test your ability to understand short dialogues. There are 5 recorded dialogues in it. After each dialogue, there is a recorded question. Both the dialogues and questions will be spoken two times. When you hear a question, you should decide on the correct answer from the 4 choices marked A, B, C and D given in your test paper. Then you should mark the corresponding letter on the Answer Sheet with a single line through the center.*

6. A. July 1st.　　　　　　　　　　　　　C. June 1st.
   B. July 21st.　　　　　　　　　　　　D. June 21st.
7. A. To a party.　　　　　　　　　　　C. To the office.
   B. To her house.　　　　　　　　　　D. To the supermarket.
8. A. A postman.　　　　　　　　　　　C. A passenger.
   B. A taxi driver.　　　　　　　　　　D. A policeman.
9. A. In a hospital.　　　　　　　　　　C. At a railway station.
   B. In a bookstore.　　　　　　　　　D. At the airport.
10. A. Pleased.　　　　　　　　　　　　C. Unhappy.
    B. Angry.　　　　　　　　　　　　　D. Surprised.

Section C

Directions: *In this section you will hear a recorded short passage. The passage is printed in the test paper, but with some words or phrases missing. The passage will be read three times. During the second reading, you are required to put the missing words or phrases on the Answer Sheet in order of the numbered blanks according to what you hear. The third reading is for you to check your writing. Now the passage will begin.*

Harrods is a famous department store in London. On December 31, its year-end sale began. Customers from _____11_____ the world came to Harrods on that day. Shoppers can get many goods at _____12_____ rates that day. In most cases the prices on that day _____13_____ by 50 to 75 percent. The sale lasts for one month. Department store sales in Britain _____14_____ by about 5 percent in 2002. But in the U.S., department store sales decreased. American shoppers think that price is very important. They don't like to shop in _____15_____ department stores.

Part II　　　　　　Vocabulary & Structure　　　　　(15 minutes)

Directions: *This part is to test your ability to use words and phrases correctly to construct meaningful and grammatically correct sentences. It consists of 2 sections.*

Section A

Directions: *There are 10 incomplete statements here. You are required to complete each statement by choosing the appropriate answer from the 4 choices marked A, B, C and D. You should mark the corresponding letter on the Answer Sheet with a single line through the center.*

16. The factory is trying to increase its profit by decreasing its _____.
    A. sales　　　　　　　　　　　　　C. cost
    B. production　　　　　　　　　　D. price
17. I won't be able to get into my office because I _____ my key.
    A. lose　　　　　　　　　　　　　C. will lose
    B. have lost　　　　　　　　　　　D. would lose

129

18. The driver should be partly _____ for the traffic accident.
    A. responsible
    B. terrible
    C. possible
    D. reliable

19. _____ a wrong telephone number, he couldn't get connected with his friends.
    A. Got
    B. To get
    C. To be getting
    D. Getting

20. He will _____ his father's business after graduating from university.
    A. take over
    B. make up
    C. put away
    D. get over

21. The team had to work overtime in order to _____ the technical problem.
    A. ask
    B. solve
    C. reply
    D. get

22. _____ the cost, the new production line will be introduced next month.
    A. In spite of
    B. Instead of
    C. In case of
    D. In terms of

23. We find _____ necessary that the controlling instrument should be put close enough to the machine.
    A. that
    B. this
    C. it
    D. what

24. Many students manage to support their college education _____ finding on-campus jobs.
    A. by
    B. on
    C. of
    D. in

25. The city library will have to close _____ the government agrees to give extra money.
    A. since
    B. when
    C. if
    D. unless

Section B

Directions: *There are also 10 incomplete statements here. You should fill in each blank with the proper form of the word given in brackets. Write the word or words in the corresponding space on the Answer Sheet.*

26. An American sportsman (hold) _____ this world record for several years.

27. (General) _____ speaking, you'd better write a thankful letter as you have received a good service.

28. I don't think Mary can be patient enough (look) _____ after the baby.

29. The plane was able to fly over the endless white plains without (difficult) _____.

30. Five people (injure) _____ in the traffic accident which happened last Friday.

31. This famous building serves as the country's national museum and is an important center of (science) _____ research.

32. This sum of money (be) _____ enough for us to buy the materials for the new factory.

33. I strongly support his (apply) _____ for the position of the sales manager.

34. The manager suggested that the meeting (begin) _____ at 10:00 Monday morning.

35. Life must be very unpleasant for those people (live) _____ near the train station.

Part III   Reading Comprehension   (40 minutes)

Directions: *This part is to test your reading ability. There are 5 tasks for you to fulfill. You should read the reading materials carefully and do the tasks as you are instructed.*

Task 1

Directions: *After reading the following passage, you will find 5 questions or unfinished statements, numbered 36 to 40. For each question or statement there are 4 choices marked A, B, C and D. You should make the correct choice and mark the corresponding letter on the Answer Sheet with a single line through the center.*

If you want something real and practical now, here is something for you! If you want to have an education but don't feel like spending all four years in college, the answer is Vocational (职业的) Education and Training (VET). Australia's VET system is often referred to as Technical and Vocational Education (TVE) in other countries. It will provide you with training that is both practical and career-based. In the end it will help you develop your own career path through study and a mix of study and work.

The VET is divided into two sections: a nationally recognized government system of Technical and Further Education (TAFE) and private schools. Private vocational schools are different in size from 50 students up to 500. Classes tend to be small with an average teacher to student ratio (比例) of 1:20. The different schools decide on their own entrance requirements, courses, and study lengths. Diploma (文凭) courses are usually over 40 weeks and certificate courses from 12 to 30 weeks.

36. VET is an educational system designed for those who want to _____
   A. learn to be qualified for a job
   B. become a college student
   C. obtain a university degree
   D. study in their spare time

37. The training that the VET system provides _____
   A. can only be taken in private schools
   B. is internationally accepted
   C. is practical and job-based
   D. lasts for four years

38. The VET's two sections are _____
   A. the TAFE system and private vocational schools
   B. theoretical education and practical training
   C. diploma and certificate courses
   D. school and company training

39. From the passage we learn that private vocational schools usually _____.
    A. charge more money for certificate courses
    B. have a class size from 50 to 500 students
    C. provide only practical diploma courses
    D. have a small class size of 20 students

40. According to the passage, diploma courses are _____.
    A. stricter in their requirements
    B. popular with college students
    C. longer than certificate courses
    D. more suitable to one's work

Task 2

Directions: *This task is the same as Task 1. The 5 questions or unfinished statements are numbered 41 to 45.*

Like all buildings, hotels can have a fire. Plan what to do when you check in. You won't have time to make a plan during a fire.

If there is any sign of fire, call the Front Desk immediately. Give your name, room number, and a brief description of the situation. If your family is with you, determine a meeting place outside the building so you'll know everyone is safe. Feel the door to see if it is warm. If it is, do not open it. If it is not warm, drop to your knees and slowly open the door, but be ready to shut it tightly if a cloud of smoke should roll in. If the corridor is clear, head for the exit.

Do not stand upright (直立), but keep low to the floor to avoid smoke. When you reach the exit, walk quickly, but carefully down the stairs. If you are unable to leave your room, make every effort to let people know that you are in your room. If you cannot reach the Front Desk, call the local fire department and explain clearly your exact location so that you may get help as soon as possible.

41. According to the passage when a hotel is on fire, you usually have no time to _____.
    A. close the door tightly
    B. call the Front Desk
    C. plan what to do
    D. explain your exact position

42. In case of a fire when you are in a hotel, the first thing you should do is to _____.
    A. call the Front Desk
    B. find your family members
    C. open the door
    D. rush out of the building

43. The purpose for you to decide where your family is to meet after getting out of the hotel is to
    _____.
    A. know if every member is safe
    B. be able to comfort each other
    C. run away from the building

D. send the injured to hospital

44. When you open the door and smoke rushes in, you should _____.

    A. open the door slowly and run out immediately

    B. close the door tightly and quickly

    C. find out if the corridor is clear

    D. call loudly for help

45. What should you do first if you are unable to leave your room during the fire?

    A. Find out where the exit is.

    B. Call the local fire department.

    C. Stand upright near the window.

    D. Let people know you are in your room.

Task 3

Directions: *The following is an advertisement. After reading it, you should complete the information by filling in the blanks marked 46 through 50 in **not more than 3 words** in the table below.*

OPEN ALL HOURS

Shoppers at The Oracle will get plenty of time to buy their Christmas presents with the center opening late almost every night.

The shopping centre is extending its opening hours for all shoppers in the run up to the Christmas period, starting tonight with late night shopping before switching to 12-hour-a-day opening hours in early December.

"By extending our opening hours over Christmas everyone can come and shop at their leisure," said Paul Briggs, Oracle customer relations' manager.

For early risers The Oracle will open half an hour earlier, at 8:30am, every Saturday from November 30.

The full extended Christmas hours come into action from Monday, December 9, when the shops will open from 9:30am until 9:30pm.

OPEN ALL HOURS

Advertiser: _____46_____

Content Advertised: extending _____47_____

Period Covered: starting from _____48_____ over the Christmas period

Extended hours: at 8:30 a.m. every _____49_____ from November 30;

_____50_____ hours a day from December 9

Task 4

Directions: *The following are some of the subjects dealt with by the new book Mastering Global Markets.*

After reading it, you are required to find the items equivalent to (与…等同) those given in Chinese in the table below. Then you should put the corresponding letters in the brackets on the Answer Sheet, numbered 51 through 55.

A — global marketing
B — opportunities and challenges
C — foreign market data
D — trading associations
E — trade payment
F — building cultural knowledge
G — cultural analysis
H — training challenges
I — trade organizations
J — export readiness
K — market survey
L — investing directly abroad
M — service areas
N — growth drivers
O — opportunity analysis
P — secondary research
Q — primary research
R — personnel management

Examples: (D) 贸易协会   (R) 人事管理

51. (   ) 全球营销   (   ) 市场调查
52. (   ) 出口前期准备   (   ) 贸易支付
53. (   ) 机遇及挑战   (   ) 培训难题
54. (   ) 文化分析   (   ) 机遇分析
55. (   ) 服务区域   (   ) 向国外直接投资

Task 5

Directions: *There are two advertisements below. After reading them, you are required to complete the statements that follow the questions (No.56 through No.60). You should write your answers in **not more than 3 words** on the corresponding Answer Sheet.*

Advertisement 1

Our company has an opening for a sales assistant position. Experience in cabinets (橱柜), windows & doors helpful. We supply building materials to custom home builders. Starting salary at $13.68/hr. Benefits included. We have a friendly office environment. Position is full time, Mon-Fri. Send resume to doug@pacsource.com or fax to 360-512-5553 or mail to Pacific Source, Postal Box 2323, Woodinville, WV98072

Advertisement 2

HyaraMaster is a local manufacturer who needs a machine operator for our workshop. If you are a machine operator who knows conventional (常规的) equipment & likes to work on the various projects of a small shop, this job may be for you. Must be able to lift up to 100 pounds, be able to read blueprints (设计图), have strong organized skills & be quality-conscious. We offer excellent benefits & a friendly environment. Send resume to HyaraMaster, 11015 47th Ave. or e-mail hr@hydramaster.com.

56. What kind of position is offered in the first advertisement?
    A position of _____

57. What is the starting salary for the position in the first advertisement?
    It is at _____.

58. Is the advertised position a full-time or a part-time job?
    It is _____.

59. What kind of person is HyaraMaster looking for in the second advertisement?
    A _____.

60. What favorable conditions are offered for the position in the second advertisement?
    Excellent _____ and a friendly environment.

Part IV   Translation — English into Chinese   (25 minutes)

Directions: *This part, numbered 61 to 65, is to test your ability to translate English into Chinese. Each of the four sentences (No.61 to No.64) is followed by four choices of suggested translation marked A, B, C and D. Make the best choice and write the corresponding letter on the Answer Sheet. Write your translation of the paragraph (No.65) in the corresponding space on the Translation/ Composition Sheet.*

61. We can meet your wish for better packing only if we increase our prices by 1%.
    A. 如果增加费用1%，我们就愿意提供更好的包装。
    B. 如果我们提高价格1%，我们就愿意提供更好的包装。
    C. 除非我们提价1%，才能满足贵公司改善包装的愿望。
    D. 除非增加1%的费用，我们难以满足贵公司包装得更好的要求。

62. If not for these difficulties, there is little doubt that the delivery terms would have been observed.
    A. 要不是因为这些困难，毫无疑问交货条件原本是可以遵守的。
    B. 尽管存在这些困难，运输条件是肯定可以实现的。
    C. 如果没有这些困难，交货条件是有可能实现的。
    D. 如果有这些困难，运输条件肯定无法实现。

63. I am beginning to see how each department works with the others to create an efficient operation.
    A. 我看到每个部门都在其他部门，以求得运转顺利。

B. 我开始看到公司每一个部门都相互合作，卓有成效地运作。

C. 我开始理解公司的各个部门是怎样配合，以创造有效的运作。

D. 我开始看到每个部门都在怎样进行工作，达到有效运作的结果。

64. If people have confidence in their own performance, they are more likely to achieve a leading position in a group.

A. 如果人们表现十分好，他们就会谋取小组领导位置。

B. 如果人们对自己的表现满意，他们就能领导小组工作。

C. 如果人们对自己的行为负责，他们就能在团队里出人头地。

D. 如果人们深信自己的表现，他们更有可能在团队里得到领导地位。

65. Welcome to the San Francisco (旧金山) International Airport, one of the leading airports in the world. It offers high quality service to Airport passengers. In order to best serve the needs of the traveling public, this San Francisco International Airport Guide is designed to introduce you to the big variety of attractive foods, goods and services provided to air travelers and airport visitors.

Part V   Writing   (25 minutes)

Directions: *This part is to test your ability to do practical writing. You are required to write a notice according to the instructions given in Chinese below. Remember to write your notice on the Translation/Composition Sheet.*

说明：以Crown Hotel 的名义于2011年6月15日写一份通告。

内容：由于本酒店的停车场面积小，因此请参加本周五晚上招待会的客人乘酒店的穿梭巴士前来。希望来宾享用此项服务，以便酒店能够安排客人住店。

Words for reference:

通告	notice
招待会	reception
穿梭巴士	shuttle bus
享用	take advantage of
招待	accommodate

Test Three

Part I　　　　Listening Comprehension　　　(15 minutes)

Directions: *This part is to test your listening ability. It consists of 3 sections.*

Section A

Directions: *This section is to test your ability to understand short dialogues. There are 5 recorded dialogues in it. After each dialogue, there is a recorded question. Both the dialogues and questions will be spoken only once. When you hear a question, you should decide on the correct answer from the 4 choices marked A, B, C and D given in your test paper. Then you should mark the corresponding letter on the Answer Sheet with a single line through the center.*

Example: *You will hear:*

You will read:　A.　New York City.

　　　　　　　　　B.　An evening party.

　　　　　　　　　C.　An air trip.

　　　　　　　　　D.　The man's job.

From the dialogue we learn that the man is to take a flight to New York. Therefore, **C. An air trip** *is the correct answer. You should mark C. on the Answer Sheet with a single line through the center.*

[A] [B] ■ [D]

Now the test will begin.

1. A. Some wine.
   B. A cup of tea.
   C. Some food.
   D. A glass of milk.
2. A. An accountant.
   B. A librarian.
   C. A secretary.
   D. A reader.
3. A. On a train.
   B. In a hotel.
   C. On a plane.
   D. In a bank.
4. A. Go dancing with the man.
   B. Go on writing a report.
   C. Give an evening party.
   D. Listen to an important lecture.
5. A. He's going to take an exam.
   B. He's happy with the test result.
   C. He's poor at history.
   D. He's an unpleasant student.

Section B

Directions: *This section is to test your ability to understand short conversations. There are 2 recorded conversations in it. After each conversation, there are some recorded questions. Both the conversations and questions will be spoken two times. When you hear a question, you should decide on the correct answer from the 4 choices marked A, B, C and D given in your test paper.*

Then you should mark the corresponding letter on the Answer Sheet with a single line through the center.

Conversation 1

6. A. It's the best physical exercise.
   B. It's everybody's favorite.
   C. It doesn't take much time.
   D. It's the easiest form of exercise.

7. A. To talk about morning exercise.
   B. To meet the new running coach.
   C. To do morning running together.
   D. To do some special training together.

Conversation 2

8. A. His passport.
   B. His schedule.
   C. His driving license.
   D. His attending card.

9. A. Far from the school.
   B. In a community.
   C. In the city center.
   D. On campus.

10. A. By bike.
    B. By bus.
    C. By car.
    D. On foot.

Section C

Directions: *This section is to test your ability to comprehend short passages. You will hear a recorded passage. After that you will hear five questions. Both the passage and the questions will be read two times. When you hear a question, you should complete the answer to it with a word or a short phrase (**in not more than 3 words**). The questions and incomplete answers are printed in your test paper. You should write your answers on the Answer Sheet correspondingly. Now listen to the passage.*

11. Who will come to visit the university?

    _____ from a group company.

12. On what day will she give a lecture?

    _____.

13. What is the lecture about?

    _____.

14. For how long will the lecture be?

    _____.

15. Who are welcome to come to the lecture?

    _____.

Part II   Structure   (15 minutes)

Directions: *This part is to test your ability to construct grammatically correct sentences. It consists of 2 sections.*

Section A

Directions: *In this section, there are 10 incomplete sentences. You are required to complete each one by deciding on the most appropriate word or words from the 4 choices marked A, B, C and D. Then you should mark the corresponding letter on the Answer Sheet with a single line through the center.*

16. Do you know the reason _____ there are so many strangers in the hall?

    A. what   C. which

    B. why   D. where

17. Only when we had finished all the work _____ realize that it was too late to take a bus to leave.

    A. we did   C. did we

    B. we can   D. can we

18. _____ the lights in the house were all out, he thought his friend was not in.

    A. Have seen   C. Saw

    B. Having seeing   D. Seeing

19. Whether you can find Mary _____ has nothing to do with what we are talking about now.

    A. or not   C. or else

    B. or so   D. or

20. If we hadn't got a lift, we _____ the top flat so early.

    A. would not reach   C. could not have reached

    B. can not reach   D. will not reach

21. No one can do anything _____ someone gives us more information.

    A. if   C. because

    B. unless   D. so

22. I don't think that place is worth _____ for hundreds of miles to visit.

    A. to travel   C. traveled

    B. travel   D. traveling

23. The pictures remind me _____ the time we spent together in the countryside.

    A. of   C. for

    B. in   D. to

24. _____ is often the case with a new idea, our discussion has produced no result.

    A. It   C. Which

    B. That   D. As

25. It is necessary that an efficient worker _____ his work on time.

    A. accomplishes   C. can accomplish

B. accomplish   D. has accomplished

Section B

Directions: *There are 10 incomplete statements here. You should fill in each blank with the proper form of the word given in brackets. Write the word or words in the corresponding space on the Answer Sheet.*

26. Most people feel that education in their country needs to be given a (high) _____ priority than anything else.

27. Most people who see a baseball game for the first time think it's pretty (bore) _____.

28. After the accident, Bill learned to walk again through his hard work and (determine) _____.

29. They will set off to deliver supplies to an (isolate) _____ village tomorrow morning.

30. A little (nervous) _____ is only to be expected when you are starting a new job.

31. The length of time (spend) _____ in doing exercise has to do with the sport you are training for.

32. Consumers may find prices higher or lower than average, (depend) _____ on where they buy gas.

33. Patients should (inform) _____ by doctors about the possible side effects of any drug they take.

34. Before (write) _____ your letter, you should know that employers desire different kinds of people for different positions.

35. It's high time we (do) _____ something about the traffic problem in this city.

Part III   Reading Comprehension   (40 minutes)

Directions: *This part is to test your reading ability. There are 5 tasks for you to fulfill. You should read the reading materials carefully and do the tasks as you are instructed.*

Task 1

Directions: *After reading the following passage, you will find 5 questions or unfinished statements, numbered 36 to 40. For each question or statement there are 4 choices marked A, B, C, and D. You should make the correct choice and mark the corresponding letter on the Answer Sheet with a single line through the center.*

One hundred and thirteen million Americans have at least one credit card. They give their owners automatic credit in stores, restaurants, and hotels, at home, across the country, and even abroad, and they make many banking services available as well. More and more of these credit cards can be read automatically, making it possible to withdraw or deposit money in scattered locations, whether or not the local branch bank is open. For many of us the "cashless society" is not on the horizon — it's already here.

While computers offer these conveniences to consumers, they have many advantages for sellers too. Electronic cash registers can do much more than simply **ring up sales**. They can keep a wide range of records, including who sold what, when, and to whom. This information allows businessmen to keep track of their list of goods by showing which items are being sold and how fast they are moving. Decisions to reorder or return goods to suppliers can then be made. At the same time these computers record which hours are busiest and which employees are the most efficient, allowing personnel and staffing assignments to be made accordingly.

Computers are relied on by manufacturers for similar reasons. Computer-analyzed marketing reports can help to decide which products to emphasize now, which to develop for the future, and which to drop. Computers keep track of goods in stock, of raw materials on hand, and even of the production process itself.

36. According to the passage, the credit card _____.
    A. is creating a society without cash
    B. has limited the function of the bank
    C. has become the only means of payment
    D. allows people to withdraw money from any bank

37. When we say something is not on the horizon, we mean that _____.
    A. it is not very far away
    B. it is not beyond our reach
    C. it seems unlikely to happen in the future
    D. it seems nowhere to be found yet

38. The phrase "ring up sales" (Para. 2) most probably means "_____".
    A. keep a record of sales
    B. call the sales manager
    C. place an order for goods
    D. keep track of the goods in stock

39. What can manufacturers do with computer-analyzed marketing reports?
    A. Open new markets in different areas.
    B. Promote the sales of new products.
    C. Make decisions on production.
    D. Calculate their annual sales.

40. What is this passage mainly about?
    A. Advantages of using credit cards in business.
    B. Approaches to the commercial use of computers.
    C. Significance of automation in commercial payment.
    D. Conveniences of doing business by electronic means.

Task 2
Directions: *This task is the same as Task 1. The 5 questions or unfinished statements are numbered 41 to 45.*

Turbo Jet offers two classes of service — super and economy. Cabins (客舱) are air-conditioned and equipped with TV and entertainment facilities. A snack bar is also available to serve light meals and drinks. Large space is reserved for passengers' luggage. Super class passengers can enjoy the comfortable waiting-room before the scheduled boarding time, as well as meals, snacks, drinks, newspapers and magazines. Luxurious (豪华的) VIP cabin for up to 6 passengers is also available.

Passengers may travel luggage-free as all luggage will be checked through to the final destination.

Turbo Jet Luggage Services Center, located at the ground floor of the Center, provides luggage handling services including luggage check-in, keeping and carrying service. Sports lovers may also store their sports bags with us here and we will deliver them all the way to the terminal.

Turbo Jet has over 100 Booking Offices in Hong Kong, Mainland of China, and Macau as well as foreign travel agencies. Passengers may choose to make their travel arrangements by telephone and online ticket reservation system, or buy them at Hong Kong International Airport. *Turbo Jet* works closely with an extensive network of travel agents to extend a wide ranging selection of travel packages for travelers.

Enquiries: Hong Kong   852-28593333

Macau   853-7907039

Shenzhen   86755-27776818

Reservations: International toll (费用) free fax: + 800 1628 1628

Mainland of China & Taiwan toll free telephone: + 800 1268 1268

E-mail: reservation@ turbol.com.hk

41. What company is *Turbo Jet*?
    A. A luggage handling service.
    B. A ticket service center.
    C. An airline company.
    D. A travel agency.

42. What is most convenient for this company's passengers?
    A. They can take as much luggage as they wish to.
    B. They can travel to their final destination directly.
    C. They can enjoy good meals before going on board.
    D. They can get their luggage at the final destination.

43. Passengers can book their *Turbo Jet* travel arrangements _____.
    A. by telephone or online
    B. at any international airports
    C. through any travel agency in the country
    D. through the *Turbo Jet* Luggage Services Center

44. Which number is free of charge for overseas passengers to book a flight?
    A. Telephone 852-28593333.
    B. Telephone 853-7907039.
    C. Telephone + 800 1268 1268.
    D. Fax + 800 1628 1628.

45. What is the purpose of the passage?
    A. To describe the functions of *Turbo Jet*.
    B. To stress the simplicity of check-in with *Turbo Jet*.
    C. To introduce the services of *Turbo Jet*.
    D. To tell about the ticket reservation of *Turbo Jet*.

Task 3

Directions: *The following is a notice. After reading it, you are required to complete the outline below it (No.46 to No.50). You should write your answers briefly **(in not more than 3 words)** on the Answer Sheet correspondingly.*

Notice

To welcome the coming New Year and to celebrate the 20th anniversary of the company, we will hold a series of celebrating activities. By pooling the creative ideas and efforts of all the staff, the company has now become one of the leading electronics companies in the country. So to express the company's gratitude to all of you who have contributed to the success of the company, the celebrating activities to be held are as follows:

1. Annual Award Meeting, 30 Dec 2006

   Welcome and Opening Speeches 8:55 – 9:00

   Review and Evaluation of 2006 Activities 9:00 – 9: 30

   Slides & Video Demonstration 9: 30 – 10:00

   Coffee Break

   2007 Schedule of Events 10:20 – 10:50

   2007 Proposed Budget 10:50 – 11:20

   Presenting Awards and Taking Photos 11:20 – 11:40

2. Dinner Party 11:40 – 12:30

3. In the afternoon, all kinds of entertainment activities will make you relaxed.

4. In the evening, New Year Party will bring you excitement.

   If you have any questions, please call the office director on 021-6843798.

Company Office

A Notice

Intended for: _____46_____ of the company

Purposes of celebration:

    1) to welcome the coming New Year

    2) to celebrate _____47_____ of the company

Activities to be held:

    1) Annual _____48_____ Meeting

    2) Dinner Party

    3) All kinds of _____49_____ in the afternoon

    4) New Year Performance in the evening

Contact Person: _____50_____

Task 4

Directions: *The following is a list of terms in Business. After reading it, you are required to find the items equivalent to (与···等同) those given in Chinese in the table below. Then you should put the corresponding letters in the brackets on the Answer Sheet, numbered 51 through 55.*

A — annual earnings

B — annual financial report

C — annual income tax return

D — annual inflation rate

E — annual interest

F — annual pay

G — annual rent

H — annual report

I — annual budget

J — annual expenditure

K — annual growth rate

L — annual general meeting of shareholders

M — annual reporting system

N — annual review

O — annual audit

P — annual sales volume

Examples: (E) 年利　　　　　　　　　　　　　　　　　　　(F) 年薪

51. (　) 年收入　　　　　　　　　　　　(　) 年租金
52. (　) 年度所得税申报表　　　　　　　(　) 年度股东大会
53. (　) 年度报告制度　　　　　　　　　(　) 年度审查
54. (　) 年度预算　　　　　　　　　　　(　) 年销售量
55. (　) 年度支出　　　　　　　　　　　(　) 年通货膨胀率

Task 5

Directions: *The following are two application letters. After reading them, you should give brief answers to the 5 questions (No.56 to No.60) that follow. The answers (**in not more than 3 words**) should be written after the corresponding numbers on the Answer Sheet.*

Letter 1

Dear Sir,

Your advertisement in this morning's *Daily Review* for a sales manager prompts me to offer you my qualifications (资格) for this position, because your requirements provide closely an equal for my working experience.

As the enclosed resume indicates, I have had five years' experience in marketing. I've kept an above-average sales record for the past five years.

I am quite happy in my present work, but foreign trade in your company sounds more appealing. I would like to have more opportunity for promotion. Regarding salary, I would leave that to you, and my present salary is $6 000 per month.

I will be glad to have an interview at your convenience, and can provide references if desired.

Yours truly,

Polly Lawrence

Letter 2

Dear Polly Lawrence,

We have reviewed your application for employment and would like to speak with you further. However, we have been unable to reach you by phone.

We would appreciate your contacting us. If we do not hear from you by the 18th, we will assume that you are not interested in pursuing this matter further.

Sincerely,

Jenny Town

56. Where did Polly Lawrence find the advertisement?

In _____ in the morning.

57. What is Polly Lawrence's present job?

He is at present working in _____.

58. Why does Polly Lawrence want to leave his present company?

Because he wishes to be _____.

59. Why did Jenny Town write to the applicant?

Because she couldn't reach him _____.

60. What was the deadline set by Jenny Town for Lawrence to contact her company?

_____.

Part IV   Translation – English into Chinese   (25 minutes)

Directions: *This part, numbered 61 through 65, is to test your ability to translate English into Chinese. After each of the sentences numbered 61 to 64, you will read four choices of suggested translation. You should choose the best translation and mark the corresponding letter on your Answer Sheet. And for the paragraph numbered 65, write your translation in the corresponding space on the Translation/Composition Sheet.*

61. People who sleep less than seven hours per night are more likely to become very fat than those who sleep seven or more hours.

A. 每晚睡眠时间不足7小时的人比超过7小时或更长的人更可能发胖。

B. 每晚睡觉7小时左右或者超过7小时的人通常都容易发胖。

C. 睡眠时间在7小时以内的人比睡眠时间超过7小时的人更担心会发胖。

D. 每晚睡眠时间超过7个小时或少于7个小时的人都没有必要担心会发胖。

62. Duties will be assigned based on the needs of the Center for Career Opportunities and interests of the Student Ambassadors.

    A. 学生大使的职责要依指导中心的就业需要来确定，也要考虑其利益。

    B. 指导中心将根据需要指定学生大使的岗位，并且使他们能得益。

    C. 学生大使的任务是根据就业指导中心的需要和本人的兴趣安排的。

    D. 学生大使的责任就是要完成就业指导中心为他们安排有趣的任务。

63. Nearly 16% of low-income families are linked to an increased risk of heart attack, compared with only 9% of families living above the poverty line.

    A. 低收入家庭中大约有16%的人会与心脏病有关，只比高于贫困线的家庭中得心脏病的人高9%。

    B. 近16%的低收入家庭与不断上升的心脏病有关，与之相对应的是生活在贫困线以上的家庭只有9%与此病有联系。

    C. 16%的低收入家庭有患心脏病的可能性，与之形成对比的是有9%高于贫困线的家庭从来都不得心脏病。

    D. 心脏病的发病率在大约16%的低收入家庭中不断增长，约比那些生活在贫困线上的家庭中患心脏病的人多9%。

64. After dropping over the past eight years, rates of smoking in the U.S. leveled off in 2006 at 1 in 5 adults, according to a survey.

    A. 根据一项报告，美国人的吸烟率已经下降了，美国打算在2006年把吸烟率降低到8年前的5比1的水平。

    B. 根据一项调查，美国人的吸烟率正在下降，2006年的吸烟率已经停留在平均水平，每5个人之中有1个人吸烟。

    C. 美国人吸烟率下降了8年，吸烟在美国一直是个棘手的问题，2006年的调查显示成年人每5人就有1人抽烟。

    D. 调查显示，在经过8年下降后，美国人的吸烟率在2006年保持在5个成年人中有1人吸烟的平稳水平上。

65. If you are going to the U.S. mainly for tourism, but want to take a short course of study of less than 18 hours per week, you may be able to do so on a visitor visa. You should inquire at the U.S. Embassy or Consulate (领事馆). If your course of study is more than 18 hours a week, you will need a student visa. Please read this information for general information on how to apply for an F1 or M1 student visa.

Part V   Writing   (25 minutes)

Directions: *This part is to test your ability to do practical writing. You are required to write an application letter according to the following information given in Chinese. Remember to do the task on the Translation/Composition Sheet.*

根据以下内容写一封求职信

1. 2010年10月10日在《中国日报》看到贵公司招聘翻译的广告。

2. 申请人：张林，家住长春市红旗路5号。毕业于中华大学，获得英语文学学士学位；在一家合资企业做翻译两年，有一定工作经验。

3. 随函附上个人简历并期待回复。

Words for Reference:

文学	literature
合资企业	joint venture

Test Four

Part I   Listening Comprehension   (15 minutes)

Directions: *This part is to test your listening ability. It consists of 3 sections.*

Section A

Directions: *This section is to test your ability to understand short dialogues. There are 5 recorded dialogues in it. After each dialogue, there is a recorded question. Both the dialogues and questions will be spoken only once. When you hear a question, you should decide on the correct answer from the 4 choices marked A, B, C and D given in your test paper. Then you should mark the corresponding letter on the Answer Sheet with a single line through the center.*

Example: *You will hear:*

You will read: A. New York City.

                             B. An evening party.

                             C. An air trip.

                             D. The man's job.

From the dialogue we learn that the man is to take a flight to New York. Therefore, **C. An air trip** *is the correct answer. You should mark C. on the Answer Sheet with a single line through the center.*

[A] [B] ■ [D]

Now the test will begin.

1. A. Tomorrow.   C. This Sunday.
    B. Today.   D. This Saturday.

2. A. She bought a beautiful dress for her daughter.
    B. She stayed at home with her children.
    C. She went out shopping by herself.
    D. She visited one of her friends.

3. A. Because he wants to save money.
    B. Because he is good at sending emails.
    C. Because he doesn't like writing letters.
    D. Because he thinks it's safe and convenient.

4. A. She doesn't think the meeting is important.   C. She is going to cancel the meeting.
    B. She doesn't want to attend the meeting.   D. She has to go to another meeting.

5. A. His friends have been to Australia for Christmas before.
    B. He is going to Australia for Christmas next week.
    C. He has been to Australia for Christmas before.
    D. He plans to go to Australia for Christmas.

Section B

Directions: *This section is to test your ability to understand short conversations. There are 2 recorded conversations in it. After each conversation, there are some recorded questions. Both the conversations and questions will be spoken two times. When you hear a question, you should decide on the correct answer from the 4 choices marked A, B, C and D given in your test paper. Then you should mark the corresponding letter on the Answer Sheet with a single line through the center.*

Conversation 1

6. A. At a restaurant.
   B. At a hotel.
   C. At a ticket office.
   D. At the train station.

7. A. On Wednesday morning.
   B. On Friday afternoon.
   C. On Saturday night
   D. On Friday morning.

8. A. It's unacceptable.
   B. It's very cheap.
   C. It's expensive.
   D. It's reasonable.

Conversation 2

9. A. He wants to know when the concert will start.
   B. He wants to find out how to get to the theatre.
   C. He wants to know if the concert is popular.
   D. He wants to book some tickets.

10. A. 64 dollars.
    B. 60 dollars.
    C. 62 dollars.
    D. 58 dollars.

Section C

Directions: *This section is to test your ability to comprehend short passages. You will hear a recorded passage. After that you will hear five questions. Both the passage and the questions will be read two times. When you hear a question, you should complete the answer to it with a word or a short phrase* **(in not more than 3 words)**. *The questions and incomplete answers are printed in your test paper. You should write your answers on the Answer Sheet correspondingly. Now listen to the passage.*

11. What is the speaker talking about?
    It is about getting an _____.

12. What are the benefits of online learning?
    It saves time and _____.

13. How can students in an online course communicate with each other?
    They can communicate with each other in _____.

14. Why is getting online learning cheaper?
    Because the students don't have to pay _____ costs.

15. What is people's biggest worry about online learning?

People worry whether the degree awarded will be acceptable to _____.

Part II   Structure   (15 minutes)

Directions: *This part is to test your ability to construct grammatically correct sentences. It consists of 2 sections.*

Section A

Directions: *In this section, there are 10 incomplete sentences. You are required to complete each one by deciding on the most appropriate word or words from the 4 choices marked A, B, C and D. Then you should mark the corresponding letter on the Answer Sheet with a single line through the center.*

16. _____ reading the story than she started laughing.

A. Not until she finished   C. Scarcely had she finished

B. Hardly had she finished   D. No sooner had she finished

17. When you come to see me next month, I _____ my term paper.

A. have completed   C. am going to complete

B. can complete   D. will have completed

18. He _____ the match if he had not hurt his leg.

A. should win   C. would win

B. could have won   D. had won

19. You could hardly imagine such a little boy _____ the way he did.

A. behave   C. behaving

B. to behave   D. to have behaved

20. It was on the train to Guangzhou _____ Mr. Li told me he should be responsible for the mistake.

A. which   C. that

B. where   D. what

21. As we know, cigarette smoking is the major factor _____ to lung cancer.

A. contributes   C. contributed

B. contributing   D. is contributing

22. Jack dare not _____ horror programs on TV when he is alone.

A. watch   C. watching

B. to watch   D. watches

23. Ms. Martin was overjoyed to hear the news _____ her daughter had got the first prize at the competition.

A. which   C. that

B. what   D. who

24. Whether you can find Mary _____ has nothing to do with what we are talking about now.

    A. or not   C. or else

    B. or so   D. or

25. I haven't got any work experience, _____ I can learn fast and I'll try my best.

    A. otherwise   C. however

    B. or   D. but

Section B

Directions: *There are 10 incomplete statements here. You should fill in each blank with the proper form of the word given in brackets. Write the word or words in the corresponding space on the Answer Sheet.*

26. Dan Jones has announced that he is going (give) _____ up his role in CBS News early next year.

27. An investigation shows that many older people express a strong desire to continue (study) _____ in university or college.

28. As Dr Wharton entered the bedroom, he heard the (die) _____ man cry out to his nurse.

29. We all think that his (behave) _____ at the party is not proper.

30. They never met again, for they (forbid) _____ to associate with each other.

31. The 1992 edition covered a range of articles (keep) _____ members up-to-date.

32. In view of the serious problem, effective measures should be taken before things get (bad) _____.

33. When it comes to job interviews, the first (impress) _____ made on the interviewer is important.

34. The police compared the suspect's fingerprints with those (find) _____ at the crime site.

35. I do not regret (tell) _____ her what I thought, and also I have no choice.

Part III   Reading Comprehension   (40 minutes)

Directions: *This part is to test your reading ability. There are 5 tasks for you to fulfill. You should read the reading materials carefully and do the tasks as you are instructed.*

Task 1

Directions: *After reading the following passage, you will find 5 questions or unfinished statements, numbered 36 to 40. For each question or statement there are 4 choices marked A, B, C. and D. You should make the correct choice and mark the corresponding letter on the Answer Sheet with a single line through the center.*

    Are you forty years old and fat? Do you look rich? If so, be careful. There is a pickpocket (扒手) looking for you. World travelers, away from home and usually carrying much money, are often troubled by pickpockets in foreign countries, but they should remember that there are pickpockets in their own country, too.

    A typical pickpocket is under forty, usually a male. He has nimble (灵敏的) fingers and has trained himself in running. Generally, he carries a newspaper or magazine in his hand. He may appear fairly clever and pretend to be calm. He has learned his job from another pickpocket, and he repays his "teacher" by giving him a certain percent of the money or things which he steals.

The skilled pickpocket always operates in crowded places. Very well-dressed men and women and slightly drunken men are the favorite objects of the pickpocket.

An average-sized department store hires about six or seven full-time detectives (侦探).They are constantly looking for pickpockets quickly. But an experienced pickpocket knows these things and is very careful. He is especially busy on buses, trains and subways, between 11:00 am and 3:00 pm, when there are many shoppers with much money to spend. He carefully remembers the payday of companies.

Pick-pocketing from a shop represents about 75% of daytime minor crimes in America. The sentence for these crimes is usually from three to five years in prison. After finishing their sentence, pickpockets and thieves seldom reform; they usually advance to more serious crimes.

36. From the first paragraph we know that targets of the pickpocket are usually those who _____.
    A. are middle-aged and wealthy
    B. appear to look quite calm
    C. are heavily drunken women
    D. come from a foreign country
37. According to the passage, a typical pickpocket looks like _____.
    A. an old gentleman
    B. a fat rich man
    C. a clever calm man
    D. a middle-aged traveler
38. A detective is employed in a department store to _____.
    A. look for the pickpockets around
    B. train people to identify pickpockets
    C. keep the store in good order
    D. recover missing articles
39. A pickpocket is especially busy on buses between 11:00am and 3:00pm because it is the time _____.
    A. when there are no detectives on watch
    B. when many shoppers carry much money
    C. when people are tired from busy shopping
    D. when more rich people take a bus
40. This passage mainly tells the reader _____.
    A. how he can identify a real thief
    B. why there are many pickpockets in the U.S.
    C. what kind of person the pickpocket is
    D. where thieves are likely to visit most often

Task 2
Directions: *This task is the same as Task 1. The 5 questions or unfinished statements are numbered 41 to 45.*

Passenger Information (Domestic Service)

Reservation   A passenger who has reserved a seat shall board the plane by his/her ticket in accordance with the reserved seat. A passenger who has reserved a seat should purchase a ticket within the time limits specified (指定的) or agreed in advance. If a passenger fails to purchase a ticket within the time limits, the reservation the passenger has made will be cancelled accordingly.

Reconfirmation of Reservation A passenger who has reserved a seat on onward or return flights shall reconfirm his/her reservations at the onward or return point 2 days before the departure of the flight if the passenger stays there for more than 72 hours, otherwise the reservation originally made will be cancelled accordingly.

Ticket The ticket can only be used by the passenger named on the ticket. A ticket cannot be transferred or altered, otherwise the ticket is no longer valid and no refund will be made.

Validity Period of Ticket The validity period of a ticket is one year. The validity period of a confirmed ticket is calculated from the date of commencement (开始) of travel. The validity period of an open ticket is calculated from zero hour of the day following the date of issue.

Children Fare A child who has reached 2 years of age and has not reached 12 years of age is charged at 50% of the adult fare and a child under 2 years of age not occupying a separate seat is charged at 10% of the adult fare.

41. According to the advertising information, after having reserved a seat, a passenger should _____.
    A. select a new seat after boarding the plane
    B. purchase a ticket any time before the flight departs
    C. confirm the reservation before the flight departs
    D. purchase a ticket within the time limit specified

42. Reconfirmation is needed for a reserved seat on _____.
    A. an onward or return flight
    B. any overseas flight
    C. any domestic flight
    D. a round trip ticket

43. According to the advertising information, the ticket reserved _____.
    A. cannot be refunded in any case
    B. cannot be used by another passenger
    C. can be used beyond its validity
    D. can be transferred to another person

44. The valid period of a confirmed ticket is calculated from the day when _____.
    A. the passenger receives the ticket
    B. reservation is made by the passenger
    C. reservation is confirmed by the passenger
    D. the passenger starts to travel

45. A 12-year-old child is charged at _____.
    A. 50% of the adult fare
    B. 20% of the adult fare
    C. 10% of the adult fare
    D. the same rate as an adult

Task 3

Directions: *The following is a piece of advice from a doctor. After reading it, you are required to complete the outline below it (No.46 to No.50). You should write your answers briefly (in not more than 3 words) on the Answer Sheet correspondingly.*

Dr. Phil gives you four steps to help manage your fears.

1.   Look at your life and identify the activities that put you in a harmful way.

According to Dr. Phil, being prepared is the key to success. Look at your lifestyle patterns. You will begin to realize that your fears can be limited to specific situations. Where do you go? What do you do? What are the areas of high risk in your life?

2.   Evaluate your highest risk areas and the associate rewards.

There are different risks involved in the various activities you participate in. Dr. Phil calls the way to evaluate them the "risk-reward ratio". In some activities the reward is worth the risk, while in others the risk far outweighs (超过) the reward.

3.   Play the "what if" game.

Ask yourself "what if?" — but answer the question realistically and honestly. "What if" you had to face your worst fear? The real answers are not nearly as bad as the imagined answers. Dr. Phil uses the following as an example of a "what if" question: "What if I am exposed to AIDS?" The answer is: I'm going to be tested.

4.   Evaluate the *rationality* (合理性) of your fears.

"When you begin to feel fear," Phil says, "You should challenge yourself by asking rational questions." Are you overreacting (过度反应), or is your fear realistic? Challenge your fears. Evaluate the rationality of each fear.

Four Steps to Help Manage Your Fear

Advisor: _____46_____
Key to success: _____47_____
Way to Evaluate risks: by the _____48_____ ratio
Game suggested to play: asking yourself _____49_____ questions
Step to challenge fears: evaluate the _____50_____ of the fear

---

Task 4

Directions: *The following is a set of library directions. After reading it, you are required to find the items equivalent to (与…等同) those given in Chinese in the table below. Then you should put the corresponding letters in the brackets on the Answer Sheet, numbered 51 through 55.*

A — Reading, Reference and Copying

B — Reading Area for Teachers and Postgraduates

C — Closed shelves for Undergraduates

D — Information Retrieval Room

E — Inter-library Loan

F — Display & Reading room for New Books

G — Multi-media Reading Room

H — Reference Department Office

I — Novelty Research
J — Reader Training & Lecture Room
K — Reading Room for Reference Books
L — Document Delivery
M — Reading Room for Chinese Social Books
N — Circulation for Foreign Books

Examples: (D) 目录检索室　　　　　　　　　　　(E) 馆际互借

51. （　）教师，研究生阅览区	（　）视听多媒体阅览室
52. （　）参考工具书阅览室	（　）中文社科图书阅览室
53. （　）读者培训与报告厅	（　）外文书刊借阅室
54. （　）咨询部办公室	（　）新书展阅室
55. （　）本科生闭架借阅区	（　）图书阅览，参考咨询和复印

Task 5

Directions: *Read the following advertising holiday brochure. After reading it, you should give brief answers to the 5 questions (No.56 to No.60) that follow. The answers* **(in not more than 3 words)** *should be written after the corresponding numbers on the Answer Sheet.*

A very warm welcome to the Summer 2005 Brochure of Switzerland (瑞士) Travel Center. Our "Grand Rail Holiday" section covers a wide range of multi-center holidays for the independent traveler. It is an ideal way to discover the variety of the country for yourself and at your own pace. For the nature lover we offer a wonderful one-week hiking (徒步旅行) package and for the cultural-minded we recommend a short break in one of Switzerland's exciting cities. They not only offer strange and beautiful lakesides but also a large variety of exhibitions and nightlife.

We are delighted to offer our biggest selection of holidays in the most beautiful regions of Europe and North America. There is a wide range of holidays on offer whether you are looking for a relaxing break or an active walking or sightseeing holiday; but if you love beautiful scenery, then Crystal Lakes and Mountains are for you. We have a large selection of accommodation in popular locations and an extensive range of 2-center holiday choices for you to create the combination that is just for you.

56. What kind of traveler is the 'Grand Rail Holiday' section especially designed for?
The _____.

57. Why is "Grand Rail Holiday" ideal for tourists to discover the variety of the country?
Because they can travel for themselves and at _____.

58. What does the organizer recommend the cultural minded tourists to do in a city in Switzerland?
To have _____ to see a large variety of exhibitions and nightlife.

59. What places does the organizer offer for the beautiful scenery lovers to visit?
Crystal _____.

60. Where does the organizer provide a large selection of accommodation for the tourists?

   In _____.

Part IV   Translation — English into Chinese   (25 minutes)

Directions: *This part, numbered 61 through 65, is to test your ability to translate English into Chinese. After each of the sentences numbered 61 to 64, you will read four choices of suggested translation. You should choose the best translation and mark the corresponding letter on your Answer Sheet. And for the paragraph numbered 65, write your translation in the corresponding space on the Translation/Composition Sheet.*

61. Even today, specific forecasts are only made for the period of 3 to 5 days in advance.
   A. 就是在目前，人们也只能提前3至5天预报天气状况。
   B. 就是在今天，预报员也只能观测到3至5天的特殊天气。
   C. 即便是今天，也只能对未来3至5天做出具体的气象预报。
   D. 即使是今天，气象台也只能播出3至5天中的天气。

62. People have to spend more time and energy on studying new skills and technology so that they can keep a favorable position in job market.
   A. 人们应把更多的精力和时间投入学习新知识和新技术上，进而能在人才市场上找到满意的工作。
   B. 人们不得不花费更多时间和精力学习新技能和新技术，以便能在就业市场上占有优势。
   C. 人们有了更多的时间和能力去研究新知识和技能，才有可能在市场找到合适的工作。
   D. 人们舍得花时间并努力去采用新的知识和技能，就是为了在市场上找到待遇好的工作。

63. Many people believe that international trade produces positive effects on economic growth and local governments should be encouraged to promote international trade.
   A. 许多人都相信，国际贸易能有效地持续带动经济繁荣，为此各级政府都重视国际贸易。
   B. 很多人相信，国际贸易对经济增长有推动作用，应鼓励各地政府提升国际贸易的地位。
   C. 很多人确信，只要国际贸易能持续影响经济发展，就能刺激当地政府开展国际贸易。
   D. 许多人认为，国际贸易对经济增长有积极作用，应鼓励地方政府发展国际贸易。

64. Along with the benefits of such machines, employees must study knowledge involved in such machines so that they are able to control them.
   A. 除了这些机器的优点之外，员工们还必须学习与之有关的知识，从而能操控它们。
   B. 这些机器能为企业带来效益，员工们一定要研究这些机器涉及的资料，以掌控它们。
   C. 这些机器确有好处，但员工们必须学习操作这些机器的知识，才能控制它们。
   D. 由于这类机器的优良特性，为了能控制它们，员工们应当弄清与其有关联的资料。

65. Bowling (保龄球) season is about to begin. Come one, come all. The only requirement is the desire to have fun. Starting October 4, lanes (球道) are reserved at Sunshine Bowl on Tuesday evenings from 7 p.m. to 9 p.m. The two best teams will represent our company at the Industrial Playoffs (Finals). Last year, the Sales Department team made the quarter finals!

   If you are interested in joining the company league, please call John Doe at extension 237.

Part V   Writing   (25 minutes)

Directions: *This part is to test your ability to do practical writing. You are required to write a letter to make an appointment according to the following information given in Chinese. Remember to do the task on the Translation/Composition Sheet.*

假设你是东方公司的总经理秘书张波，请你为总经理草拟一封约见信。

1. 写信日期：2010年8月10日
2. 被约见人：公司销售部经理李洋先生
3. 事宜：在公司下个月召开年会之前，谈谈下一年度的销售计划。请李洋先生带上今年的销售报告和下一年的销售计划表等相关资料。
4. 约见时间：下周一上午10:00
5. 约见地点：总经理办公室
6. 如不方便，请打电话021-66324321，以便另约时间。

注意书信格式必须完整。

Keys & Translations

UNIT 1

Section I Maintaining a Sharp Eye
译文
Passage I

失物招领困惑旅馆业

　　所有大宾馆的客房服务员都知道，顾客离开时常常把东西忘在宾馆里。在美国一家旅馆，存放遗忘物品的壁橱里装满了袜子、领带和内衣，同时也有一些不寻常的东西被遗忘在那里，如迷你裙、韩国扇、音乐盒等。

　　几乎该宾馆里所有的人都听说过在小冰箱里发现了活龙虾的事。也有宠物被忘记带走的，包括一只宠物鼠。它的主人在提及此事时显得有点不好意思。表面上他问人们是否看到一件老鼠形状的衣服。在伦敦那些颇有趣味的丢失物品中有某种疾病的DNA样本，有几个特大的烤青豆罐头，还有一只小兔子被遗忘在床下的鞋盒子里。

　　每一家宾馆都有奇特的故事可讲。一家希尔顿酒店的客房服务员不知道该如何解释不断增多的假牙遗忘现象。仅一个月内就有四套假牙被忘在酒店里，有两套假牙过了两个月后才被取走。"你可以想得到，一旦他们咀嚼早餐时，他们才会意识到丢了点什么，"经理笑着说道。

　　大多数酒店都把丢失的物品保留三个月，如果没有人认领，就送给慈善机构。有些酒店就送给拾到物品的人。这会鼓励他们在清扫房间时发现丢失物就上交。如果遗忘的东西不是很贵重的话，酒店经理通常等待客人来认领。他们不愿意去联系失主。

　　如果说客人忘在酒店里的东西很有趣的话，他们选择偷偷带走的东西也很有趣。有些酒店每年要花一万美元来补充木衣挂。"没钉在墙上的东西旅客都拿，"一位经理说。"我们丢过熨斗、浴衣，枕头也越来越受到青睐。酒店发现，有酒店标识的东西比没有标识的东西更受欢迎。

　　旅客拿这些东西似乎是想纪念他们在这里住过。有些酒店印有卡片，放在卫生间里，告诉客人浴衣可以购买。烟灰缸对那些入住香港太平洋皇家酒店的客人来说是一件很受欢迎的纪念品。客人顺手牵羊的动机常常不仅仅是怀旧。正如希尔顿酒店公关部经理所说，有些旅客认为房价太高，"他们应该不花钱拿点东西。"

Passage II

6号汽车旅馆订房须知
订房规定

- 所有订房旅客必须年满18岁，并出示身份证明。
- 办理住宿时间：随到随办。结账退房时间：中午12点。
- 17岁及小于17岁者跟成年家人同住一室不另收费。

158

- 住宿要遵守当地的法令。一般说来，有一张床的房间可以住一至二人；有两张床的房间最多不能超过4人。如果旅客人数达到5人以上，要为多出的人加订房间。
- 婴儿可以包括在房间所允许入住的人数之内，条件是经理可提供能承受婴儿体重的活动婴儿床。
- 任何旅客不得将睡袋、帆布床及任何家具放入6号汽车旅馆的房间内。
- 6号汽车旅馆的各地旅馆均为残疾人提供所需设备。请同预订中心或您打算入住的6号汽车旅馆确认。

个人订房

- 拨打1-800-4-6号汽车旅馆的订房中心电话（1-800-466-8356），即可预订6号汽车旅馆的各地旅馆的客房。
- 可以给您想要入住的6号汽车旅馆打电话或写信预订房间。也可亲自去任何一家6号汽车旅馆，他们可为你电话联系订房。
- 如果用信用卡担保，房间可以整夜保留直至您到达。如不能担保，则房间只能保留至晚6点（大多数各地旅馆）。
- 如果要取消已预付了租金或已担保了的预订房间，则必须要在到达之日晚6点之前通知已为你预订了房间的6号汽车旅馆，还要收到取消预订的号码方可生效。
- 要取消通过订房中心预订的房间，需打电话给订房中心，而不是给所订房间的那家6号汽车旅馆。

团体订房

- 请给团体订房部打电话，号码1-800-544-4866.
- 美国、加拿大境外的旅客可发传真：614-601-4052 或网上咨询，发至_groupsales@motel6.com_。
- 团体订房（10个以上房间）要求预付第一宿的全部房费的押金。押金需在达到之日前至少30天交付。
- 有关儿童团体订房的特殊规定请与团体订房部联系。
- 取消订房必须提前30天通知。

---

1. 1) a   2) c   3) d   4) b   5) b   6) b   7) a   8) c

2. 1) great value   2) reclaimed   3) nostalgia   4) aware   5) public relations
   6) live   7) souvenir   8) popular   9) depart   10) property

3. 1) The crowd overflowed the hall and some had to stand outside.
2) Has anyone claimed the suitcase you found?
3) The police were at a loss to explain the affair.
4) The father encouraged his children to learn painting.
5) He tried several different jobs, but ended up as a lawyer.

4. 1) F   2) T   3) F   4) F   5) T
   6) T   7) F   8) F   9) T   10) F

5. 1) cancellations, cancel   2) add, additional / added   3) reservation, reserved

    4) confirm, confirmation   5) arrival, arrive   6) notify, notification

    7) available, availability   8) inquired, inquiry

6. 1) She may go with us provided that she comes here in time.

    2) Children may stay free if they occupy the same room with their parents.

    3) Notification of cancellation of a reservation must be made 30 days prior to the arrival date.

    4) Group reservation requires advance payment of the deposit.

    5) The room may be held for the whole night if a guest guarantees it with a credit card.

Section II Trying Your Hand

样例1:

旅馆订房卡

客人姓名：雷诺思·丹

入住时间：12月28日   结账时间：1月2日

房间种类：双人房间

房　　费：每晚125美元

付款方式：成功卡 934 243 132342

旅行代理：珍尼·威廉

旅行代理传真号：(914)　997–8115

样例2:

马歇尔宾馆

价格表

（ 所有价格包括早餐和附加税。）

	不带浴室的单人房间	带浴室的单人房间	不带浴室的双人房间	带浴室的双人房间
每晚房价	49镑	59镑	78镑	89镑
每周房价	144镑	162镑	196镑	210镑

1.

>

> **校内住宿须知**
>
> **校公寓**

>
>
> 　　学校为已经被学校录取并已注册获准学习学业课程的大学生和研究生提供有限住房。
>
> 　　学校公寓为学生提供的住房包括有传统宿舍式的住房，设单人间和双人间，有合用公共区域的套房，和公寓套房。使用期为本学年（250天）。250天的房费为3 975美元，359天的房费为5 153美元。所有房间都配有家具。公共设施费用， 如水、电和煤气（电话费除外）等均包括在房费之内。

2. 1) 深夜返回旅馆，请走正门。

2) 贵重物品请存放在旅馆保险箱内。

3) 全世界千千万万家宾馆都每天换洗床单。

4) 如果计划有变动，请拨打预订房间时所拨打的同一电话号码取消预订。

5) 有些景点的宾馆在旅游高峰季节需预付押金以确保所预订的房间。

3. 1) who　　2) of whom　　3) when　　4) that　　5) whose

6) which　　7) in which　　8) why　　9) where　　10) who

4. 1) which → that　　2) which → who　　3) which → in which

4) which → that / who / whom　　5) that → whom　　6) which → where

7) that → whom　　8) which → in which　　9) that → which

10) which → whose

5. 1) He is the cleverest man (that) I have ever met in my life.

2) I've always longed for the time when I should be able to be independent.

3) I told the story to John, who later told it to his brother.

4) The first place that I'll visit in China is Beijing.

5) We have returned all the books, which are written in English, to the library.

6) Commercials are one of the things that we have to endure when we watch TV.

UNIT 2

Section I Maintaining a Sharp Eye

译文
Passage I

在餐馆用餐

了解美国人在家里吃什么是很有趣的，但从这里也许了解不到很多东西。美国的居民来自世界各地，而世界各地的传统习俗又各不相同，从而我们也许会发现世界各地的饮食在此融合。然而，只有当人们走出家门到外面就餐时，他们的饮食习惯才会发生变化，变得相互类似。最近的一项调查向我们展示了许多关于美国人在饭店就餐的饮食习惯。

美国人经常外出吃饭。98%的美国家庭平均每月至少到饭店吃一次饭，多数家庭一周在外吃饭达九次以上。尽管人们在饭店吃饭并非都是正餐 —— 早餐、午餐和晚餐，但这也说明人们在饭店就餐的比例超过三分之一。你能猜出人们在饭店最常吃的是哪顿饭吗? 毫不奇怪，是午餐。从下表中可以看出人们在饭店早中午饭就餐的比例:

午餐: 38%
晚餐: 30%
间餐: 20%
早餐: 12%

美国人到什么样的饭店就餐是第二个有趣的问题。快餐店是美国现代生活的真正象征。在快餐店里通常没有餐桌服务，人们自己拿取食品，有时可以坐在汽车里从外卖窗口取食品，而食品往往是在你到达之前就准备好的。最受欢迎的快餐是汉堡包，而最受欢迎的快餐店则是汉堡包快餐店。

第三个问题是美国人为什么要外出就餐。要回答这个问题首先得看他们选择什么样的饭店。快餐店似乎已经取代了许多家常饭菜，人们在那里吃饭图的是方便。多数美国人说在快餐店吃饭是为了不用做饭。另一个原因是节省吃饭时间。尽管现在还有许多全方位服务的餐厅，但只有在有特殊的活动的时候人们才到那里就餐，例如过生日，庆贺各种纪念日，或是为了休闲放松。在全方位服务的饭店里吃饭的那种休闲感觉与在快餐店是完全不同的，吃快餐就是为了快。

美国确实是一个饭店林立的社会，但我们要问: 饭店是否真的那么好，在那里就餐是否卫生健康。饭店一定很不错，因为它们是那么受欢迎，但是看一看人们点的菜就会发现，油炸食品和软饮料是他们最喜欢的。既然我们知道脂肪和糖过多不利于人体健康，那么看起来美国人是宁肯吃快餐也不顾自己的健康了。

Passage II

聚会上的祝酒词

1. 新娘对参加婚宴的朋友们的衷心感谢
朋友们:

任何语言都无法恰当地表达出我对今天在座的各位朋友对我所说和所做的一切的谢意。多年来，我和大家彼此相知，请让我就道一声"谢谢"吧。

今天，我见到了许多好朋友。你们能来参加我和彼得的婚礼，这对我们来说实在不同寻常。

看到在我们成长的岁月里给予过我们帮助的人们来参加我们的婚礼，使得今天更有意义。当我们最需要帮助的时候，在座的各位多次鼓励我们，伸出援助之手，给我们提出建议。对此真的无以为报，只能以我们的爱心回报你们，就像你们慷慨地给予我们的一样。

为准备今天的婚礼，彼得的家人和我的家人都费尽了心机，并且在我们订婚期间一直在支持我们，他们是这样说的，更是这样做的。我们拥有世界上最好的父母，在过去的几周里，跟他们在一起充满了欢乐。

亲人们，朋友们，请允许我举杯以表达我对各位真诚的爱和谢意。

2. 商业聚会祝酒词

女士们，先生们：

我们邀请各位参加今天的答谢宴会，以表达对我们诚信可靠的贸易伙伴们的谢意。

我们都清楚，做生意并不是一件容易的事情。做生意的方法各不相同：有的是追逐利润，有的则是为了造福社会。然而，不论为了什么目的，有一点是必须要记住的：就是要心存感激之情。后悔和怨恨无论何时都无济于事。对所有人心存感激之情会使我们生意兴隆。

这就是我们今天邀请大家来聚会的目的。我们非常感谢各位能成为我们的合作伙伴。祝大家今天度过一个愉快的夜晚。

让我们为生意兴隆干杯。

1. 1) a   2) b   3) b   4) c   5) c

2. 1) similar   2) habit   3) at least   4) regular   5) surprisingly
   6) percent   7) pick up   8) is celebrating   9) convenience   10) appears

3. 1) Their victory was celebrated with music and dancing.
   2) It's a great convenience to live in this building.
   3) I use my own symbols for "true" and "false".
   4) Whether the meeting can succeed or not depends largely on the Chairman's efficiency.
   5) The books that have been damaged will be replaced.
   6) Each of us has personal preferences for certain types of entertainment.

4. 1) T   2) F   3) F   4) T   5) F   6) F   7) T   8) T

5. 1) adequate   2) engagement   3) reliably   4) appreciate   5) endless
   6) specially   7) encourages   8) kindness   9) meaningful   10) express

6. 1) 很难用语言来恰当地表达我的谢意，感谢今天在座的各位朋友对我所说和所做的一切。
   2) 看到在我们成长的岁月里给予过我们帮助的人们来参加我们的婚礼，使得今天更有意义。
   3) 当我们最需要的时候，在座的各位多次鼓励我们，伸出援助之手，给我们提出建议。
   4) 我们拥有世界上最好的父母，因为在过去的几周里，他们关怀备至，跟他们在一起充满了欢乐。
   5) 我们邀请各位参加今天的答谢宴会，以表达对我们诚信可靠的贸易伙伴们的谢意。

6) 然而，不论为了什么目的，有一点是必须要记住的：就是要心存感激之情。

7) 对所有人心存感激之情会使我们生意兴隆。

8) 让我们为生意兴隆干杯。

Section II Trying Your Hand

样例1：

爱博尼斯餐厅

戴温伯特西街1246号

晚餐时间：周二—周六 晚5:30—10:30

订餐电话：245-2886

汤类

家常汤，滚烫、美味

一杯 .... 1.5 美元　　　　一碗 .... 2.0 美元

色拉

主厨色拉 3.95美元

蔬菜色拉，配车达和瑞士奶酪片，以及切片火鸡和火腿肉

家常色拉 .... 2.25 美元

覆盖西红柿片和紫苜蓿芽

调料自选

酒类

本店特备上等精选国内外名酒。请查看酒单。

晚餐

配有色拉、蔬菜和各种本店自制的面包

特瑞亚克鸡 5.59美元

以淡味调料浸泡，炭火自烤

鱼片 5.59美元

大比目鱼片，以大蒜和香菜调味，配有本店制作的调料

上等牛腰肉和大虾 10.59美元

两者均是最佳品

上等排骨 12.59美元

本店著名的排骨，焦嫩、多汁

甜点

柠檬奶酪饼 1.75美元

酪乳巧克力饼 1.50美元

样例 2:

> **早餐**
>
> 薄煎饼 (3张) .... 1.40美元 　　热麦片粥........ 0.85美元 　　烤面包片...... 0.15美元
> 鸡蛋 (1个) .... 0.5 美元 　　酸奶............. 0.35美元 　　小松饼.......... 0.65美元
> 鸡蛋 (2个) .... 0.80美元 　　水果色拉........ 0.60美元 　　甜面包......... 0.60美元
> 熏猪肉 (3块) 1.30美元
>
> **营业时间**
>
> 周一 ~ 周五：早6:30—晚9:00 　　　　周六：早7:00—晚9:00
> (早餐至上午10:30) 　　　　　　　　　(早餐至中午12:00)

1.

> **金龙饭店**
> * 以中餐和特色烈性酒而著名。
> * 提供各式菜肴。
> * 点四道菜以上者免费提供色拉或甜点。
>   　　　　　营业时间：上午11:30—晚11:30
>   　　　　　订餐电话：233-9768
>   　　　　　地　　址：卡特大街325号

2. 1) 你喜欢什么，咖啡还是牛奶？
　　2) 我再给你夹点烤鸭，好吗？
　　3) 有些中国人喜欢吃饭时先喝汤。
　　4) 在快餐店你得自己给自己服务。
　　5) 如果顾客需要，那家饭店可以为每位顾客单独做菜。

3. 1) while　　　　2) in that　　　　3) provided that　　4) lest　　　　5) as
　　6) Wherever　　7) Although　　8) if only　　9) So long as　　10) so that

4. 1) As young she is → Young as she is　　2) after → before
　　3) Where → When / Whenever　　　　4) as → than
　　5) in order to → in order that　　　　6) so that → in case
　　7) so that → that　　　　　　　　　8) so → lest

5. 1) As all the seats were occupied, he had to stand.
　　2) People do not realize the value of health until they lose it.

165

3) I would give up my job before I'd agree to be transferred.

4) We didn't buy anything because we were short of money.

5) Turn off the switch when/in case anything goes wrong with the machine.

6) They came to see us last month. But it was two years since we had last met each other.

UNIT 3

Section I Maintaining a Sharp Eye

译文

Passage I

家中购物电视网络：未来的潮流吗？

你在电视上看过在家里购物的节目吗？你能描述一下在家里通过电视来购物是怎样的吗？你是否曾经面临过这样的抉择：在周末上街采购，还是待在家中看电视？如今这两件事你可兼而有之了。家中购物电视网络成了许多人无需走出家门便可购物的途径。

一些购物者厌倦上商场和购物广场 —— 在人群中挤挤攘攘，排长队等候，甚至有时还买不到想买的东西。他们宁愿静静地在家里坐在电视机前，观看和蔼可亲的主持人对某个产品的描述，同时还有一位模特将它展示出来。他们可以昼夜24小时购物，要买哪个商品，只需简单地打个电话，就可以用信用卡付款。家庭购物网深知热情主持人的影响力，还有名人顾客赞许该商品的魅力，以及价格便宜的情感吸引力。

主要的时装设计师、大商场，甚至邮购公司也热衷于参加到家庭购物这一成功的活动中来。有些大百货公司正在尝试建立自己的电视频道，而一些零售商则计划在未来推出互动式电视购物。这样，电视观众就可以与他们自己个人的商店购物代理联系，询问产品情况并订购商品，而所有这一切都是通过他们的电视进行的。

电视购物能取代商场购物吗？一些商业界人士宣称，家庭购物网络代表着"未来的电子购物大商场"。然而对众多人来说，走出家门，在一家真正的商店购物乃是放松休闲的一种方式，甚至也是一种娱乐。还有，在许多购物者看来，摸一摸或试穿一下他们想要买的商品，仍是重要的。正因如此，专家们说，将来在家购物会与商场购物并存，但决不会完全取代商场购物。

Passage II

伦敦之夏

大多数人一想到伦敦，便联想起大本钟、威斯敏斯特教堂和特拉法加广场。但是伦敦远远不止拥有这些著名的旅游景点。夏季的几个月里尤其如此。那时博物馆和剧场的通常"节目单"会增添许多特别的活动和展览，从而使游览变得更加丰富多彩。

爱好文学的人不应错过的一个地方便是道蒂大街的查尔斯·狄更斯的故居，离大英博物馆不过几步之遥。你可以穿过狄更斯的餐厅、卧室和客厅，一路来到一间小书房，这里是这位伟大的英国作家完成他最著名的两部小说的地方，即《匹克威克外传》和《雾都孤儿》。房间里还有狄更斯的手稿和信件等藏品。

对文化探索者来说，另一个有意思的去处是泰晤士河南岸的莎士比亚球型剧场展览馆。参观者可以通过摆放在那儿的伊丽莎白时代的手稿、绘画和服饰去探究17世纪戏剧的迷人天地。

如果你爱喝英国啤酒，那么你一定要在8月1日至5日去伦敦西区的奥林匹亚，参加那里的"大不列颠啤酒节"。那时300多种号称"正宗麦芽啤酒"的传统的英国啤酒要斟满数千只一品脱大的酒杯。但是要注意，去一次恐怕是不够的！用一位组织者斯蒂芬·考克斯的话说，"正宗麦芽啤酒需要在不同的日子分别品尝才能喝出味道来。啤酒的酒质、颜色，甚至口味都会一天一个样儿。这有点像赛马：当天的表现至关重要。"

在八月最后一个周末的两天里，诺丁山便成了伦敦最激动人心的活动场所之一，即诺丁山狂欢节。整个地区都是加勒比狂欢节的世界，100多个乐队走上街头，乐手们身着五颜六色的盛装，数千人随着雷盖乐、爵士乐、摇摆乐和室内乐纷纷起舞。

如果你的音乐品味更传统一些，不喜欢雷盖乐或者摇摆乐，你就不应错过在皇家阿尔伯特纪念堂举办的举世闻名的BBC音乐会的演出季节。人们熟知的"漫步"古典音乐会从7月底到9月中旬每周7个夜晚都有表演。

在文学、啤酒、狂欢节和古典音乐之余，如果你还想获取特别一点的体验，最好的办法便是自己去找。伦敦有数千个去处和活动，适合各种口味的需要，只等着你去发现。不论你是谁，也不论你想要什么，在伦敦你都有极好的机会找到它。

1. I. Advantages and disadvantages of store shopping

    Advantages:

    a. relax; be entertained

    b. touch

    Disadvantages:

    a. fighting

    b. in long lines

    c. finding

II. Advantages and disadvantages of home shopping TV Networks

    Advantages:

    a. stay; sit

    b. described; displayed

    c. phone call; credit card

    Disadvantages:

    a. touch

    b. chance; enjoy yourself

III. The future of Home Shopping TV Networks

    a. communication; interactively

    b. electronic shopping malls

    c. shopping

2. 1) networking   2) in line   3) around the clock   4) shopping

   5) bargain   6) credit cards   7) go out   8) is experimenting with

9) alongside   10) placed a ... order

3. 1) I have long been tired of sitting in an office all day.

2) For customers, credit cards permit the purchase of goods and services even when funds are low.

3) If the words "Charge it to the credit card" sound familiar, it is no wonder.

4) The debate will become even more heated if she joins in.

5) I am very eager to continue my education at your college.

4. 1) a   2) b   3) d   4) c   5) c

5. 1) take over   2) from day to day   3) missed   4) taste   5) enriched

6) wandered   7) study   8) suit   9) make sure   10) dates back

6. 1) A delegation will come to explore the environmental conditions of our city next week.

2) There were at least two thousand people who watched the performance that day.

3) Jane has a large collection of foreign coins.

4) Now it is the football season, and the basketball season starts next month.

5) This is the scene of the accident which happened last night.

Section II Trying Your Hand

样例 1:

> **Minolta AF—E照相机**
> 　　下次旅行时，请带上一个Minolta AF—E照相机。它自动上卷，自动回卷，设计精巧，是一部轻便的能自动对焦的35毫米照相机。只要你轻轻一按，就能拍出高质量的照片。

样例 2:

> **学生旅游**
> **这是你自己的旅游**
> **千万别错过**
>
> | | |
> |---|---|
> | 伦敦 | $242 |
> | 巴黎 | $239 |
> | 法兰克福 | $286 |
> | 阿姆斯特丹 | $258 |
> | 马德里 | $294 |
> | 圣何塞 | $370 |

机票费用含往返机票。

五星旅行社
唐宁街 10号　　　　　　　　　　　电话：212-325-3411
百老汇街 2381号　　　　　　　　　电话：223-345-1256
第三大道　　　　　　　　　　　　　电话：212-346-6100
网址：www.sattravel.com

1.

佳能ESO型相机
　　这种最新式的ESO-IN RS型相机具有持续可视的取景影像，其超快连续摄影的速度可达每秒10幅照片，从而可使专业摄影师能够精确地捕捉重大的瞬间。

2. 1) 中国的长城始建于公元前214年。它是目前世界上最长的遗迹。

　　2) 印度的泰姬陵建于1630年到1652年之间。它是印度王妃之墓。

　　3) 埃菲尔铁塔于1889年建成。为纪念法国大革命100周年而建。

3. 1) nodding　　2) wounded　　3) exciting　　4) pleased　　5) written
　　6) planned　　7) giving　　8) studying　　9) ordered　　10) satisfied

4. 1) led → leading　　　　　　　2) surprising → surprised
　　3) gaining → gained　　　　　　4) concerning → concerned
　　5) using → used　　　　　　　　6) using → used
　　7) studied → studying　　　　　8) played → playing
　　9) painting → painted　　　　　10) run → running

5. 1) She doesn't like the new book written by the young author.

　　2) The young man sitting between my parents is a painter.

　　3) He noticed the concerned look in his mother's eyes.

　　4) Read the instructions written on the box before using it.

　　5) All people involved in this matter have been questioned.

　　6) I saw a string of pearls hanging around her neck.

UNIT 4

Section I Maintaining a Sharp Eye

译文

Passage I

我们可以向谁求助？

在过去的7年里，我一直和一个已经不同于以往的儿子生活在一起。他在一次头部重伤中侥幸活了下来，但是一直处于昏迷之中。现在，虽然他的智力仍然存在，但是他的行为却受到身体的限制。他再也不能说话，只能通过使用一部有声音附件的计算机来表达他的意思。他再也不能用嘴吃任何东西，只能靠插在胃里的一根喂食管进食。他再也不能走路，只能在轮椅中度过一天的大部分时光。

按理说，我们可以请一位护理员来帮助我们照料儿子，但是那只是说笑而已。从来没有人答应长期定时地来照料。他们干一段时间，然后就被"煎熬"跑了。儿子需要的照料是每时每刻持续不断的，他一天24小时身边都需要有个人。他通过计算机告诉我说我在烧的饭闻起来味道好极了，他希望自己可以吃。他也渴望能够说话，他告诉我他是那么向往能够和人们交谈。他的"朋友"一个也没有来过，他们看到他这个样儿"不知所措"。他们说"看见他那副样子我觉得太难过了"。

有人劝我找一个助残团体来宣泄一下我的情绪。但是我到处都搜寻遍了，也没有找到一个。没有任何一个团体是属于我儿子这一类型的。大部分脑部受伤的人已经有所康复，即使他们仍然是坐在轮椅中，但是却能够说话或吃东西。我的儿子不是属于那个类型。看到儿子日复一日地努力去做大多数的人根本不当回事儿的事情，我的心都要碎了。在这几年里，全家人都在盼望，在祈祷。我们可以向谁求助啊？

Passage II

他的生命在继续

1999年2月28日标志着日本首例对一个法律上承认的脑死亡捐赠人捐出的器官进行移植手术的日子。经过两轮由有行医执照的医生遵照器官移植法进行的合法检测之后，一位高知县的病人被诊断为脑死亡。

虽然这是日本的首例，但却不是第一次牵涉到日本人。对于千叶太根这位64岁东京的珠宝商来说，高知县的这例器官移植病例又一次唤起他对于大儿子的历历在目的回忆。1987年3月,他在美国学习的23岁的儿子严山，在一次意外事件中不幸摔出宿舍的窗户，头盖骨碎裂。在事故发生5天之后，医生们回天乏术，宣布他为脑死亡。他们花费了20分钟的时间向这位父亲解释脑死亡的含义。

在那时千叶对于脑死亡或器官移植一无所知,但是他却表示可以捐赠他儿子的器官。他的妻子也同意这一决定。就这样，他儿子的心脏、肝脏、肾脏和角膜分别捐献给了6位危重的病人。

在回家之后，千叶收到美国一位器官移植官员写来的一封信，告诉他说他儿子的捐献已经挽救了6个人。严山这位年轻人实际上继续活在其他人的生命中。尽管严山从未讲到过捐赠器官的事，但是千叶可以肯定，他的儿子一定会很乐意帮助他人。

千叶说高知县脑死亡病人的家属一定同他当年一样悲痛欲绝。他也高度称颂这个家庭所表现出的深厚的爱和勇气：他们尊重了病人的夙愿，将器官捐赠给那些需要的人。千叶还说，媒体应该体谅这家人的感情，特别注意为他们保密，因为他们承担了巨大的压力。

千叶担心人们只从需要器官的人的立场看问题，他认为宣布脑死亡不应该仅仅为了器官移植。 在目前的制度下，脑死亡被视为一种特殊类型的死亡，而不是简单意义上的生命结束。他担心，如果从这个角度看问题，很少会有人愿意捐赠他们的器官。

1. 1) d   2) a   3) b   4) c

2. 1) is committed to   2) get across   3) even if   4) on the basis of

5) once   6) via   7) for a while   8) praying for

9) no longer   10) turn to   11) for granted   12) gains

13) is limited to   14) burn out

3. 1) helpful, help   2) food, feed   3) laugh at, laughter   4) care, careless, carefully

5) cooking, cooked   6) burning, burnt   7) emotional, emotion

4. 1) F   2) T   3) T   4) F   5) T   6) F   7) T   8) T   9) T   10) F

5.　　An organ transplant from a legally brain-dead donor was performed for the first time in Japan. It reminded me vividly of my eldest son.

In March 1987, my 23-year old son, Genzan, lost consciousness after breaking his skull in an accidental fall from a dormitory window while studying in the United States. When he failed to recover, doctors declared him brain dead five days after the accident. They gave me a 20-minute explanation of brain death.

I knew nothing about brain death or transplants at the time, but offered to donate my son's organs. My wife agreed with the decision. As a result, our son's heart, liver, kidneys and eyes were given to six seriously ill patients respectively.

After returning home, I received a letter from a U.S. transplant officer who said that my son's gift had saved six persons — Genzan actually continued his life in other people's lives. Although Genzan had never spoken about organ donation, I'm certain that my son would have been happy to help others.

6. 1) 由于在车祸中失血过多，这位乘客已经失去了知觉。

2) 他在遗嘱中写道，他将非常乐意死后将器官捐献给需要的人。

3) 在一位捐献者的肾脏被成功地移植到这位病人的体内之后，他的生命得救了。

4) 这种倾心的谈话能帮你解脱忧虑和悲伤。

5) 病人出院后仍需卧床休息几天。

6) 医生诊断后再给你开处方。

Section II Trying Your Hand

样例 1：

芬必得胶囊

适 应 症： 各种剧烈疼痛和炎症。

服用方法： 早晚各口服一次，每日两粒。

注　　意： 12岁以下儿童须遵医嘱。超量服用可引起头痛及恶心。

有 效 期： 3年。

生产厂家： 中美天津史克制药有限公司。

样例 2：

红花油

成　　分： 红花油及各种消炎剂。

功　　能： 治疗各种骨痛、肌肉痛及骨折引起的肿痛，扭伤等。

服用方法： 外用。经常在患处涂抹并按摩。

注　　意： 不要直接接触眼睛。

有 效 期： 2年。

保　　存： 存放于阴凉处，盖子拧紧。

1.

云南白药

适 应 症： 主治妇女病及各种伤痛。

功　　能： 止血愈伤，活血散淤，消炎消肿。

用　　法： 妇科症用温开水送服，外伤用酒调匀敷于患处。

用　　量： 成人每次2颗，一日4次。儿童减半。

注　　意： 服药一日内忌食鱼类及生冷食物。

储　　藏： 置于干燥处。

制药单位： 云南白药集团有限公司。

---

2. 1) The usual dose is 2-4 tablets, 3 times daily, taken after meals.

2) Indications: This drug is for the relief of fatigue and weakness in various causes.

3) Form: The drug is suspended in white solution.

4) For pregnant women, please consult a doctor about the dosage.

5) Storage: Kept in refrigerator and out of children's reach.

6) This medicine is clinically approved for relieving headache and lowering temperature.

3. 1) Although the doctor was very kind, the patient was still very nervous.

2) Mid-Autumn Festival is a time when family members enjoy the moon together.

3) Whoever comes is welcome. / No matter who comes, he is welcome.

4) One of the reasons (why) he failed is his carelessness.

5) We'll go for a walk when/after the rain stops.

6) Whether the experiment is successful (or not) is still a secret.

7) She loves sweet food better than her mother does.

8) The Chinese player did as good as, if not better than, the foreign player.

9) It is widely accepted that practice makes perfect.

10) The new product that they showed at the fair still needs improvement.

4. 1) Some say the doctor is merciful, *while* others say he is killing people.

2) *The saying* "in Rome do as the Romans do" works for every overseas student.

3) *What I said* hurt her so deeply.

4) *Whether* he comes or not makes no difference.

5) He who laughs last laughs best.

6) We went to the museum, *which* was very crowded. / We went to the museum, *where it was* very crowded.

7) Jimmy is not *as good* at skating as his brother (is).

8) He'll answer her letter as soon as he *receives* it.

9) The presents will be given to those *who* come early./ The presents will be given to *whoever* come early.

10) The day will come *when* peace-loving people enjoy a world without war.

UNIT 5

Section I Maintaining a Sharp Eye

译文

Passage I

再见了，中国朋友!

女士们，先生们：

我们十分高兴今晚有机会相聚在此，向中国朋友表达我们的感激之情，同时与你们告别。

我们刚刚结束在你们这个非凡国家的旅行，贵国给我们留下了极其深刻的印象。美国人有赞赏进步的传统；而中华人民共和国正是前进发展的杰出榜样。在过去的52年里，你们国家取得了令人惊叹的成就。

在我们逗留期间，在中国国际旅行社经验丰富而干练的导游引导下，我们在你们的伟大国家游历了8 000多公里。在中国旅行中，中国人民表现出的那种果敢和自信，以及到处大兴土木的景象都给我们留下了印象。它展示出你们在经济发展计划的指引下，正在大力推进各项全国性项目。

中国人民谦虚谨慎，勤劳勇敢，聪明智慧。我用我的笔和相机记录了这次访问中我亲眼目睹的最动人的情景。回国后，我将让我国人民知道我所记录下来的一切。我深信，这对他们来说将是巨大的鼓舞。

在我们访问的世界各地中，从文化角度而言，对贵国的访问是最有收获的。热情、好客、精美的食品、舒适的住宿以及优美的风景融为一体，使得这次旅行令我们永远难以忘怀。

明天我们都要离去。请你们相信，我们将永远珍惜对贵国以及贵国可亲可敬的人民美好的记忆。的确，中国是一个我们愿意再度返回的地方 —— 在这儿一个人能学到许多东西。与此同时，我们也期待着在我国有机会迎接你们，我们的中国朋友，以回报你们的友情和好客。

谢谢大家。再见。

Passage II

初到中国

我现在仍然十分清楚地记得抵达北京那天的情景。那是一个阳光明媚的秋日，可是对我们这些习惯了家乡气候的人来说，显得冷了一点。一些菲律宾朋友来机场接我们，因为我们的确不熟悉周围的路，并且当时连一句中国话也不会讲。我们很快便取到了行李，这给我留下了很深的印象。我们接着就前往北京语言文化大学。在未来的11个月里，它既是我们的学校也是我们的家。北京的一切都是我梦想中的样子，而且还要更好。

在北京居住是我一生中最最愉快的一次经历。我该怎样来描述这段经历呢？它是我曾经去过的让我感到宾至如归的为数不多的地方之一。我去过新加坡、泰国、文莱、印尼和马来西亚。它们确实是美丽的地方。可是在那里待了几个星期以后我便想着要回家。与在那些地方不同，我在这里已经住了三个月，仍然好像是昨天刚到。

对我来说，北京是一个极其诱人的地方。它把现代与传统的世界融为一体。我可以毫不迟疑地说，北京是一座完全合格的现代化城市。你能清楚地看到耸立在城市上空的高层建筑；纵横交错的道路上，每天都有数以千计的汽车在行驶；为迎接2008年奥运会而筹建的令人赞叹的基础设施正在施工；以及大型娱乐设施，如公园、博物馆以及动物园等。还有便捷的地铁和交通系统可送你到各个地方。到了农村，又是另一番景象：你会观赏到许多旧砖瓦房和农田。清晨和傍晚，你还会看到老人们聚集在公园里进行通常的锻炼和彼此闲聊。有时看到他们，我会情不自禁地赞赏他们从日常生活的简单活动中所获得的那种满足和快乐。尽管时代在进步，但有些东西的确是不变的，你仍能看到许多往日的痕迹。

我对平民百姓的印象是，他们大多数都是热心肠的。老人仍受到年轻一代的尊重，而且对社会活动都很积极。但是坦率地说，目前中国人对我仍是个谜；例如传统的保守与年轻人有时的无拘无束的态度融为了一体。这里的人们受到了西方的诱惑，但与此同时，他们做事的方式仍遵循着传统。我想，我要真正了解中国的文化和社会，得花上好几年的时间。我认为，要做到更好地了解中国，第一步就是要学会说当地的语言。

1. 1) c   2) c   3) d   4) a   5) a

2. 1) In the meantime   2) make a journey   3) scene   4) farewell
    5) prudent   6) brave   7) friendliness   8) returning his kindness

9) encouragement   10) sure

3. 1) The clock struck nine; she quietly bade farewell to her mother.

2) We look forward to your company's exciting growth in the years ahead.

3) I was deeply impressed by what I saw and heard during this visit.

4) We are witnessing the birth of a new and more efficient way to use computers.

5) Upon completing my graduate study, I will return to China and seek a job in a business firm.

4. 1) F   2) T   3) F   4) T   5) T   6) T   7) T   8) T   9) F   10) T

5.   The author could still remember quite clearly the day he arrived in Beijing. It was a sunny autumn day. Some Filipino friends met him at the airport. He was quite impressed by how fast they were able to get his luggage. In no time they were proceeding to Beijing Language & Culture University, where he would study for the next eleven months. Beijing was everything that he dreamed it would be, and more.

His stay in Beijing was one of the most enjoyable experiences in his life. To him, Beijing was a mixture of the modern and traditional worlds. The people, the buildings, the transportation system, the traces of the past, and the combination of traditional and modern cultures were very attractive to him. He had been to Singapore, Thailand, Brunei, Indonesia and Malaysia. Those were really beautiful places, but after a few weeks at those places he was itching to go back home. Unlike there — it had been three months in Beijing and it seemed just like yesterday.

6. 1) 那是一个阳光明媚的秋日，可对我们这些习惯了家乡气候的人来说，显得冷了一点。

2) 在北京居住是我一生中最最愉快的一次经历。

3) 对我来说，北京是一个极其诱人的地方。它把现代与传统融为一体。

4) 尽管时代在进步，但有些东西的确是不变的，你仍能看到许多往日的痕迹。

5) 老人仍受到年轻一代的尊重，而且对社会活动都很积极。但是坦率地说，目前中国人对我仍然是个谜。

6) 这儿的人们受到了西方的诱惑，但与此同时，他们做事的方式仍遵循着传统。

Section II Trying Your Hand

样例 1：

约翰逊先生：

　　昨天没能去机场为您送行，十分遗憾。我由衷地感到您已经尽了最大的努力。没有您的合作，我们的生意不可能会取得这样丰硕的成果。

　　希望我们以后经常联系并更加密切地合作。

张林敬启

2010年4月6日

样例 2:

汤恩先生:
　　自从你为我送行以来，一周已经过去了，但机场分别的情景仍然历历在目。你和我的其他朋友一起把我从家里一直送到机场。您对我的亲切关怀我永远不会忘记。
　　不久我还打算回来。那时就会登门拜访。
　　再次表示谢意。

夏平

2010年3月18日

1.

August 20, 2010

Dear Wang Fang,
　　I have completed all my business here. I sincerely thank you for all the trouble you have taken for my sake. I am going home by air at two this afternoon. This is to say goodbye to you. Please remember me to your wife.

Yours ever,

White

2. 1) 承蒙接待，十分感激, 希望将来有机会再相会。

2) 最后，我们借此机会请大卫转达我们深厚的友谊。

3) 祝您旅途愉快，希望玩得痛快!

4) 非常感谢您来为我送行。

5) 女士们，先生们：中国民航飞往伦敦的127次航班就要起飞了。

6) 为您送别，我们感到十分难过，祝您回家一路顺风。希望您明年再次来此做客。

3. 1)　　It is the well-known Chinese cuisine that has a long history.

2) a.　It is this food manufacturer who / that has supplied the market with sugar-free food.

b.　It is sugar-free food that this food manufacturer has supplied the market with.

3) a.　It is a thank-you letter that must include proper praise of the hostess.

b.　It is proper praise of the hostess that a thank-you letter must include.

4) a.　It was she who didn't finish the course at college because of her illness.

b.　It was the course at college that she didn't finish because of her illness.

c.　It was because of her illness that she didn't finish the course at college.

4. 1)　Never before have I seen such a beautiful park.

2)　There came Professor Black.

3) Hardly had he passed the interview.

4) Only in this way can they carry out their plan successfully.

5) Were there no electricity, there would be no modern industry.

6) No sooner had they got to the plant than they started to work.

7) Scarcely did he speak about the difficulties in his work.

8) Not only is he a scientist but a great artist.

9) Had it not been for your help, we couldn't have finished the experiment on time.

10) Only after they had performed hundreds of experiments did they succeed in solving the problem.

5. 1) Wood gives much smoke while burning.

2) When in trouble, I always turned to her for help.

3) He speaks English much better than French.

4) Read the text again, please.

5) See you next week.

6) Can you do this work?

— I'm afraid not.

7) They came from America and we from England.

8) She is as tall as I.

9) Have you ever been to Xinjiang?

— Never.

10) When did you meet him?

— Two days ago.

6. 1) It is his car key that he is looking for.

2) It is the red color that they have chosen.

3) It was because he did very well in the interview that he got the job.

4) It was Peter who taught us English last term.

5) Only when he got home did he know what had happened.

6) If he can do it, so can you.

UNIT 6

Section I Maintaining a Sharp Eye

译文

Passage I

我的第一份工作

我的第一份工作是在一个叫巴特卡面包房的本地饭店里找到的。我在那里工作了七年，受益匪浅，尤其是从一位女招待那里学会了很多东西。

海伦60多岁，长着一头红发，非常自信，这一点正是我极其缺乏的。我非常尊重海伦，因为她做她喜爱的工作 —— 做招待 —— 在这方面还没有人能赶得上她。她能让每一位顾客和同事露出笑容，并感觉良好。

我还从她那儿懂得，为生活中的每一点小小的成绩而自豪是多么重要。当我在厨房里帮忙时，把两个鸡蛋放在烤炉上，轻轻地翻动，端上桌去的蛋正好是顾客要求的那样，那种美好的感觉再好不过了。

当女招待改变了我的生活。我的一位常客是弗雷德·哈斯布鲁克，他是一位电子产品推销员。他到餐馆来总是要一份墨西哥煎蛋饼。每当看到他朝饭店走来时，我就尽可能在他一坐下就把他的煎蛋饼摆放到他的餐桌上。

由于我从海伦那里学到了自信，我梦想着自己开饭店。但当我打电话向父母借钱时，他们说："我们没有这笔钱。"第二天，弗雷德看见我时问道："出什么事了，快乐姑娘？你今天怎么不笑了？"我将我的梦想讲给他听，然后说："弗雷德，我知道如果有人信任我，我会做得更好。"

他就去找了其他一些饭店里的常客。第二天，他给我几张支票，共计5万美元，还有一张我至今保存着的便条，上面写着："此贷款的唯一担保就是我对你作为一个诚实的人的信任。有梦想的好人应该有机会去实现梦想。"

我拿着支票来到美林金融服务集团 —— 这是我第一次走进股票交易所，在这里我把钱投了进去。我仍然在巴特卡工作，筹划着自己开饭店的事。然而，投资落空了，我的钱赔光了。

我不由自主地想如果我做一个股票经纪人会是什么样子。经过深思熟虑之后，我决定在美林金融服务集团申请一份工作。尽管我没有工作经历，但还是被雇佣了。并终于成为一名不错的经纪人。我最后还清了弗雷德和其他顾客的5万美元加上14%的年利。五年之后，我就能够开自己的公司了。

弗雷德给我一封感谢信让我永远铭记在心。他一直在生病。在信中他说我的支票帮他偿还了他日益增加的医药费。他在信中写道："这笔贷款是我一生中最好的投资。还有谁能够在一个具有百万美元人格魅力的'女招待'身上投资，并看到这笔投资使她成为一名非常成功的职业妇女！能有这样机会的'投资人'又有多么少啊？"

Passage II

你在工作中找到乐趣了吗？

根据专家们的看法，工作中缺少幽默确是一种憾事。研究表明，心情愉快的人工作成果大，能产生更多的效益。

当今工作场所里常有压力是因为不开玩笑。如果你学会了逗笑，那么你和周围的人都会更好地承受压力的风暴。

专家们说，良好的幽默感会有助于你在以下几方面获得成功：

1. 适应变动。当今工作中角色和责任在迅速地变换。幽默感能为你提供应付这种变换所需要的韧劲。

2. 提高领导水平。随着事业的发展，可能会让你在机构中承担更多的领导责任，做出更多的决定。培养幽默感会使你具有更有成效的领导能力。

3. 应付加大的压力。如前面所提到的，压力伴随着所有的工作。你承担的责任越大，你经受的压力就越大。而幽默是应付周围压力的一个强有力的工具。欢笑声能帮你消除肌肉紧张，缓解愤怒，增强你克服恐惧及控制忧虑的能力，使你保持一种更为积极的心态。

4．加强改革和创新的能力。良好的幽默感能提高你创造性思维的能力。

5．提高交际技能。你机构中的每一个成员都需要有这些技能。幽默既能使他人对你所说的内容更加感兴趣，同时还能有助你被团队中的其他人所接受。

好了，你已经准备好要开怀大笑并且鼓励你的同事们也大笑吗？以下建议有助于你逐渐学会幽默起来：

第一步：为自己创造幽默的环境，并培养自己的幽默感。怎么做呢？多看喜剧电影；从杂志和报纸上寻找卡通画看；多与你最风趣的朋友和同事在一起。

第二步：要多开玩笑，不要太严肃。多花点时间陪你的孩子玩，把你认为风趣的事情拟出一张表，每天做一件。

第三步：要经常开心大笑，学会讲笑话。

第四步：玩一些有关语言、双关语及其他用词方面的游戏。

第五步：在日常生活中寻找幽默。寻找生活中意想不到的、不协调的、稀奇古怪和可笑的东西。

第六步：不要和自己过不去，要学会对自己的错误不以为然。

第七步：在压力中寻找幽默。

1. 1) b   2) c   3) d   4) a   5) b

2. 1) looked up to 2) alike   3) took ... pride in 4) regular   5) had faith in
6) invest   7) hired   8) annual   9) personally   10) has matured

3. 1) Thanks to him, I began to love my career.
2) He was so excited about his idea that he felt he had to share it with someone.
3) The party ended up with Mary's dance.
4) I'll give you a cheque to cover the cost of your journey.
5) He is one of the regular customers at the village bar.
6) It might be a better investment to buy stock.

4. 1) T 2) T 3) F 4) F 5) T 6) T 7) T 8) F 9) T 10) T

5. 1) responsible 2) positive 3) laughter 4) manage 5) decide
6) humor   7) ridiculous 8) angry   9) increasingly 10) power

6. 1) 根据专家们的看法，工作中缺少幽默确是一种憾事。
2) 如果你学会了逗笑，那么你和周围的人都会更好地承受压力的风暴。
3) 现今工作中角色和责任在迅速地变换。幽默感能为你提供应付这种变换所需的韧劲。
4) 欢笑声能帮你消除肌肉紧张，缓解愤怒，增强你克服恐惧及控制忧虑的能力，使你保持一种更为积极的心态。
5) 你机构中的每一个成员都需要有这些技能。幽默既能使他人对你所说的内容更加感兴趣，同时还有助于你被团队中其他人所接受。

6) 为自己创造幽默的环境，并培养自己的幽默感。

7) 寻找生活中意想不到的、不协调的、稀奇古怪和可笑的东西。

Section II Trying Your Hand

样例 1:

就 业 申 请 表

（就业前调查问卷）（就业机会均等）

日期：2011年7月20日

姓名（姓在前）：约翰逊·麦克尔　　　　　　　　　社会保险号：621-01-8866

地址：加州洛杉矶艾斯伯瑞路423号　　邮编：90043　　电　　话：555-6432

你申请何种工作？ 广告设计

你有何种特殊资格？ 注册程序员

你会使用何种办公设备？ 计算机

你是否年满18岁？ 是： √　　　　　　　　　　否:

学 历

学校	年限	学校名称	城市	课程	是否毕业
高中	4	洛杉矶高中	洛杉矶		是
大学	4	圣地亚哥学院	圣地亚哥	职业培训	是
其他					

工作经历

公司名称 和地址	日期 从	日期 至	说明工作 职责	起始 工资	最终 工资	辞职 原因
琳安·爱帕尔公司	2005	2011	协助广告设计	$2 500	$4 000	需要全职工作

证明人

姓名	地址	职业
泰德·安德森	康门斯区14923号 琳安·爱帕尔公司	经理

样例 2:

个人简历

王威力

洪源市怒江街235号

电话：8687954

电子邮件: wlwrd@hotmail.com

求职意向：

　　秘书、接待员或行政助理

学历：

2007	毕业于洪源应用技术学院商务管理专业
2008	获得洪源市商务培训学校秘书资格证书
2009	受过下列计算机培训 —— DOS, dBase IV, WordPerfect, Windows, Excel

就业情况：

2009年9月　　在新计算机园公司任行政助理（全职工作）

至现在　　　职责: 保证办公室工作顺利进行；保证工作按质、按时完成；安排会议；订购物品；培训新员工；办公设备故障的检修。

　　　　　　使用过下列办公软件：Microsoft Office、Excel及WordPefert

2007年9月　　在泰恒路高中做秘书和接待员（兼职工作）

至2009年7月　职责：打印报告、考卷、课程计划和日常信函；参加会议并作会议记录；保证办公室工作顺利进行；安排会议；设置并保管学生成绩档案系统。使用过下列办公软件: Microsoft Word、Microsoft Outlook、Dos、Windows

个人爱好：

　　音乐、小说、游泳

证明人：

　　1. 方明: 新计算机园公司人事部主任。电话：86493367

　　2. 李达军博士: 泰恒路高中校长。电话：28281360

1.

Resume

Ma Hongguang

No. 135 Huanghe Street, Binhai City

Telephone: 86856793

E-mail: mhg88@sohu.com

Objective:

To work in a position related to agricultural machinery

Education and training:

2009   Graduated from Binhai College of Agricultural Technology

2010   Trained at Binhai Agricultural University for 6 months, taking courses on agricultural machinery

Work experience:

Aug. 2011—present   assistant engineer, Dongfang Research Institute of Agricultural Machinery

Sep. 2009—Jul. 2010   laboratory assistant, Binhai College of Agricultural Technology

Personal data:

Date of Birth: May 12, 1976

Sex: Male

Marital Status: Single

Health: Good

Interest: Sports, music, reading

2. 1) 写个人简历时，应提供有关个人的主要情况。

    2) 我正在找一份能充分利用我的电子知识的工作。

    3) 下列人员同意提供有关我的资历和工作能力的证明。

    4) 在传统的简历中，首先列出每一位雇主的名字，并加下划线，然后写出省、市的名称。

    5) 雇主们对应聘者工作之余的活动和爱好尤其感兴趣。

3. 1) d   2) c

4.

English Study

English is a popular language in the world. No matter where you are, no matter where you come from, you can hear people talk in English or see people read newspapers, magazines, textbooks or novels in English. Almost at all the important international meetings, people communicate with each other in English. The wide use of English has made it the important language in the world.

As we know, language is one of the most useful communication tools. English, as an international language, is especially so. Unless you are good at English, you can hardly work very well, only because you cannot keep up with the rapid progress in science and technology. Furthermore, if you cannot speak and write fluent English you will have little chance to attend in advanced studies in other countries.

What shall we do in order to study English well? In order to study English well, we should, first of all, have perseverance. Even when we meet great difficulties, we should not be discouraged and stopped. Persistence and patience will help us make greater progress. Secondly, practice is the golden key to success. We should not be afraid of making mistakes. If there is no mistake, there is no progress. Actually, we should grasp every opportunity to speak, to write, to listen or to read.

Based on your perseverance and diligent practice, plus proper study methods, you can surely grasp this very useful language.

5. 1) The speaker didn't know his subject, nor did he speak well. In brief, he was disappointing.

   2) From what I have observed, I can come to the conclusion that he is suitable for the job.

   3) Obviously (Clearly), there is no need to say again how important this work is.

   4) My elder brother thought he couldn't go to the party because he had too much homework. But he went after all.

   5) No doubt, John will call us if he comes to the town.

UNIT 7

Section I Maintaining a Sharp Eye
译文
Passage I

销售：推出畅销书的关键
在上个月那些阳光灿烂的日子里，昆明充满了纸和油墨的芳香。从 9 月 15 日到 25 日，第 12 届全国图书展销会在这座风景如画的边陲城市举行，全国各地的出版商们带着 10 多万种书籍聚集在这里，在展销会上搭建起 1 300 多个图书交易摊位。

在展销会上展销的 10 多万种图书中，畅销书几乎是最引人注目的。其中，经济类图书、教育类图书和因特网图书最受欢迎。这次图书大聚会不仅带来了巨大的经济效益 —— 仅前 4 天就收入 6 亿 7 千多万元 —— 同时还显示出中国出版业的最新趋势。

热情的书迷们排着长队在销售畅销书的书摊前呈之字形向前移动。在这些书摊前几乎找不到任何空位，销售人员们一刻不停地忙着将新书朝书架上搬。这次书展定会使那些对销售策略持非常乐观态度的出版商们感到高兴。

图书的畅销与否常常取决于其促销方式，而并非因为书写得好。至少有些小说是这样的。在每一本畅销书后面，都有一个成功的促销活动，有一大笔资金会投入到促销活动中去。就拿《富爸爸，穷爸爸》来说吧。这本书在中国出版之前，世界图书出版公司仅一个月内就在报纸杂志上刊登了 40 多则广告，并在 600 多个网站上推销。他们为此投资了相当大的一笔钱。"至于他们花费了多少，又赚了多少，那是个商业秘密，但是我可以告诉你，其收益说明投资是值得的。"

图书与其他商品的区别在于书是文化产品，但是与其他商品一样，要想为公众所知，图书也需要做广告。

然而，中国的出版业直到 20 世纪 90 年代被推向市场后才认识到这一点。市场上有如此多的图书在竞争，如果不进行促销，仅靠口头宣传，就注定要失败。要推销一本书，出版社首先要选定一个好的题材，然后请作家去写。如果你找到了恰当的题材，即读者感兴趣的题材，你就找到了市场，这就使你的书成功了一半。出版商们还会从每年的出版计划中挑选一些可能畅销的图书，为它们举办促销活动。

一旦定下要推销什么图书，出版商们便会为它们找出卖点，制订促销计划并组织促销活动。第一步便是在报纸杂志上登广告。让作家在现场签名售书已是读者们十分熟悉的促销活动。

如今，为吸引读者而举办的活动多种多样。但是读者们一定要小心，不能盲目地被那些促销活动所误导。人们已逐渐意识到，他们不应过多注意广告宣传。有些人相信声誉，可有些人则不。因此，人们首先应该仔细看一看、想一想。

Passage II

生意就是生意，全世界都是如此吗？

史密斯先生是美国一家饮料公司的老板，他要与日本一家食品公司就向日本出口啤酒的事进行谈判。他已与这家日本公司的美国代表进行过意向性商讨，现在，史密斯先生要飞往日本与之商讨细节，希望最好能获得一份可供双方签字的协议。

在美国，史密斯先生通常能成功地在一两天内将类似的交易搞定。他的习惯是尽早进入正题，不在准备工作上花许多时间。他想在东京也用同样的办法，因此他只打算在东京待 3 天。"生意就是生意，"他常常这样说，而且有人告诉他，他的日本伙伴跟他一样，对这项计划中的合作很感兴趣。

刚到东京的第一个晚上，史密斯先生就利用吃晚饭的机会谈起这项计划中的交易的要点。然而，除了对方友好但并不承担义务的谈话，史密斯先生没有听到任何明确的说法。第二天，他在与这家日本公司领导们的第一次会晤中，情况依然如故。尽管史密斯先生曾几次努力想开始商讨正题，可对方却闭口不谈这项计划，只是一个劲地谈他们公司的历史、传统和信念。让史密斯先生感到沮丧的还有，这些日本人当中，只有一个人会说英语。

史密斯先生生气了，"时间就是金钱"这一原则毕竟任何地方都应该适用。最后，当他听说那天下午的安排不是商务谈判而是观光时，他再也耐不住了。在绝望中，他向那些日本人严厉地请求马上开始谈商务。经过短时间的磋商，这些日本人终于同意了他的请求。然而，与他的期望相反，谈判并未获得预期的进展。没有谈出任何明确的说法，更不用说承诺了，最终谈判毫无结果。尽管他提出了具体的建议也没起作用。经过 3 天令人沮丧的、几乎毫无进展的谈判，史密斯先生飞回了美国，没有达成任何协议，或者他感觉是这样。他觉得他做好了充分的准备来商谈交易的任何方面，可是什么也没做成。

然而，准备不仅仅是生意上的，文化上的准备也是必需的。正是在如下几个可能出现的问题上史密斯先生没有做好准备：（1）未充分理解不同的思维方式；（2）未充分注意为对方留面子的必要性；（3）对东道国的历史、文化、政府以及外国人在他们头脑中的形象了解和认识不足；（4）对决策过程、人际关系和个性的作用等认识不足；（5）留给谈判的时间不足等。

1. 1) d   2) b   3) d   4) a   5) d

2. 1) flocks   2) was published   3) to reveal   4) has invested
5) commodities   6) optimism   7) blinded   8) sign

3. 1) Experts flocked in to discuss the marketing strategies of the new products.
2) A powerful launching campaign resulted in the large sales of the new type of air-conditioner.
3) All countries concerned must take a stand on this issue.
4) It is quite wrong to believe in the idea that money does everything.
5) Mr. Miller is a good professor, and he is very popular with his students.
6) Never expect that customers will depend on word of mouth; they only believe in what you really do and offer.

4. 1) F   2) T   3) F   4) F   5) T   6) F   7) F   8) F

5. 1) Producing beverage / drinks.
2) To get down to business as soon as possible.
3) Three days.
4) He is probably an interpreter.
5) Because he knows little about how Japanese do their business.
6) Preparations in a cultural sense / Cultural preparations.

6. 1) image   2) preferred   3) ending   4) conversational
5) was devoted / devoted herself   6) impatient   7) progressive   8) frustrated

Section II Trying Your Hand

样例 1

王牌空气冷却器是 Toto 电器公司的新产品。该产品用进口橡胶制成，比电扇更实用，也更安全。该空气冷却器有一个水蒸发冷却系统向外鼓吹凉爽清风。它可用在任何地方：书桌、餐桌、床头柜上，甚至汽车或小艇上均可使用。您只需将水灌进去，然后打开电源即可。无需安装！换一次水，可连续制冷 5 个小时。重量轻，便于携带，耗电低，只需 4 节小号电池或一个交流电配电器。

欲知详情，请拨电话：1-402-464-0044。

样例 2

> 　　*阳光窗帘*是太阳家用产品有限公司的新产品。该产品用特制原料聚乙烯制成，夏日能遮挡阳光，冬日又能保暖。您只需将其挂在窗帘杆上，置于窗户与您的窗帘之间。阳光窗帘能保护您的家具不受阳光照射而褪色，还能增加私密感 —— 您能够看到外面，但外人看不到里面。
> 　　颜色有：紫色、绿色、红色、蓝色、银灰色。
> 　　尺寸有：# 29017　阳光窗帘　30x63
> 　　　　　　 # 29033　阳光窗帘　30x81
> 　　　　　　 # 29041　阳光窗帘　36x63
> 　　　　　　 # 29058　阳光窗帘　36x81

1.

> 　　*苗条牌系列短裤*是卡森斯服装公司的新产品。用 70% 的精制橡胶和 30% 的尼龙制作，*苗条牌系列短裤*设计特别，利用人体的自然热量增加腰部、腹部、臀部及腿部的排汗量，有效地减少你体内多余的水分，收到快速减肥的效果。可水洗，男士和女士均宜。
> 　　尺寸有：24 至 44 英寸。
> 　　颜色有：黑色、蓝色和灰色。

2. 1) treated　　　　　　2) keep sunrays out　　3) prevent heat loss　　4) curtain rod

　　5) your furniture　　6) privacy　　　　　　7) see out　　　　　　8) see in

　　9) families and hotels　10) more information

3. 1) is designed　　　2) features　　　　　　　　3) adapted　　　4) stylish

　　5) (should) warn　　6) approaches / is approaching　7) to take care of

4. 1) convenient → convenience　　　　2) especially → special

　　3) dirty-removing → dirt-removing　　4) handhold → hand-held

　　5) excited → exciting　　　　　　　　6) breathtaken → breathtaking

　　7) hold → holds　　　　　　　　　　8) importing → imported

5. 1) Dressed up in these pretty costumes, your little dog will be the center of attention on the streets.

　　2) Made of genuine leather, this easy-to-carry shoulder bag never goes out of style.

　　3) These socks are made of 100% cotton, which gives you a soft-as-silk feeling.

　　4) Made of specially-treated material, the coat is light in weight and machine washable.

　　5) This colorful *Talking Parrot* has a hidden recording device that enables him to repeat everything you say and in your own voice!

　　6) This handsome pocket watch has an accurate quartz movement device.

UNIT 8

Section I Maintaining a Sharp Eye

译文

Passage I

绝对公平的交易

它像是一块琥珀。它像是一颗富有暖感的暗红色宝石。我一见到它就知道，它必须属于我。

当然那就是一把乔达诺。我一看见就知道那是乔达诺。乔达诺小提琴在全世界仅存有很少的几把。纽约的一位专家说只有 12 把。现在我知道那位专家说错了。我发现了第 13 把。

6 个月前，我去了意大利。我应邀参加在伊斯基亚岛举行的古典音乐节。

音乐节很乏味。这些演出通常没有什么值得一提的地方。他们演奏了巴赫和珀塞尔的作品，演奏得很好，但也没有什么与众不同。

就在下一曲刚开始的时候我看到了这把小提琴。我不知道我为什么我没早发现。也许小提琴在这首曲子里才更为重要。

音乐会刚一结束，我就走上舞台来到年轻的小提琴手面前。我没看小提琴手，我看的是那把小提琴。

"这把琴很不错，是吧？"他对我说。我吃了一惊——他英语讲得很地道。

"你怎么知道我是英国人？"我问道。

"你是霍布斯先生，对吧？"

"对，我是霍布斯。"我够出名的，我想。

"我叫弗兰克。"

"很高兴见到你，弗兰克。现在告诉我你这把小提琴的事。你是在哪儿得到这把琴的？"

"哦，我不记得了。这是我父亲的。他有很多的旧乐器。我觉得这把琴相当古老，但我不敢肯定。这把琴很不错，是吧？"

"哦，对，对。是不错。确实不错。"

我不敢相信这是真的！我运气真好——这个年轻人，我觉得他相当愚蠢，不知道他演奏的这把小提琴是一件极其罕见、极其珍贵的古董！

"我可以看一下吗？"我问道。

"当然可以。"他把小提琴递给我。在琴把的背后，我发现了字迹极小极小的拉丁文题铭：乔当思，那不勒斯，1722 年制作。一点没错！我太激动了，我不知道怎么办才好。我尽量控制住自己，又问了弗兰克几个问题。

"我可以见一下你父亲吗？"

"当然可以。为什么不和我们一起共进晚餐呢？"

"那太好了，谢谢。"

5 分钟后，我已坐在他的汽车里，一起沿着岛上狭窄蜿蜒的道路驶向弗兰克父亲的家。

我知道说谎是不对的。但是如今的世道有时候要想取得进展你就得不择手段。

"我想买你那把旧的小提琴！"我对弗兰克的父亲说。"我开价很大方。"

"这个，霍布斯先生，"老人说，"我在这方面是业余爱好，我不是专家。我对古董乐器知道得

187

不多。"

"我是这方面专家,"我告诉他,"我觉得这把旧琴挺吸引人,但也许不是太值钱。也许 200 英镑是一个公道的价钱。"

老人摇摇头。

"我父亲不想让人家觉得不懂礼貌,"弗兰克说,"但是他觉得 200 英镑不算是很大方!"

我们都笑了。

"我看得出来你父亲是个聪明人,弗兰克,"我说。"他知道怎样做生意!我出 250 英镑,但不能再多了。"

老人和他儿子又开始商量。

"你出的价钱确实慷慨大方,霍布斯先生,"老人说,"我很乐意接受这个价钱!"

我不敢相信我的运气有多好!我只花 250 英镑就买下一把能卖到 25 000 英镑的小提琴!趁他们还没改变主意之前我匆忙开了一张支票,拿起小提琴,叫了辆出租车就往回走。

"再见!见到你真高兴!"

"希望能够再见到你,"弗兰克说。我却希望永远不再见到你,我想。

(待续)

Passage II

绝对公平的交易(续)

第二天我醒得很早,收拾好手提箱就赶往机场。得到这件令人难以置信的便宜货,我感到异常兴奋,但同时又有点担心。我来解释一下其中的缘由。虽然现在欧洲是一个单一市场,但仍有一些东西不准由一个国家带往另一个国家。一切我们称之为"艺术或文化遗产"的东西 —— 譬如说,艺术品或古董 —— 都在禁止之列。这就是为什么我在到达机场时感到担心的原因。我办理了手提箱的托运手续,将小提琴作为手提行李,我不想让这把贵重的小提琴在安全检查时通过 X 线机。我不得不打开琴盒,让海关人员查看这把乐器。

三个海关人员拿起小提琴仔细查看,他们在认真讨论。他们叫来了一个级别更高的海关官员,这位官员仔细地查看了小提琴,然后又查验了我的护照。他将我仔细地打量了一番,又和其他海关人员交谈了一阵。最后他把小提琴放回琴盒,将我放行上飞机。我又一次不敢相信我的好运。我舒了一口气,觉得我是世界上运气最好的人了。但事情还没有完,现在我还得通过英国海关。

下飞机的时候,我的心脏已经跳得很快了。它跳得就像在敲鼓 —— 我觉得肯定谁都听得见。我在行李认领处等我的行李,觉得警察或海关人员随时都会来逮捕我。因为这是欧洲航班,我可以决定是否要将带入这个国家的东西报关。机场有两个出口,如果我走绿色出口,我暗自考虑,我可以什么也不说就离开机场,虽然这是违法的!如果我走红色出口,我的小提琴就必须接受检查,我也就有可能被逮捕!

我选择了绿色出口,什么也没说就走出了机场。我去叫了一辆出租车。我正要上车,觉得有一只手搭在我的肩膀上。

"对不起,先生,"一个声音说。完了!我想。我就要被逮捕,坐牢!

"我想你忘记了你的箱子。"我转过身,看见我的一只箱子还在地上。

"谢谢!"我说。

我确实是世界上运气最好的人。

当我终于回到家的时候,我松了一口气。我从口袋里掏出钥匙开门……我发现门已经开了。

"啊，不可能！"我自言自语地说。"有贼！"

我慢慢地小心翼翼地走进房门，怕人还在里面。我想的不错，房子里确实有人，房子里有两个人。那个年轻的小提琴手弗兰克和他的老父亲坐在我的客厅里。

"你好啊，我们又见面了，霍布斯先生！"他们说，"我们正在等您。"

我大吃一惊。这不可能。他们怎么可能先来到这里呢？他们想干什么？他们怎么知道我住在这里？

"我必须再一次说谢谢您，霍布斯先生。"那个老人说，"但不是谢您那 250 英镑！你真的以为我那么傻吗？"

我什么也没说。我无言以对。

"我们已经知道您的古董乐器生意做得不错，我们还知道您做生意不总是特别诚实。我们一直想把这把乔达诺小提琴带进英国，在这里我们可以把它卖给一个有钱的收藏家，但我们知道带着它通过海关很危险。再一次感谢您，霍布斯先生，谢谢您给我们帮了忙。不必担心！我们不会把您做的事情告诉任何人！既然我们已经知道您干得有多漂亮，将来我们就能请您给我们帮更多的忙。"

也许我的运气并没有我起初想的那么好！

1. 1) He found it at a musical festival on the island of Ischia, Italy.

2) The young violinist had no idea of the value of the antique violin.

3) It was made in 1722.

4) Because he felt he needed an excuse for his telling lies.

5) £250.

6) Because he didn't like to be discovered that he had told a lie in the deal.

7) Open.

2. 1) is expected 2) valuable 3) is controlled 4) rare 5) miss

6) attended 7) cheque 8) impolite 9) acceptable 10) has left

3. 1) They made an offer to help us in getting the loan.

2) He wasn't invited to attend last week's party.

3) They were excited with joy at the victory of the city team.

4) This is only one of many possible solutions.

5) We are sorry to have taken up much of your valuable time.

6) He prepared the report with remarkable speed.

4. 1) T 2) F 3) F 4) T 5) T 6) T 7) F 8) T

5. 1) musical 2) sounds 3) woke up 4) restrict

5) breathed 6) forgot / has forgotten 7) deals 8) dangerous

6. 1) I was horrified at the news.

2) I don't think it's wise to carry too much hand luggage.

3) The company deals in computer hardware and software.

4) I was extremely happy about the decision they had made.

5) She breathed a sigh of relief when she found her son was safe.

6) He went out of the room without saying anything.

Section II Trying Your Hand

样例1

> Geokon 有限公司位于美国新汉普夏市，在世界范围开展经营活动。公司成立于 1979 年，现有员工 60 余人。数年来，Geokon 公司作为一系列优质工业测量仪表的一家主要设计和生产厂商脱颖而出。尤其是 Geokon 公司依靠创新和经验，已开发出一系列世界领先水平的传感器。这些可靠性极高的装置为在世界范围内更广泛地应用传感装置技术作出了不小的贡献。

样例2

> C&A 工具工程有限公司（美国印第安纳州）
>
> C&A 工具工程有限公司总部设在印第安纳州东北部的一个人口只有 1 800 人的楚鲁布斯科镇。1969 年公司成立时只有两个人，但现在已有大约 230 名员工。C&A 公司从来没有解雇过一名员工，这在美国公司里是很少见的。
>
> 公司成立时是一家为金属铸造业服务的工具和模具公司，但后来扩展到生产多种配件和工程用具。这些零部件和工程用具包括柴油机燃油喷射系统、医疗设备配件和汽车配件。现在 C&A 公司与大约 300 家客户公司签有合同。

1. 1) The company was founded in 2010.

2) The company is a manufacturer of diesel engines.

3) We are a small company with over 80 employees.

4) The company's annual sales were RMB 6 million *yuan* in 2010.

5) The sales are up 10 percent over last year.

6) Our head office is located in Beijing.

7) We have developed several new products.

8) We can produce according to the customers' specifications.

2. 1) manufacturer   2) are located   3) was founded   4) became   5) began

6) changed   7) include   8) received   9) passed   10) employs

3. 1) is based   2) to record   3) are expected   4) publishes

5) located   6) provides   7) is growing   8) specializing / specialized

4. 1) established → was established

     2) more → more than

     3) found → founded

     4) provide → providing; relate → related

     5) is → was

     6) manufacture → manufactures

     7) provide → to provide

     8) are → is

5. 1) We are a small firm located in Wenzhou and specializing in computers.

     2) We have been in business since 1987.

     3) Now we have over 200 employees in Dalian, China.

     4) The center consists of three divisions, with the R&D section as the largest.

     5) Our mission is to improve the health of the patients.

     6) Friends of the Third World is a nonprofit volunteer group.

UNIT 9

Section I Maintaining a Sharp Eye

译文

Passage I

我的购物经历

最近在 NEXT 购物之后，我觉得最好让大家都知道，因此写了如下的看法。

故事最初从我和太太到位于 Milton Keynes 的 NEXT 去买东西开始。我想买几套上班穿的新西装，并且好容易发现了 3 套我很喜欢的。但是有一个问题，就是我个子矮，有时候很难找到合适的尺寸。果然，NEXT 的 Milton Keynes 分店没有我的尺寸。询问了售货员之后，我最后报名参加了 NEXT 产品目录 —— 既然那里有西装，我就可以直接订我的尺寸了。

第一次寄来产品目录时，那上面的好东西之多使我感到吃惊 —— 男装、鞋类、女服饰品、室内陈设品，等等。我开始有点担心，怕妻子看见会不停地花信用卡上的钱。

好，接着往下说。我为自己订了 3 套尺寸合适的西装，而电话另一端的女士是再客气不过、再友好不过了。在这期间我觉得真舒服。她说我的尺寸是现成的，7 天之内就会送到。一连串麻烦事便由此开头…

过了 14 天还没见西装，我决定与 NEXT 联系，看出了什么问题。他们告知我作为新顾客，我有 250 英镑的信贷限额。而我的订货总额有 450 英镑，所以他们不能发货。我对此没有过多疑虑，但是我不理解他们为什么不早点与我联系，或者在我当初订货时就告诉我。不管怎么说，为了避免麻烦，客户服务部的小姐建议我用信用卡付款。为了使他们能够发货，我就照办了。又一次，他们告诉我 7 天之内西装就会到。

又过了 12 天后，衣服终于到了。打开包装，我发现其中一件尺寸不对，而另外两件与我订的货不同，就又打电话与服务部联系。他们让我把衣服寄回去，他们将重新受理这次订货。

5 天后我终于收到我订的 3 套西装，尺码全都正确。我心里想，麻烦终于过去了。错。

收到正确无误的西装一星期之后，信用卡账单也寄到了，但向 NEXT 公司支付了两次各 450 英镑。结果是虽然我把前一次寄错的衣服退了回去，他们却忘了将货款退还到我的信用卡上。我就又回到电话机前给 NEXT 打电话，而这次我发现客户服务部不如以前那样友好了。在向两个人说明情况之后，我又不得不向一位主管重复了第 3 遍，他们才承认是他们错了。他们说需要 7 个工作日货款才会来到我的账上。因为我还得等 3 周信用卡账单才会寄到，我自然认为到那时钱肯定已经付给我了。又错了。

终于，这笔钱出现在我的信用卡账单上，但付款的日期是在我通知他们 5 个多星期之后。

所以，根据我的经验，我对所有各位 NEXT 的顾客的建议是：尽量到商店购买所需物品，而只把产品目录作为最后的选择。

Passage II

方便最重要

像当今快节奏世界上的多数人一样，我没有时间去商店买东西。如果你浪费我的时间，我会永远恨你。

问多数的零售商店店员，什么对顾客最重要，他们会回答你"价钱便宜"。而随便问一个顾客，他们都会说"方便"。

这就是为什么我发现自己越来越多地在网上购物的原因。我没有时间去商业街，就是去了，还不得不和无知的、粗鲁的、待人冷淡的售货员打交道。我没有时间那样做。我宁愿登录网站，多花一点钱，就把事情办了。让我来告诉你们我最近的购物经历：

星期五晚上，我去了商业街。我不喜欢到商业街去。商业街拥挤、嘈杂、地方太大，而且没有一份将就够用的店名录来帮助我找到路。

虽然如此，但我才搬到一间大办公室，需要一些摆放计算机的家具和挂在墙上的艺术品。一位朋友推荐了商业街的一家快速配框店。她说那里供选择的商品很多，而且价钱很合理。好，我喜欢"非常合理"的价钱，而且供选择的商品多总是一个优点。

当我终于找到那家商店，我又高兴又惊奇。那里可选择的商品确实很多，而且价钱非常合理。很快环视了一周后，我走近柜台（在过了比我愿意等候的时间更久之后，来了一位售货员）说："我要买那一幅和那一幅，就像墙上的那样装框。哦，还有，你们有鲍里斯·瓦利乔吗？"

"从来没听说过这个人。"

"噢。那么，你们有一个天使朝着孩子睡觉的床俯下身来的那幅画吗？我不记得这位艺术家的名字了，但那是一幅名画。我觉得是叫《守护天使》…或其他类似的名字。"

"我觉得没见过 —— 你到那边名画柜找找看。"她用红色的长指甲指着我肩膀后面的一个地方。

"哪儿？哪边？是那里吗？"

"不，不 —— 是那边。"

得，没有鲍里斯·瓦利乔，也没有守护天使。经过到处打听，又进进出出几次之后，她找到这两幅画合适的衬边和画框，接着给我登记。

"你什么时候取？"

对了，我说过没有？他们柜台的后面有一块硕大的招牌，上面写着："配框立等可取"。

"噢，我还需要去买几件家具，所以大约一小时左右。"我回答。

"呀，不行。"她说，"我们明天下午之前不可能做出来。"

"可是…那牌子上写的是'配框立等可取'。"我表示不同意。

"是的，但是我们很忙。"她解释说，"你前面还有其他顾客。明天下午。"

"可是牌子上写着…"

"两点钟以后，什么时候都行。"

"好，你听我说，我明天来不了…后天也不行…大后天也不行。就把墙上挂的那两幅给我吧，那也行。"

"哎呀，对不起，我不能给你。那不符合商店的规定。"

"可是牌子上写着…"

"对不起，先生。可是我说过了，我们很忙。"她重复说道。

"当然，生意好我很高兴，"我跟她说，"你真好运气。我跟你说，我们算了吧。"

"算了…？你是说你全都不要了？！"

她似乎生气了，因为我浪费了她的时间。可你知道 —— 真太可惜了！因为她浪费了我一个小时的生命，而空闲时间对我来说是非常难得的。

在你觉得我真是一个怪人之前，让我来谈一下我的生活。从星期一到星期五我5点钟起床。6点半去上班，8点钟到达办公室。我工作到4点半，然后6点钟回到家里。周末我不上班，在家里工作，通常要干到凌晨3、4点钟。

我可没有一个小时的空闲，让既要说谎（通过招牌），又对出售的商品一无所知，还要给我引用"商店规定"的店员去浪费。

假如，她觉得自己忙，在浪费我的时间之前就该跟我说明情况，我是会理解的 —— 或者，假如他们头脑还算清醒，自己先把招牌摘掉！这些人不是中学生做钟点工，这些人（从表面上看来）是受过教育的成年人。

我永远不会再去那家商店。

我后来在网上挑选了几幅画，订购了其中的一幅，比在商业街买多付了75美元。

1. 1) The name of a shop.

2) The suits that he liked.

3) A list of products that a customer could buy through telephone.

4) Because there were so many items that his wife would like to buy.

5) Send off.

6) Four.

7) It was the least reliable way to buy things.

2. 1) resort   2) definitely   3) Initially   4) charge   5) recent

6) delivered   7) Eventually   8) managed   9) consultations   10) notify

3. 1) I think we all share your concern about this matter.

2) Details of the competition are available from our head office.

3) It marked a new stage in the history of the Internet.

4) The driver was obviously in the wrong in going ahead against the red light.

5) We waited for two hours, but he did not show up.

4. 1) F   2) T   3) T   4) F   5) T   6) F   7) F   8) T

5. 1) ignorance   2) convenient   3) pace   4) selected

    5) reasonable   6) approached   7) proceedings   8) mention

6. 1) He explained that he had been delayed by a traffic jam.

2) There is no use wasting time in discussing the matter.

3) Jobs are hard to come by with so many people out of work.

4) Perhaps you can recommend me another hotel.

5) There's very little selection of winter clothes in the spring.

6) The police put up a sign that the rode was closed.

Section II Trying Your Hand

样例 1

加利福尼亚银行

不可撤销跟单信用证

跟单信用证号码：99 / 80000

签发日期：2007 年 6 月 20 日

有效日期和地点：2007 年 8 月 15 日于 上海

申请开证人：安吉利斯进口股份有限公司

          美国加利福尼亚洛杉矶西 9 路 3710 号，邮政区码 90019

受益人：万通商贸股份有限公司

       中国上海 1267 号信箱

货币代号及数额：美元 950 000.00 元整

汇票种类：见票 60 天付款

分批装运：不允许

转船：不允许

装运：2007 年 7 月 31 日前自中国上海至洛杉矶

装运货物：500 台电冰箱 型号 DRF–F600

须附有下列单据：

     发票一式 5 份

     全套以发货人为抬头并注明"货已装船"、"运费已付"的可转让清洁提单

费用：所有在美国以外的银行收费由受益人账户支付。

John F. William
有权签字人的签字
加利福尼亚银行

样例 2

商业银行
美国伊利诺伊州惠顿繁荣街88号
邮政区码：60187-2553

通知行编号：MB-5432
开证行备查编号和日期：SBRE-777　2007 年 1 月 26 日

致
杜佩奇运输公司
美国伊利诺斯州惠顿农场北路 421 号

亲爱的先生们：

　　本行受中国广州中国银行委托通知贵公司，中国银行广州分行已开具以我行为付款人，由中国广州阳光路 7 号的德远进口公司账户支付，以贵公司为受益人的 SB-87654 号不可撤销跟单信用证，金额为不超过贰万五千美元 (USD $25 000.00)，按发票金额 100% 开立的即期汇票付款，并须附有下列单据：

1. 经签署的发票一式 5 份,证明货物属 2007 年 1 月 10 日第 DEF-101 号定购单项下。
2. 装箱单一式 5 份。
3. 全套"货已装船"、以中国广州中国银行为抬头、日期最迟为 2007 年 3 月 19 日、注明"运费已付"的可转让清洁提单。

证明装运：100 套 "ABC" 牌风动工具，CIF 广州
装运：自美国伊利诺伊州惠顿　至中国广州
分批装运：不允许
转船：允许

单据须于装运之后 15 日内提交。

本行保证,在符合本证条款的单据于 2007 年 3 月 26 日(或之前)提交本行时,即予付款。

詹姆斯·波拉
敬上

1. 1) 我们已开出以贵方为受益人的保兑信用证。

2) 本信用证于2010年7月15日止在中国议付有效。

3) 单据需在装船后15天内交给议付行。

4) 货物不得迟于（或于）2010年7月30日装运。

5) 他们希望贵方将上述信用证的有效期延长10天。

6) 提单日期不得迟于2010年8月15日。

7) 随附下列单据一式两份。

8) 我行保证兑付所有按照本条款开具的汇票。

2. 1) agreed   2) supplying   3) done   4) required   5) be obtained

6) assembles   7) include   8) documents   9) commonest   10) sent

3. 1) shall be working   2) writing   3) appointed   4) found

5) has made   6) were   7) seen   8) covers

4. 1) kilometers area → kilometers in area

2) for → on

3) and → by

4) read → reading

5) lived → have lived

6) ten-year → ten years'

7) meet → met

8) enlarged → was enlarged

5. 1) This room is ten meters long.

2) The negotiations are extending into next month.

3) How long does it take to fly from Beijing to Guangzhou?

4) The factory is about a half-hour drive from the station.

5) It's a very long way from here to Canada.

6) The store is three times the size of a football field.

UNIT 10

Section I Maintaining a Sharp Eye

译文

Passage I

我在兰卡斯特大学的留学经历

伊丽莎白·卡斯特兰

大学二年级时，我的美术摄影系的同学都纷纷忙于申请出国留学。从他们那儿，我了解到了各种各样出国学习的信息。于是，在反复思考并征求我的导师和其他教授的意见后，我认识到出国留学可以促进我的艺术成长和个人发展，进一步提高我的绘画技艺并形成我的个人风格。

在到达兰卡斯特大学之前，为了进出方便，我曾要求分配在宿舍一楼靠门口的房间居住。这个要求很容易就得到了应允。但是，宿舍生活管理办公室却忘了告诉我，一楼就是底层，出于安全原因，女生都不安排住在这里。因此，当我发现和我分在同一公寓的另外 3 人全是男士时，我感到很吃惊！开始时，大家都感到非常尴尬，好在我有单用的浴室，只需要和他们合用厨房。由于我的情况特殊，宿舍生活管理办公室和大学服务员采取了特别的安全防范措施。

就我而言，最困难的就是在我选修的版画复制、摄影和绘画实践等三门绘画摄影课中所面临的文化和学术适应问题。最初，系里对接收一个有视力障碍的学生有些顾虑。正如我在其他地方所遇到的情况一样，我是美术系第一个有视力障碍的学生。

美术专业的学生都必须到图书馆或野外作大量的独立研究。教授会给学生推荐一些艺术家去研究，但也希望学生不要局限于教授的建议而进行独立的研究。因此，我花了很多时间在兰卡斯特大学图书馆，研究那些在我到达英国以前就对我有过影响的艺术家。此外，我还研究了 20 世纪拉美绘画、非洲绘画、亚洲绘画和印度绘画。我还说服了我的许多新朋友作我的绘画和摄影模特，让我能从生活中取材。 我还在业余时间参观了各种博物馆和艺术馆。

在我的狭小公寓间里无法完成这么多工作，我被迫自己认路走到画室去工作。我的老师们为我推荐了一位画工罗伯。他帮助我熟悉这幢建筑及其设施，并给我提供了必要的帮助。罗伯教我如何独立地在复制室和摄影室工作。我开始在没有人帮助的情况下在这两个地方工作。渐渐地，我适应了周围的环境，来去都轻松自如了。

国外留学的经历对于个人成长、学术发展和事业成就都有极大的益处。我感到到国外留学极大地拓展了我的艺术才能，丰富了我的艺术史知识。我了解了关于版画复制和摄影的创新技巧，学会了如何进行独立研究。另外，我在绘画、认路和走动、日常起居以及外出旅行等诸多方面都能独立了。我增强了独立适应环境和取得成功的信心。这一切使我能更加清晰地认识到自我的价值、目标和毅力。此外，我对英国文化有了广泛深入的了解，学会了如何与各种不同的人相处。最后，我还结交了终生不渝的朋友，拥有了终生难忘的美好记忆。我将永远珍惜我在兰卡斯特大学的那段经历。

Passage II

继 续 学 习

在知识经济时代，只有不断学习，我们才能更好地武装自己以适应明天。新加坡学习节和学习博览会已经进入了第三个年头。它适时应运而生，也是我们积极准备迎接明天的证明。继续教育和再培训并非解决我们失业问题的灵丹妙药，却为我们将来的经济繁荣奠定了坚实的基础，并且在调节劳动大军使之适应不断变化的世界并增强其竞争力方面，扮演着举足轻重的角色。

这里谈谈我个人的一段学习经历。高中未毕业我便辍学，因学历不高，我只找到了一份办公室勤杂工的工作。后来战争爆发，我没有了工作，有人鼓励我学日语以维持生计。通过自学我熟练地掌握了日语，能够担当口译工作。战后，我决定一边工作一边自学完成高中学历。随后，我进入了新加坡马来亚大学学习，并且在 30 岁时获得了社会学文凭。

然而，我并未就此止步。在后来的 40 多年工作生涯中，我担任过各种职务，并从事过各种工作。我曾经做过社会工作，也曾经在工人运动办事处工作过，还做过外交官。另外，我也在私人企业干过一段，担任过《海峡时报社》的总裁。还在学术界干过，创办了南洋理工大学防御与策略研究所。不管做哪项工作，在学习上我从未懈怠。

我倾听内心情感并认真对待，不过我却没有因为生活的奔波而怨天尤人；恰恰相反，我更加主动地去学习知识掌握技术，为的是做得更好。我必须通晓我所做的工作并能应对自如。因为我明白，现实是无法改变的，天上不会掉馅饼。我必须竭尽全力武装自己来履行好我所承担的职责。我需要在工作中学习并在我所从事的每项工作中向别人学习，甚至在我事业上取得了相当的成就之后，我也一如既往地坚持学习。这已经成为我的习惯了。这个习惯，甚至到今天依然让我获益匪浅。

我以我自己的经历来说明，所有的人，无论处于什么样的环境下，无论多大年龄，无论有无受过正规教育，也无论工作有多么繁忙，一生一世都必须不断地吸取新知识，学习新技术。

世界的变化很快。个人、公司乃至国家都需要不断学习，才能跟得上发展。为了使新加坡保持持续繁荣，并在国际竞争中立于不败之地，我们的人民必须掌握知识、技术和应变能力。我们需要人民和劳动大军能够坚持继续学习，认识到这一点十分重要。

尽管学习的经济效益更为明显，但是我们不应该仅仅为提高就业能力而学习。在不断发展变化的社会里，学习的愿望关系到能否跟上生活的节奏，能否融入社会并且在社会中获得一席之地。由于医学的发展，我们的寿命得以延长，所以我们必须终生坚持学习，这样才能始终与下一代保持联系与一致。

1. 1) b   2) b   3) c   4) d   5) a

2. 1) equivalent   2) adjustments   3) conflict   4) insight
5) shares   6) provides   7) assign

3. 1) The minister granted the journalists an interview.
2) I can recommend him to you as an extremely good accountant.
3) I'll always treasure the memory of our first meetings.
4) Learning some rhymes and songs can help parents interact with their babies.
5) Though his father was the company's manager, he got the position on his own.

4. 1) T   2) F   3) T   4) F   5) T   6) F   7) T   8) T   9) F   10) T

5. 1) economy   2) prosperity   3) Competition   4) knowledgeable
5) responsible   6) education   7) employed   8) interpreted

6. 1) The young generation behaves quite differently from their fathers' and grandfathers'.

2) The new regulations will be of great benefit to us all.

3) We feel as if we couldn't keep up with the fast changes in computer technology.

4) He undertook the organization of the whole scheme.

5) She picked up French soon after she went to live in France.

6) His interests ranged widely from chess to boating.

Section II Trying Your Hand

样例 1

神州大学外国语学院

2010 年 5 月 10 日

滨海外国语大学

约瑟夫·伍德教授

亲爱的伍德教授：

您的新作《英语语调研究》给我院英语教师留下了深刻的印象。我们希望能聆听您对英语语调及其他问题的见解。可否在您方便的时候来我校给我校教师作一次讲座。

我们会给您提供规定的费用作为您来往的旅费和其他开支。

您如果能来的话，请尽早告知我们，并说明来的时间。

院办秘书 张红谨启

样例 2

上海中医学院

2010 年 3 月 17 日

罗伯特·霍普金斯先生

普林斯顿大学医学院

敬爱的霍普金斯教授：

由上海中医学院发起的"传统中医治疗法学术研讨会"将于 2010 年 5 月 20 日在上海举行。我们十分乐意邀请您参加此次学术研讨会。我们将负责您的食宿费用，但不承担您的往返机票费用。

如果您有论文，或者有您希望在学术会上报告的选题，请您尽快通知我们，因为会议日程安排即将最后确定。

请尽快确定您能否来参加会议。此致

敬礼

上海中医学院

院办秘书 刘风谨启

1.

> 亲爱的克拉申教授：
>
> 　　由滨海大学发起的"中国英语教学研讨会"将于 2010 年 6 月 12 日在滨海召开。
>
> 　　您是英语教学方面的知名专家。我们非常高兴邀请您参加本次学术研讨会，而且我们真诚地希望您能对提高中国的英语教学质量提出建议。
>
> 　　我们希望您能接受我们的邀请，如果您能告诉我们到达时间，我们将安排到机场迎接。
>
> 　　　　　　　　　　　　　　　　　　　　　　　　　办公室秘书 谢怡谨启

2.
1) It gives us the greatest pleasure to invite you to come to our symposium.
2) We'd like to invite some famous scholars like you to come to the conference and present their proposals for this project.
3) We really hope that you will attend this conference and all the travel fares and accommodation costs will be for our account.
4) You are cordially invited to the most important academic conference of this year.
5) I will be away on business travel during that period so that I cannot accept your kind invitation.

3.
1) Four "A" size cells are used to power this set.
2) There are two knobs on the right side of the set to control the speed and volume.
3) Push the button on the right side and you can get the medium wave band.
4) The Reset Button is used for setting calendar and time.
5) The stopwatch's Start / Stop Key allows the unit to be used as a stopwatch and controls the start / stop of timing.
6) Do not leave dead batteries in the battery-box as this may cause malfunction.
7) This set is highly sensitive and should be handled with care.
8) An external antenna is provided to improve the short-wave reception.

4.
1) (1) has undergone　(2) has been found　(3) meet　(4) guaranteed　(5) will be done
2) (1) is read off　(2) works　(3) can　(4) is stored　(5) total of

Self-Assessment

Test One

1. B	2. C	3. C	4. D	5. A
6. A	7. A	8. C	9. B	10. D
11. sizes	12. more than	13. at all	14. whole	15. put in
16. B	17. C	18. B	19. A	20. A
21. C	22. A	23. D	24. B	25. D

26. decision   27. going   28. is / was   29. service   30. be returned
31. (un)reasonable   32. (should) inform 33. were waiting   34. particularly   35. to speak
36. A   37. A   38. B   39. C   40. C
41. B   42. A   43. B   44. D   45. D
46. report   47. experience   48. ability   49. address   50. 24th December
51. C, Q   52. H, A   53. B, P   54. G, M   55. I, K
56. Industrial Attachment Program   57. (the) real world 58. 12   59. practice
60. company culture

	2分	1分	0.5分	0分
61	C	B	A	D
62	A	B	C	D
63	D	A	B	C
64	B	C	A	D

65. 参考译文：

　　女士们、先生们，下午好！机长约翰逊和所有乘务员欢迎您乘坐英国航空公司197次航班飞往纽约。我们现在的飞行高度为30 000英尺，飞行速度为每小时600公里左右。飞行5个半小时后我们将到达纽约。纽约现在的气温为零下3摄氏度。我们的乘务员将在半小时后为您提供午餐。

　　谢谢大家。

评分标准参考：

1. 本题按综合方式评分，从格式、内容和语言三方面全面衡量，只给一个分数，即给总体印象分 (global/impression marking)。

2. 评分时应以考生应得 (rewarding) 分数评定，不要以扣分 (penalty) 方式评定。

3. 分数可分5个等级，即：

　　1) 14分：内容完整，表达清楚；语言上仅有个别小错。

　　2) 11分：内容较完整，表达尚清楚；语言错误不多，可以有个别句子结构上的错误。

　　3) 8分：　内容大体完整，表达可勉强理解；有较多的语言错误，包括一些严重错误。

　　4) 5分：　内容不完整，但是没有离题；表达有较大困难；语言错误多，其中较多是严重错误。

　　5) 2分：　内容表达不清楚；语言支离破碎，仅有个别句子尚正确。

4. 如果试卷的得分可高于或低于某一等级分，则应加1分或减1分。

5. 如果不按提示写作文或语言表达完全无法理解，应给0分。

6. 格式错误酌情扣1~3分。

7. 评分应力求准确，防止趋中倾向。

Scripts:

Section A

1. What are you going to do at the weekend?

2. Excuse me, can you tell me where the post office is?

3. Do you think the weather will be fine tomorrow?

4. Is Peter coming to our Christmas party?

5. How long have you been in Hong Kong?

Section B

6. M: Can I help you, madam?

   W: Er …, I want a tape recorder and some tapes.

   Question: Where does the conversation most likely take place?

7. M: How many tickets have you bought?

   W: I wanted to buy 5, but there were only 2 left.

   Question: How many tickets has the woman bought?

8. M: Did you come for the lecture yesterday?

   W: No. I missed it because I had a fever.

   Question: What happened to the woman?

9. M: What do you think of this kind of food?

   W: It's bad for the heart because it contains too much fat.

   Question: What does the woman think of the food?

10. M: I've got a pain in my neck.

    W: You shouldn't have been working so long on the computer.

    Question: What does the woman think the man should do?

Section C

Houses come in all shapes and <u>sizes</u>. They may be new or old. They may be large or small. Houses usually have two bedrooms or more. Larger houses often have <u>more than</u> one bathroom. Modern houses are often built with a garage. Many houses have no garage <u>at all</u>. If people have cars, they will park them on the street.

Nowadays most people like central heating. This is heating through the <u>whole</u> house. It means that all the rooms can be heated at the same time. Modern houses are built with central heating. A lot of older houses have had it <u>put in</u> later.

Test Two

1. D	2. A	3. B	4. A	5. C
6. C	7. D	8. B	9. D	10. A
11. all over	12. lower	13. come down	14. increased	15. expensive
16. C	17. B	18. A	19. D	20. A
21. B	22. A	23. C	24. A	25. D
26. has held	27. Generally	28. to look	29. difficulty	30. were injured
31. scientific	32. is / was	33. application	34. (should) begin	35. living

36. A   37. C   38. A   39. B   40. C

41. C   42. A   43. A   44. B   45. D

46. The Oracle   47. its opening hours   48. tonight   49. Saturday

50. 12   51. A, K   52. J, E   53. B, H   54. G, O

55. M, L   56. (a) sales assistant   57. $13.68/hr ($13.68 an / per hour)

58. a full-time job   59. machine operator   60. benefits

	2分	1分	0.5分	0分
61	C	D	B	A
62	A	C	D	B
63	C	B	D	A
64	D	B	A	C

65. 参考译文：

    欢迎您来到世界主要机场之一的旧金山国际机场！本机场为乘客提供优质服务。为了最好地满足旅行公众的需要，这本《旧金山国际机场指南》专门为您介绍机场为顾客和来访者提供的各种诱人的餐饮、货物和服务。

评分标准参考：

1. 本题按综合方式评分，从格式、内容和语言三方面全面衡量，只给一个分数，即给总体印象分 (global/impression marking)。

2. 评分时应以考生应得 (rewarding) 分数评定，不要以扣分 (penalty) 方式评定。

3. 分数可分5个等级，即：

    1) 14分：内容完整，表达清楚；语言上仅有个别小错。

    2) 11分：内容较完整，表达尚清楚；语言错误不多，可以有个别句子结构上的错误。

    3) 8分：内容大体完整，表达可勉强理解；有较多的语言错误，包括一些严重错误。

    4) 5分：内容不完整，但是没有离题；表达有较大困难；语言错误多，其中较多是严重错误。

    5) 2分：内容表达不清楚；语言支离破碎，仅有个别句子尚正确。

4. 如果试卷的得分可高于或低于某一等级分，则应加1分或减1分。

5. 如果不按提示写作文或语言表达完全无法理解，应给0分。

6. 格式错误酌情扣1~3分。

7. 评分应力求准确，防止趋中倾向。

Scripts:

Section A

1. Where will you take your winter holiday?

2. Could you please tell me the way to the railway station?

3. Will you show me around the factory?

4. What kind of job would you like to do?

5. Would you like to sit down over there, Miss Brown?

Section B

6. W: Remember Lily's birthday is June 1st.

   M: Thanks for reminding me. I thought it was sometime in July.

   Question: When is Lily's birthday?

7. M: Can you stay for dinner with us?

   W: I'd like to. But I have to go to the supermarket.

   Question: Where is the woman going?

8. M: Let me help you with your luggage.

   W: Thank you. Please drive me to the hotel.

   Question: What is the man?

9. W: Excuse me, is there still any flight for Beijing today?

   M: Sorry, all flights are gone.

   Question: Where does the conversation most probably take place?

10. M: You look beautiful in the new dress!

    W: Thanks. I bought it a month ago at a 30% discount.

    Question: How does the woman feel about the new dress?

Section C

     Harrods is a famous department store in London. On December 31, its year-end sale began. Customers from all over the world came to Harrods on that day. Shoppers can get many goods at lower rates that day. In most cases the prices on that day come down by 50 to 75 percent. The sale lasts for one month. Department store sales in Britain increased by about 5 percent in 2002. But in the U.S., department store sales decreased. American shoppers think that price is very important. They don't like to shop in expensive department stores.

Test Three

1. C	2. B	3. B	4. B	5. C
6. D	7. C	8. D	9. B	10. A
11. A president / President Jean Smith	12. On Monday	13. International Trade		
14. Two hours	15. All the students	16. B	17. C	18. D
19. A	20. C	21. B	22. D	23. A
24. D	25. B	26. higher	27. boring	28. determination
29. isolated	30. nervousness	31. spent	32. depending	33. be informed
34. writing	35. did	36. A	37. C	38. A
39. C	40. D	41. C	42. D	43. A
44. D	45. C	46. the whole staff	47. the 20th anniversary	
48. Award	49. entertainment activities		50. Office Director	

51. A, G   52. C, L   53. M, N   54. I, P   55. J, D

56. Daily Review   57. marketing   58. a sales manager   59. by phone   60. the 18th

	2分	1分	0.5分	0分
61	A	C	B	D
62	C	D	A	B
63	B	C	A	D
64	D	B	C	A

65. 参考译文：

如果你去美国主要是为了旅游，但还想上一个每周18小时以下的短期培训课程，办理旅游签证就可以了。你应该去美国大使馆或领事馆咨询。如果你的课程在每周18小时以上，你就需要办理学生签证。请阅读本资料以便大体了解申请F1或M1学生签证的做法。

评分标准参考：

1. 本题按综合方式评分，从格式、内容和语言三方面全面衡量，只给一个分数，即给总体印象分 (global/impression marking)。

2. 评分时应以考生应得 (rewarding) 分数评定，不要以扣分 (penalty) 方式评定。

3. 分数可分5个等级，即：

    1) 14分：内容完整，表达清楚；语言上仅有个别小错。

    2) 11分：内容较完整，表达尚清楚；语言错误不多，可以有个别句子结构上的错误。

    3) 8分： 内容大体完整，表达可勉强理解；有较多的语言错误，包括一些严重错误。

    4) 5分： 内容不完整，但是没有离题；表达有较大困难；语言错误多，其中较多是严重错误。

    5) 2分： 内容表达不清楚；语言支离破碎，仅有个别句子尚正确。

4. 如果试卷的得分可高于或低于某一等级分，则应加1分或减1分。

5. 如果不按提示写作文或语言表达完全无法理解，应给0分。

6. 格式错误酌情扣1~3分。

7. 评分应力求准确，防止趋中倾向。

Scripts:

Section A

1. W: What would you like, a cup of tea or a glass of milk?

    M: Neither, thanks. I think I'd like something to eat.

    Question: What does the man want?

2. M: I'd like to borrow this book. This is my library card.

    W: OK, would you please sign your name here?

    Question: Who is the woman?

3. W: Hello, I made a room reservation two weeks ago.

    M: Yes, ma'am, your name and telephone number, please.

Question: Where are the two speakers now?

4. M: Would you like to go dancing with me this evening, Susan?

W: I'd love to. But the annual report has kept me busy.

Question: What might the woman be going to do this evening?

5. W: Robbie looks sad today. He even doesn't want to talk to me!

M: He failed in the history examination again.

Question: What do we know about Robbie?

Section B

Conversation 1

M: Do you do morning exercise every day?

W: Yes. Doing morning exercise is good for health.

M: Which sport is your favorite?

W: Running is my favorite sport.

M: How long have you been in the habit of doing morning running?

W: Twenty years.

M: Why do you choose running as your favorite exercise?

W: It seems to be the easiest form of physical exercise.

M: Easiest?

W: You see, it needs no special training. People can do it at any place and at any time.

M: OK. See you tomorrow morning at the sport field.

Q6. What does the woman think of running?

Q7. Why will the two people meet at the sport field tomorrow morning?

Conversation 2

W: Welcome to have a Chinese training class with us. May I see your class-attending card?

M: Sure, here you are.

W: Thank you. How long do you plan to be here?

M: Three months.

W: You look hurried. Would you please tell me where you live?

M: In Xinxing Community.

W: Is it far from here?

M: Not very. In this same district.

W: How do you get here every weekend?

M: In most cases, by bike.

W: And how, if it rains heavily?

M: By bus.

Q8. What should the man present when he wants to attend the Chinese training class?

Q9. Where does the man live?

Q10. How does the man get to the training class in most cases?

Section C

May I have your attention, everyone? Here is the good news that may interest you. President Jean Smith from Askan Import and Export Group Company is now attending a meeting in our city. We have invited her to give us a lecture on international trade when she comes to visit our university on Monday. Mrs. Jean Smith is famous in the area of international trade. She will be giving the lecture on Monday afternoon from 2 to 4 pm at Lecture Hall No. 6 in the Computer Building. There will also be a Question and Answer time after the lecture. The lecture is open to all the students. Be sure not to be late if you're interested. Thank you.

Q11. Who will come to visit the university?
Q12. On what day will she give a lecture?
Q13. What is the lecture about?
Q14. For how long will the lecture be?
Q15. Who are welcome to come to the lecture?

Test Four

1. B	2. C	3. A	4. B	5. C
6. C	7. A	8. D	9. D	10. A
11. online degree	12. money	13. chat rooms	14. extra	15. future employers
16. D	17. D	18. B	19. C	20. C
21. B	22. A	23. C	24. A	25. D
26. to give	27. study / studying	28. dying	29. behavior	30. were forbidden
31. to keep	32. worse	33. impression	34. found	35. telling
36. D	37. C	38. A	39. B	40. C
41. D	42. A	43. B	44. D	45. D
46. Dr. Phil	47. being prepared	48. risk-reward	49. "what if"	50. rationality
51. B, G	52. K, M	53. J, N	54. H, F	55. C, A
56. independent traveler		57. their own pace	58. a short break	
59. Lakes and Mountains		60. popular locations		

	2分	1分	0.5分	0分
61	C	A	D	B
62	B	A	C	D
63	D	B	C	A
64	C	B	A	D

65. 参考译文：

        打保龄球的季节就要开始了。希望大家都来参加。唯一的要求就是想玩得开心。10月4日起，每个星期二晚上7:00至9:00，我们包租了"阳光保龄球馆"的球道。最优秀的两支球队将代表我们公司参加行业联赛的最后决赛。去年，销售部球队打进了四分之一决赛！

        如果您有兴趣参加公司联赛，请给约翰·多伊打电话，分机号码为：237。

评分标准参考：

1. 本题按综合方式评分，从格式、内容和语言三方面全面衡量，只给一个分数，即给总体印象分 (global/impression marking)。

2. 评分时应以考生应得 (rewarding) 分数评定，不要以扣分 (penalty) 方式评定。

3. 分数可分5个等级，即：

    1) 14分：内容完整，表达清楚；语言上仅有个别小错。

    2) 11分：内容较完整，表达尚清楚；语言错误不多，可以有个别句子结构上的错误。

    3) 8分：内容大体完整，表达可勉强理解；有较多的语言错误，包括一些严重错误。

    4) 5分：内容不完整，但是没有离题；表达有较大困难；语言错误多，其中较多是严重错误。

    5) 2分：内容表达不清楚；语言支离破碎，仅有个别句子尚正确。

4. 如果试卷的得分可高于或低于某一等级分，则应加1分或减1分。

5. 如果不按提示写作文或语言表达完全无法理解，应给0分。

6. 格式错误酌情扣1~3分。

7. 评分应力求准确，防止趋中倾向。

Scripts:

Section A

1. W: When shall we meet, this Saturday or this Sunday?

   M: I think it will be a little too late. Why not today?

   Question: When does the man suggest for their meeting?

2. M: Did you get what you wanted? You've been out all the afternoon.

   W: I looked all over the store but didn't find any dress appealing to me.

   Question: What did the woman do the whole afternoon?

3. W: You can email your friends abroad.

   M: That's a great idea. I really want to save some money.

   Question: Why does the man say emailing is a great idea?

4. M: The meeting is very important. You'd better attend it.

   W: That's true. But I feel sleepy. I didn't sleep well last night.

   Question: What does the woman imply?

5. W: I'm going to Australia for Christmas with some friends next week.

   M: Great. Now you can have a look at my pictures taken there during Christmas.

   Question: What can we learn from the man's words?

Section B

Conversation 1

M: Good morning, madam. Can I help you?

W: Yes, I want to fly to Chicago on Wednesday 7th and return on Friday 9th. How much is the ticket?

M: Tickets are cheaper if you stay over Saturday night.

W: Thanks. But unfortunately I've already arranged some business here that Friday.

M: What time of day would you prefer? Morning or afternoon?

W: Morning, because I have to be there by early afternoon. Is there a meal?

M: Yes, they'll be serving breakfast, and you'll also see a film.

W: Sounds good. But what's the total cost?

M: Eight hundred and fifty dollars round trip.

W: Ha! I thought it might be rather expensive.

Q6. Where does this conversation probably take place?

Q7. When does the woman plan to leave?

Q8. What does the woman think of the traveling cost?

Conversation 2

W: Good morning, Cambridge Theater. Can I help you?

M: Good morning. Are there any tickets for the pop concert on Saturday night?

W: Certainly, sir. You want to have tickets for the pop concert on the night of the 13th?

M: I'm not sure of the date. Is it Saturday and the 13th?

W: Yes, it is.

M: What time does the concert start?

W: At 8:00 p.m. How many tickets would you like?

M: Three tickets, please. How much altogether?

W: 64 dollars, sir.

M: OK. We'll be there 15 minutes before the concert begins.

Q9. Why does the man call the theater?

Q10. How much does the man have to pay?

Section C

Getting an online degree through distance learning is an option that has become available because of the increased use of the Internet throughout the world. The most popular reasons for trying to get an online degree are time and money. With an online course, you can enroll in a class, do assignments on the Internet, and even communicate with classmates in chat rooms or on bulletin boards. Getting such a degree can, in some cases, be cheaper because you don't have to pay the extra costs related to an overseas adventure.

For all these benefits, there are a number of worries about this kind of learning. Above all else, you have to consider how a degree from an online school will be received by future employers. In some countries, companies might feel that the academic standards of such an online institution are not as challenging or strict as a regular program.

Q11. What is the speaker talking about?

Q12. What are the benefits of online learning?

Q13. How can students in an online course communicate with each other?

Q14. Why is getting online learning cheaper?

Q15. What is people's biggest worry about online learning?

Vocabulary

A

abruptly /ə'brʌptlɪ/ ad.	突然地		u5
accessory /ək'sesərɪ/ n.	附件		u3
accommodation /əkɒmə'deɪʃən/ n.	食宿		u1
accomplishment /ə'kʌmplɪʃmənt/ n.	成就		u6
accounting /ə'kaʊntɪŋ/ n.	会计		u8
adequately /'ædɪkwɪtlɪ/ ad.	充分地		u2
adjustment /ə'dʒʌstmənt/ n.	调整		u10
admire /əd'maɪə/ v.	钦佩		u5
adolescent /ˌædəʊ'lesənt/ n.	青少年		u6
advance /əd'vɑːns/ v.	进，推进		u3
affectionate /ə'fekʃənɪt/ a.	充满深情的		u5
agent /'eɪdʒənt/ n.	代理人		u6
airline /'eəlaɪn/ n.	航空公司		u6
ale /eɪl/ n.	麦芽酒		u3
alike /ə'laɪk/ a.	同样的		u6
allocation /ˌæləʊ'keɪʃən/ n.	分配，安置		u7
alongside /əˌlɒŋ'saɪd/ prep.	与…并行		u3
aluminum /ə'ljuːmɪnəm/ n.	铝		u9
amateur /'æmətə/ n.	业余爱好者		u8
amazing /ə'meɪzɪŋ/ a.	惊人的		u5
amber /'æmbər/ n.	琥珀		u8
ambition /æm'bɪʃən/ n.	志向；抱负		u6
anniversary /ˌænɪ'vɜːsərɪ/ n.	周年纪念		u2
announcer /ə'naʊnsə/ n.	解说员		u3
annual /'ænjʊəl/ a.	年度的		u6
annual /'ænjʊəl/ a.	每年的		u8
anticipate /æn'tɪsɪpeɪt/ v.	预期，期望		u7
antique /æn'tiːk/ n.	古董		u8

anxiety /æŋˈzaɪətɪ/ n.	忧虑	u6
apparently /əˈpærəntlɪ/ ad.	表面上地	u1
appear /əˈpɪə/ v.	出现	u2
applaud /əˈplɔːd/ v.	拍手喝彩	u4
appreciation /əˌpriːʃɪˈeɪʃən/ n.	理解，欣赏	u7
approve /əˈpruːv/ v.	赞成，批准	u1
approximately /əˈprɒksɪmɪtlɪ/ ad.	大约	u8
argue /ˈɑːgjuː/ v.	争论	u4
article /ˈɑːtɪkəl/ n.	物品，商品	u9
ashtray /ˈæʃtreɪ/ n.	烟缸	u1
aspect /ˈæspekt/ n.	方面	u6
assignment /əˈsaɪnmənt/ n.	分配，任务	u1
assign /əˈsaɪn/ n.	分配；指派	u6
athletics /æθˈletɪks/ n.	运动	u6
attachment /əˈtætʃmənt/ n.	附件	u4
attend /əˈtend/ v.	出席	u8
availability /əˌveɪləˈbɪlətɪ/ n.	可用性	u1
avoid /əˈvɔɪd/ v.	避免	u4

B

baked /beɪkt/ a.	烘烤的	u1
balcony /ˈbælkənɪ/ n.	阳台	u1
band /bænd/ n.	乐队	u3
basis /ˈbeɪsɪs/ n.	基础	u4
bathrobe /ˈbɑːθrəub/ n.	浴衣	u1
beef-kabob /biːf kəˈbɔb/ n.	烤腌牛肉串	u2
benefit /ˈbenɪfɪt/ n.	利益	u9
beverage /ˈbevərɪdʒ/ n.	饮料	u7
bizarre /bɪˈzɑː/ a.	古怪的	u6
blindly /ˈblaɪndlɪ/ ad.	盲目地	u7
boost /buːst/ v.	提高	u6
brief /briːf/ v.	摘要，简要说明	u7
brokerage /ˈbrəukərɪdʒ/ n.	经纪业	u6
broker /ˈbrəukə/ n.	经纪人	u6
Brunei /ˈbruːnaɪ/ n.	文莱	u5

| button /ˈbʌtn/ *n.* | 按钮 | u3 |

C

camcorder /ˈkæmkɔːdə/ *n.*	数码摄像机	u3
cancellation /ˌkænsəˈleɪʃən/ *n.*	取消	u1
capable /ˈkeɪpəbl/ *a.*	有能力的	u5
capacity /kəˈpæsɪtɪ/ *n.*	生产能力	u8
carnival /ˈkɑːnɪvl/ *n.*	狂欢节	u3
catalogue /ˈkætəlɒg/ *a.*	商品目录	u9
celebrate /ˈselɪbreɪt/ *v.*	庆祝	u2
celebrity /sɪˈlebrɪtɪ/ *n.*	名人	u3
champagne /ˌʃæmˈpeɪn/ *n.*	香槟酒	u2
charity /ˈtʃærətɪ/ *n.*	慈善机构	u1
check /tʃek/ *n.*	账单	u2
check /tʃek/ *n.*	支票	u8
cherish /ˈtʃerɪʃ/ *v.*	珍惜	u5
chew /tʃuː/ *v.*	咀嚼	u1
circulation /ˌsɜːkjʊˈleɪʃən/ *n.*	流通	u6
classified /ˈklæsɪfaɪd/ *a.*	分类的	u6
client /ˈklaɪənt/ *n.*	客户	u8
closing /ˈkləʊzɪŋ/ *v.*	结束语	u5
collateral /kɒˈlætərl/ *n.*	担保品	u6
colleague /ˈkɒliːg/ *n.*	同事	u6
comedy /ˈkɒmɪdɪ/ *n.*	喜剧	u6
commercial /kəˈmɜːʃəl/ *n.*	商业广告	u7
commission /kəˈmɪʃən/ *n.*	佣金	u6
commodity /kəˈmɒdətɪ/ *n.*	日用品，商品	u7
completely /kəmˈpliːtlɪ/ *ad.*	完全	u8
conclude /kənˈkluːd/ *v.*	结束	u5
conference /ˈkɒnfərəns/ *n.*	会议	u1
confidence /ˈkɒnfɪdəns/ *n.*	信心	u6
confident /ˈkɒnfɪdənt/ *a.*	自信的	u6
confirm /kənˈfɜːm/ *v.*	核实	u1
considerate /kənˈsɪdərɪt/ *a.*	体贴的	u4
construction /kənˈstrʌkʃən/ *n.*	建设	u5

consultation /ˌkɒnsəl'teɪʃən/ n.　　磋商，商榷　　u7

consult /kən'sʌlt/ v.　　咨询，查阅　　u4

contentment /kən'tentmənt/ n.　　满足　　u5

control /kən'trəʊl/ v.　　控制　　u8

convenience /kən'viːnjəns/ n.　　便利　　u9

convenience /kən'viːnjəns/ n.　　方便　　u2

conversational /ˌkɒnvə'seɪʃənl/ a.　　会话的　　u6

convey /kən'veɪ/ v.　　传达，传递　　u5

cope /kəʊp/ v.　　应付　　u6

costume /'kɒstjuːm/ n.　　服饰　　u3

cot /kɒt/ n.　　帆布床　　u1

counsel /'kaʊnsəl/ v.　　向 … 建议　　u6

counterpart /'kaʊntəpɑːt/ n.　　配对物；对方　　u7

co-worker /ˌkəʊ'wɜːkə/ n.　　同事　　u6

crank /kræŋk/ v.n.　　转曲柄；曲柄　　u3

creativity /ˌkriːeɪ'tɪvətɪ/ n.　　创造性　　u6

crib /krɪb/ n.　　儿童床　　u1

crucial /'kruːʃəl/ a.　　极重要的　　u3

cupboard /'kʌbəd/ n.　　壁柜　　u1

customs /'kʌstəms/ n.　　海关　　u8

D

dealer /'diːlə/ n.　　经销商　　u4

decision /dɪ'sɪʒən/ n.　　决定　　u6

declare /dɪ'kleə/ n.　　申报应纳税的　　u8

deed /diːd/ n.　　行为　　u2

definitely /'defɪnɪtlɪ/ ad.　　肯定　　u9

deliberation /dɪˌlɪbə'reɪʃən/ n.　　考虑　　u6

delightful /dɪ'laɪtf(ʊ)l/ a.　　可爱的　　u5

demand /dɪ'mɑːnd/ n.　　需求　　u6

deny /dɪ'naɪ/ v.　　否认　　u4

department /dɪ'pɑːtmənt/ n.　　部门　　u6

depart /dɪ'pɑːt/ v.　　离开　　u1

describe /dɪs'kraɪb/ v.　　描述　　u3

diagnose /'daɪəgnəʊz/ v.　　诊断　　u4

diner /'daɪnər/ n.	廉价餐馆	u6
directory /dɪ'rektərɪ/ n.	姓名地址录	u9
disabled /dɪs'eɪbld/ a.	残疾的	u1
discount /'dɪskaʊnt/ n.	折扣	u9
discount /dɪs'kaʊnt/ n.	折扣	u3
dispatch /dɪ'spætʃ/ v.	发货	u9
display /dɪs'pleɪ/ v.	展示	u3
distribute /dɪ'strɪbjuːt/ v.	分送	u8
DNA (deoxyribonucleic acid)	脱氧核糖核酸	u1
doom /duːm/ v.	注定	u7
dormitory /'dɔːmɪtri/ n.	宿舍	u4
dotcome /'dɒtkəm/ n.	网站	u3
drawing-room /'drɔːɪŋ-rʊm/ n.	客厅	u3
dressing /'dresɪŋ/ n.	调料	u2
duty /'djuːtɪ/ n.	职责	u5

E

economic /ˌiːkə'nɒmɪk/ a.	经济(上)的	u8
eject /ɪ'dʒekt/ v.	喷出；弹出	u3
elaborate /ɪ'læbərɪt/ a.	精致的	u3
embrace /ɪm'breɪs/ v.	拥抱；欢迎	u5
emotional /ɪ'məʊʃənl/ a.	情绪的	u4
employability /ɪmˌplɔɪə'bɪlətɪ/ n.	可雇用性	u10
employee /ˌemplɔɪ'iː/ n.	雇员	u8
encouragement /ɪn'kʌrɪdʒmənt/ n.	鼓励	u2
endemic /en'demɪk/ a.	特有的	u6
endorse /ɪn'dɔːs/ a.	认可	u3
endowment /ɪn'daʊmənt/ n.	人寿保险	u10
engagement /ɪn'geɪdʒmənt/ n.	订婚	u2
enhance /ɪn'hɑːns/ v.	提高	u6
enrich /ɪn'rɪtʃ/ v.	使丰富	u3
enroll /ɪn'rəʊl/ v.	招收	u1
entertain /ˌentə'teɪn/ v.	期待	u3
entrance /'entrəns/ n.	入口	u3
envy /'envɪ/ v.	羡慕	u10

essential /ɪ'senʃəl/ a.	必要的	u9
ethos /'iːθɒs/ n.	精神，气质	u7
exchange /ɪks'tʃeɪndʒ/ n.	交流	u8
exclaim /ɪk'skleɪm/ v.	呼喊，惊叫	u1
executive /ɪg'zekjʊtɪv/ a.	行政官的，经理的	u1
exit /'eksɪt/ n.	出口	u8
exotic /ɪg'zɒtɪk/ a.	奇异的	u5
expand /ɪk'spænd/ v.	扩大	u8
expert /'ekspɜːt/ n.	专家	u5
expert /'ekspɜːt/ n.	专家	u8
explain /ɪk'spleɪn/ v.	解释	u8
exploratory /ɪk'splɒrətərɪ/ a.	探索的，探险的	u7
explore /ɪk'splɔː/ v.	探求	u3
express /ɪk'spres/ v.	表达	u2
extremely /ɪk'striːmlɪ/ ad.	极端地	u1

F

facility /fə'sɪlɪtɪ/ n.	设施	u1
faith /feɪθ/ n.	信任	u6
farmland /'fɑːmlænd/ n.	农田	u5
fascinate /'fæsɪneɪt/ v.	迷住	u5
fascinating /'fæsɪneɪtɪŋ/ a.	迷人的	u3
feast /fiːst/ n.	盛宴，宴会	u7
Filipino /ˌfɪlɪ'piːnəʊ/ n.	菲律宾人	u5
flip /flɪp/ v.	翻转	u6
flock /flɒk/ v.	聚结	u7
focus /'fəʊkəs/ v.	集中	u8
formula /'fɔːmjʊlə/ n.	套话	u5
fragrance /'freɪgrəns/ n.	芬芳，香气，香味	u7
fragrant /'freɪgrənt/ a.	香的	u2
frame /'freɪm/ n.	框架	u6
frame /freɪm/ n.	精神状态	u6
frame /freɪm/ n.	框架	u9
franc /fræŋk/ n.	法郎	u1
frank /fræŋk/ a.	坦诚的	u5

friendliness /'frendlɪnɪs/ n.	友好	u5
fringe /'frɪndʒ/ a.	额外的，边缘的	u10
fruitful /'fruːtfʊl/ a.	富有成果的，收效很多的	u5
fund /fʌnd/ n.	资金	u8
furnishing /'fɜːnɪʃɪŋ/ n.	服饰品	u9
furnish /'fɜːnɪʃ/ v.	(用家具等)布置	u1

G

gallery /'ɡæləri/ n.	艺术馆	u10
gargle /'ɡɑːɡl/ n.	嗽口	u4
garment /'ɡɑːmənt/ n.	衣服	u1
gather /'ɡæðə(r)/ v.	聚集	u5
general /'dʒenərəl/ a.	普通的	u5
generous /'dʒenərəs/ a.	慷慨的	u8
gentleman /'dʒentlmən/ n.	绅士	u2
germ /dʒɜːm/ n.	细菌	u4
glamour /'ɡlæmə(r)/ n.	魅力	u3
grant /ɡrɑːnt/ v.	允许	u10
greet /ɡriːt/ v.	招呼	u6
groan /ɡrəʊn/ v.	呻吟	u4
guarantee /ˌɡærən'tiː/ v.	担保	u1
guardian /'ɡɑːdjən/ n.	护卫者	u9
guidance /'ɡaɪdns/ n.	引导	u5

H

habit /'hæbɪt/ n.	习惯	u2
hamburger /'hæmbɜːɡə/ n.	汉堡包	u4
handicraft /'hændɪkrɑːft/ n.	手工艺品	u3
hanger /'hæŋə/ n.	衣挂	u1
heritage /'herɪtɪdʒ/ n.	遗产	u8
high-tech /haɪ-tek/ a.	高科技的	u8
hire /'haɪə/ v.	雇佣	u6
horrify /'hɒrɪfaɪ/ n.	震惊	u8

I

identification /aɪˌdentɪfɪˈkeɪʃən/ n.	身份，鉴别	u1
ignorant /ˈɪɡnərənt/ a.	无知的	u9
illegal /ɪˈliːɡəl/ n.	违法的	u8
impaired /ɪmˈpeəd/ a.	有障碍的	u10
impolite /ˌɪmpəˈlaɪt/ a.	无礼的	u8
impressive /ɪmˈpresɪv/ a.	令人难忘的	u5
imprint /ɪmˈprɪnt/ v.	铭刻	u6
incongruous /ɪnˈkɒŋɡruəs/ a.	不协调的	u6
incredible /ɪnˈkredəbl/ n.	难以置信的	u8
incredibly /ɪnˈkredəblɪ/ ad.	不能相信地	u8
indication /ˌɪndɪˈkeɪʃən/ n.	指出，指示，迹象，暗示	u7
indifferent /ɪnˈdɪfərənt/ a.	冷淡的	u9
Indonesia /ˌɪndə(ʊ)ˈniːzjə/ n.	印度尼西亚	u5
infant /ˈɪnfənt/ n.	婴儿	u1
infrastructure /ˈɪnfrəstrʌktʃə/ n.	基础设施	u5
initially /ɪˈnɪʃəlɪ/ ad.	最初	u9
injury /ˈɪndʒərɪ/ n.	受伤	u4
innovation /ˌɪnəʊˈveɪʃən/ n.	创新	u6
innovative /ˈɪnəʊveɪtɪv/ a.	革新的	u10
inquiry /ɪnˈkwaɪərɪ/ n.	查询	u1
inscription /ɪnˈskrɪpʃn/ n.	题字	u8
instructor /ɪnˈstrʌktə/ n.	指导者，教员	u1
instrument /ˈɪnstrʊmənt/ n.	乐器	u8
insufficient /ˌɪnsəˈfɪʃənt/ a.	不足的，不充分的	u7
intelligence /ɪnˈtelɪdʒəns/ n.	智力	u4
interactive /ˌɪntəːˈræktɪv/ a.	互动的	u3
inviting /ɪnˈvaɪtɪŋ/ a.	诱人的	u2
involve /ɪnˈvɒlv/ v.	包括	u4
issue /ˈɪsjuː/ n.	争议；问题	u4
itch /ɪtʃ/ v.	渴望	u5
item /ˈaɪtəm/ n.	产品	u3
item /ˈaɪtəm/ n.	条，项；商品品种	u9

J

jerk /dʒɜːk/ n.	性情古怪的人	u9

K

keen /kiːn/ a.	强烈的，渴望的	u9
kidney /ˈkɪdni/ n.	肾	u4
knick-knack /ˈnɪknæk/ n.	小装饰品	u3

L

lament /ləˈment/ v.	痛惜	u10
landmark /ˈlændmɑːk/ n.	著名景观	u3
laughter /ˈlɑːftə/ n.	笑声	u6
leftover /ˈleftəuvər/ n.	遗忘的物品	u1
legal /ˈliːgəl/ a.	合法的	u4
level /ˈlevl/ n.	楼层	u3
liberal /ˈlɪbərəl/ a.	不拘泥的	u5
light-fingeredness /ˈlaɪtˈfɪŋgədnɪs/ n.	扒窃	u1
linen /ˈlɪnɪn/ n.	亚麻布织物	u1
limelight /ˈlaɪmlaɪt/ n.	聚光；引人注目的中心	u7
limit /ˈlɪmɪt/ v.	限制	u4
liquor /ˈlɪkə/ n.	白酒，烈性酒	u2
liver /ˈlɪvə/ n.	肝脏	u4
live /laɪv/ a.	活的	u1
loan /ləun/ n.	贷款	u6
location /ləuˈkeɪʃən/ n.	场所	u1
logo /ˈləugəu/ n.	标识语	u1
luggage /ˈlʌgɪdʒ/ n.	行李	u5

M

maid /meɪd/ n.	清扫房间的女服务员	u1
make /meɪk/ n.	品牌	u3
Malaysia /məˈleɪzɪə/ n.	马来西亚	u6

mall /mɔːl/ *n.*	商业街	u9
management /'mænɪdʒmənt/ *n.*	管理	u6
manager /'mænɪdʒə/ *n.*	经理	u6
manufacture /ˌmænjʊ'fæktʃə/ *v.*	生产	u8
manuscript /'mænjʊskrɪpt/ *n.*	手稿	u3
massive /'mæsɪv/ *a.*	大规模的	u5
mature /mə'tjʊə/ *v.*	成熟	u6
mat /mæt/ *n.*	(画与镜框之间的)衬边	u9
meantime /'miːntaɪm/ *n.*	其间	u5
media /'miːdɪə/ *n.*	媒体	u4
memento /mɪ'mentəʊ/ *n.*	纪念品	u1
menswear /'menzweə/ *n.*	男服	u9
methodology /ˌmeθə'dɒlədʒɪ/ *n.*	方法	u6
midst /mɪdst/ *n.*	中间	u6
million /'mɪljən/ *n.*	百万	u6
minimum /'mɪnɪməm/ *a. & n.*	最小的；最小限度	u1
missing /'mɪsɪŋ/ *a.*	丢失的	u1
motivation /ˌməʊtɪ'veɪʃən/ *n.*	动机	u1
mount /maʊnt/ *v.*	增加	u6
mutual /'mjuːtʃʊəl/ *v.*	相互的	u9

N

nail /neɪl/ *v.*	钉	u1
native /'neɪtɪv/ *a.*	本地的	u5
noncommittal /ˌnɒnkə'mɪtəl/ *a.*	不明朗的，不承担义务的	u7
non-monogrammed /nɒn-'mɒnəgræmd/ *a.*	无标识语	u1
normal /'nɔːml/ *a.*	正常的	u9
nostalgia /nɒ'stældʒə/ *n.*	怀旧	u1
notification /ˌnəʊtɪfɪ'keɪʃən/ *n.*	通知	u1
notify /'nəʊtɪfaɪ/ *v.*	通知	u1

O

occasion /ə'keɪʒən/ *n.*	场合	u2
occupancy /'ɒkjʊpənsɪ/ *n.*	占用	u1

omelet /ˈɒmlɪt/ n.	煎蛋饼	u6
opposite /ˈɒpəzɪt/ prep.	对面的	u1
ordinance /ˈɔːdɪnəns/ n.	法令	u1
organ /ˈɔːgən/ n.	器官	u4
original /əˈrɪdʒənəl/ a.	最初的	u9
output /ˈaʊtpʊt/ n.	产量	u8
overcome /ˌəʊvəˈkʌm/ v.	克服	u4
overflow /ˌəʊvəˈfləʊ/ v.	充满	u1
overlook /ˌəʊvəˈlʊk/ v.	眺望	u1
overseas /ˌəʊvəˈsiːz/ a.	外国的，海外的	u8
oyster /ˈɔɪstə/ n.	牡蛎	u2

P

panacea /ˌpænəˈsɪə/ n.	灵丹妙药	u10
park /pɑːk/ v.	停放(车辆等)	u1
partner /ˈpɑːtnə/ n.	伙伴	u2
passenger /ˈpæsɪndʒə/ n.	旅客	u6
passport /ˈpɑːspɔːt/ n.	护照	u8
peculiar /pɪˈkjuːljə/ a.	奇怪的	u1
pedal /ˈpedl/ v.	踩踏板，蹬自行车	u7
peer /pɪə/ n.	同学	u10
percent /pəˈsent/ n.	百分比	u2
performance /pəˈfɔːməns/ n.	业绩	u10
perform /pəˈfɔːm/ v.	进行，运行	u4
permanently /ˈpɜːmənəntlɪ/ ad.	永久地	u5
perplex /pəˈpleks/ v.	困惑	u1
personnel /ˌpɜːsəˈnel/ n.	人事部门	u6
personnel /ˌpɜːsəˈnel/ n.	人员	u9
persuade /pəˈsweɪd/ v.	劝告	u5
persuasion /pəˈsweɪʒən/ n.	劝告	u5
pet /pet/ n.	宠物	u1
picturesque /ˌpɪktʃəˈresk/ a.	风景如画的，独特的	u7
pint /paɪnt/ n.	品脱	u3
player /ˈpleɪə/ n.	唱机	u3
pleasing /ˈpliːzɪŋ/ a.	令人高兴的，愉快的，合意的	u7

plus /plʌs/ *n.*	有利因素	u9
plus /plʌs/ *prep.*	加上	u6
population /ˌpɒpjʊ'leɪʃən/ *n.*	人口	u2
positively /'pɒzɪtɪvlɪ/ *ad.*	完全地	u2
prawn /prɔːn/ *n.*	大虾	u2
preference /'prefərəns/ *n.*	偏爱	u2
preliminary /prɪ'lɪmɪnərɪ/ *a.*	预备的，初步的	u7
prepay /ˌpriː'peɪ/ *v.*	预付	u1
presentable /prɪ'zentəbl/ *a.*	像样地	u2
pressure /'preʃə(r)/ *n.*	压力	u4
pride /praɪd/ *n.*	自豪	u6
private /'praɪvɪt/ *a.*	私人的	u8
proceed /prəʊ'siːd/ *v.*	继续下去	u9
processor /'prəʊsesə/ *n.*	处理器	u10
productive /prə'dʌktɪv/ *a.*	多产的	u6
profit /'prɒfɪt/ *n.*	利润	u8
progress /'prəʊgres/ *n.*	进步	u5
promenade /ˌprɒmə'nɑːd/ *n.*	漫步	u3
prompt /prɒmpt/ *a.*	迅速的	u9
propose /prə'pəʊz/ *v.*	提议	u2
prosperous /'prɒspərəs/ *a.*	繁荣的	u2
prudent /'pruːdnt/ *a.*	谨慎的	u5
psychology /saɪ'kɒlədʒɪ/ *n.*	心理学	u6
pulse /pʌls/ *n.*	脉膊	u4
pun /pʌn/ *n.*	双关语	u6
purchase /'pɜːtʃəs/ *v.*	购买	u3
pursuit /pə'suːt/ *v.*	追求	u2
pyjamas /pɪ'dʒɑːməs/ *n.*	绣花睡衣	u3

Q

qualification /ˌkwɒlɪfɪ'keɪʃən/ *n.*	资格	u6
quality /'kwɒlɪtɪ/ *n.*	质量	u8
qualm /kwɑːlm/ *n.*	疑虑	u9
quit /kwɪt/ *v.*	停止，离开	u5
quotation /kwəʊ'teɪʃən/ *n.*	报价	u9

quota /'kwəʊtə/ n.   配额   u9

R

realization /ˌrɪəlaɪ'zeɪʃən/ n.   真正认识   u10

receipt /rɪ'siːt/ n.   收到   u9

recipe /'resɪpi/ n.   食谱   u4

reclaim /rɪ'kleɪm/ v.   索回   u1

recommend /ˌrekə'mend/ v.   推荐   u10

recreational /ˌrekrɪ'eɪʃnl/ a.   娱乐的   u5

refrigerator /rɪ'frɪdʒəreɪtə/ n.   冰箱   u1

reggae /'regeɪ/ n.   雷盖乐(舞)   u3

register /'redʒɪstə/ v.   注册   u9

regret /rɪ'gret/ v.   遗憾   u2

regular /'regjʊlə/ n.   经常的   u9

reimburse /ˌriːɪm'bɜːs/ v.   偿还   u9

reinforce /ˌriːɪn'fɔːs/ vt.   加强   u10

reliable /rɪ'laɪəbl/ a.   可靠的   u2

remarkable /rɪ'mɑːkəbl/ a.   不平常的   u8

replace /rɪ'pleɪs/ v.   代替   u1

reputation /ˌrepjʊ'teɪʃən/ n.   名誉   u9

resentment /rɪ'zentmənt/ n.   怨恨   u2

reservation /ˌrezə'veɪʃən/ n.   预订   u2

resilience /rɪ'zɪlɪəns/ n.   毅力，韧劲   u6

resourceful /rɪ'sɔːsfʊl/ a.   足智多谋的   u5

respectively /rɪ'spektɪvlɪ/ ad.   分别地   u4

responsibility /rɪˌspɒnsə'bɪlɪtɪ/ n.   责任   u6

restricted /rɪ'strɪktɪd/ a.   受限制的   u8

resume /'rezjuːmeɪ/ n.   简历   u6

retailer /riː'teɪlə/ n.   零售商   u3

retail /'riː teɪl/ n.   零售   u9

rewarding /rɪ'wɔːdɪŋ/ a.   有收获的   u5

ridiculous /rɪ'dɪkjʊləs/ a.   可笑的   u6

rob /rɒb/ v.   剥夺，抢夺   u4

roof /ruːf/ n.   屋顶   u3

routine /ruː'tiːn/ n.   常规   u5

S

salary /'sælərɪ/ *n.*	工资	u6
satellite /'sætəlaɪt/ *n.*	卫星	u1
satisfactory /ˌsætɪs'fæktərɪ/ *a.*	满意的	u9
scallop /'skɔləp/ *n.*	干贝	u2
scenery /'siːnərɪ/ *n.*	景色	u5
security /sɪ'kjʊərətɪ/ *n.*	安全	u8
seemingly /'siːmɪŋlɪ/ *ad.*	从表面上看来	u9
separate /'sepəreɪt/ *a.*	分开的	u2
separate /'sepərɪt/ *a.*	单独的	u9
shoot /ʃuːt/ *v.*	拍摄	u3
shrimp /ʃrɪmp/ *n.*	虾	u2
shy /ʃaɪ/ *a.*	害羞的	u1
signal /'sɪgnəl/ *v.*	表示	u5
sirloin /'səːlɔɪn/ *n.*	牛上腰部肉	u2
skull /skʌl/ *n.*	头颅	u4
sleeve /sliːv/ *n.*	袖子	u3
snack /snæk/ *n.*	快餐，小吃	u2
sneeze /sniːz/ *n.& v.*	打喷嚏	u4
soap /səʊp/ *n.*	肥皂	u1
sojourn /'sɒdʒɜːn/ *n.*	逗留	u5
solely /'səʊ(l)li/ *a.*	独自地	u4
sophomore /'sɒfəmɔː/ *a.*	（大学）二年级的	u10
sorely /'sɔːlɪ/ *ad.*	非常地	u6
sour /'saʊə/ *v.*	变坏	u6
sovereign /'sɒvrɪn/ *n.*	主权	u3
specialty /'speʃəltɪ/ *n.*	特色	u2
special /'speʃəl/ *a.*	特殊的	u8
spirit /'spɪrɪt/ *n.*	烈酒	u2
stall /stɔːl/ *n.*	货摊，出售摊	u7
starve /stɑːv/ *v.*	挨饿	u2
stern /stɜːn/ *a.*	严厉的	u7
stint /stɪnt/ *n.*	任期	u10
stockbroker /'stɒkbrəʊkə/ *n.*	股票经纪人	u6
stomach /'stʌmək/ *n.*	胃	u4

stress /stres/ *n.*	压力	u6
stretch /stretʃ/ *v. & n.*	伸展，扩张；一段路程	u1
stuff /stʌf/ *n.*	东西	u9
subsidiary /səbˈsɪdɪərɪ/ *n.*	分公司，子公司	u7
subway /ˈsʌbweɪ/ *n.*	地铁	u5
suite /swiːt/ *n.*	套房	u1
sun		
superb /sjuːˈpɜːb/ *a.*	精美的	u5
supervisor /ˈsjuːpəvaɪzə/ *n.*	主管人	u9
super /ˈsjuːpə/ *a.*	极好的	u2
surprisingly /səˈpraɪzɪŋlɪ/ *ad.*	令人吃惊地	u2
survey /ˈsəveɪ/ *n.*	调查	u2
switchboard /ˈswɪtʃbɔːd/ *n.*	交换台，总机	u1
system /ˈsɪstəm/ *n.*	系统	u4

T

tasty /ˈteɪstɪ/ *a.*	好吃的	u4
towel /ˈtaʊə/ *n.*	毛巾	u1
tower /ˈtaʊə/ *v.*	高耸	u5
trace /treɪs/ *n.*	痕迹	u5
traditionally /trəˈdɪʃənlɪ/ *ad.*	传统地	u5
tradition /trəˈdɪʃən/ *n.*	传统	u2
transcript /ˈtrænskrɪpt/ *n.*	抄本；副本	u6
transportation /trænspəˈteɪʃən/ *n.*	交通	u5
treat /triːt/ *v.*	款待	u2
tremendous /trɪˈmendəs/ *a.*	巨大的	u5
triple /ˈtrɪpl/ *v.*	增至3倍	u8
tube /ˈtjuːb/ *n.*	管子	u4
typically /ˈtɪpɪkəlɪ/ *ad.*	典型地，独特地	u5

U

uncommon /ˌʌnˈkɒmən/ *a.*	不寻常的	u4
underwear /ˈʌndəweə/ *n.*	内衣	u1
unfortunate /ʌnˈfɔːtʃənɪt/ *a.*	不幸的	u4

225

utility /juːˈtɪlətɪ/ *n.*　　　　　　　　　公用，效用　　　　　　　　　u1

V

varied /ˈveərɪd/ *a.*　　　　　　　　　多样的　　　　　　　　　u2
VAT /ˌviːeɪˈtiː, væt/ (Valued-Added Tax)　增值税，附加税　　　　　u1
verbal /ˈvəbəl/ *a.*　　　　　　　　　口头的　　　　　　　　　u6
via /ˈvaɪə, ˈviːə/ *prep.*　　　　　　　经由　　　　　　　　　u4
volt /vəʊlt/ *n.*　　　　　　　　　　伏特　　　　　　　　　u1

W

walnut /ˈwɔːlnʌt/ *n.*　　　　　　　　胡桃　　　　　　　　　u2
warm-hearted /ˌwɔːmˈhɑːtɪd/ *a.*　　热心的　　　　　　　　u5
weather /ˈweðə/ *v.*　　　　　　　　经受　　　　　　　　　u6
window-shopping /ˈwɪndəʊʃɒpɪŋ/ *n.*　逛商店　　　　　　　u3
wind /waɪnd/ *v.*　　　　　　　　　卷起　　　　　　　　　u3
wing /wɪŋ/ *n.*　　　　　　　　　　侧翼；边楼　　　　　　u3
witness /ˈwɪtnɪs/ *v.*　　　　　　　目击　　　　　　　　　u5

Useful Expressions

eat out	外出吃饭	u2
electric razor	电动胡须刀	u1
enjoy outdoor	享受户外活动	u6
equal to	等于	u2
even if	就算	u4
executive suite	办公套房	u1
fail to	没能	u4
fast-food restaurant	快餐店	u2
feet square	平方英尺	u1
get ... across	使…理解	u4
get ... off	休息	u6
get down to business	着手干正事	u7
get rid of	摆脱，弄掉	u4
go horseback riding	骑马	u6
go on	继续	u4
hair dryer	吹风机	u1
have a sip	尝一口	u2
have faith in	相信	u6
have fun at	在…中感到乐趣	u6
high season	高峰期	u1
hip hop	摇摆乐	u3
hold on to	坚守	u5
home meals	家常饭	u2
house ware	家用物品	u6
humor skills	幽默技巧	u6
in despair	绝望	u7
in need of	需要	u4
in no time	马上	u5
in the meanwhile	与此同时	u5
in the shape of	以…为形状	u1
know better than	不仅懂得	u4
knowledge-based economy	知识经济	u10
laugh heartily	开心大笑	u6
laugh up	谈笑	u6
leave behind	忘带	u1
let alone	更不用说…了	u7